A New Season

A New Season

Using Title IX to Reform College Sports

Brian L. Porto

PRAEGER

Westport, Connecticut
London

Library of Congress Cataloging-in-Publication Data

Porto, Brian L.
    A new season : Using title IX to reform college sports / Brian L. Porto.
        p.   cm.
    Includes bibliographical references and index.
    ISBN 0–275–97699–8 (alk. paper)
    1. Women athletes—Government policy—United States.   2. Sex discrimination in
sports—Law and legislation—United States.   3. College Sports—United States.   1. Title:
Title IX and the reform of college athletics.   II. Title: Title nine and the reform of
college athletics.   III. Title.
GV709.18.U6P67   2003
796'.082—dc21   2003048216

British Library Cataloguing in Publication Data is available.

Library of Congress Catalog Card Number: 2003048216
ISBN: 0–275–97699–8

First published in 2003

Praeger Publishers, 88 Post Road West, Westport, CT 06881
An imprint of Greenwood Publishing Group, Inc.
www.praeger.com

Printed in the United States of America

The paper used in this book complies with the
Permanent Paper Standard issued by the National
Information Standards Organization (Z39.48–1984).

10 9 8 7 6 5 4 3 2 1

For Sherrie—hiker, skier, and kayaker—
who taught me that the joy of sports
lies not in achievement, but in participation.

CONTENTS

PREFACE

Nothing invites a critique like hypocrisy in high places, and there is no institution in America today that is more hypocritical than "big-time" college sports. Article I of the Constitution of the National Collegiate Athletic Association (NCAA) states that the NCAA believes that college sports should be "an integral part of the educational program" at its member institutions.[1] In reality, college sports are commercial and semiprofessional entertainment enterprises, largely because of the NCAA's efforts, and they have little to do with higher education. To make matters worse, colleges' attempts to earn revenue and to gain visibility through athletic success have financial, academic, and social consequences that do them more harm than good.

I have observed college sports closely for thirty years, as a participant, a professor, a lawyer, and an author. My observations began during my undergraduate years at the University of Rhode Island, a second-tier member of the NCAA's prestigious Division I, where I had an undistinguished career as a distance runner in the early 1970s. They continued during doctoral studies in political science from 1974 until 1979 at Miami University of Ohio, which also occupies the second tier of Division I. A teaching job at Macalester College in Minnesota introduced me to the NCAA's Division III, where athletic scholarships are prohibited, and member colleges do not view sports as a source of revenue. In 1984 my enrollment in law school at Indiana University at Bloomington enabled me to see college sports in their most commercial and professional form.

Today, I live in Vermont, where college sports are not important sources of entertainment, the flagship state university does not field a football team, and hiking is just as popular as tailgating is in the fall. The major college closest to my home is Dartmouth, which does not offer athletic scholarships.

The best athletes at Dartmouth often participate in sports such as lacrosse, squash, and cross-country skiing, which attract few spectators and promise little or no financial reward after graduation.

My observations of college sports have taught me two principal lessons. One lesson is that sports can be a valuable part of a college education when they are secondary to the academic curriculum. Sports, like musical recitals and theatrical performances, force students to discover and to confront their fears, their limitations, and the adequacy of their preparation in public, which academic work rarely does. This probably explains why a high percentage of my cross-country and track teammates in college entered graduate and professional schools after graduation, and then built successful careers in business, education, government, and scientific research. The other lesson is that when sports are primarily a means of earning money and gaining public visibility, they do not belong on college campuses. This is because colleges (a term that includes universities in this book) are nonprofit institutions, and their primary mission is to promote long-term human development. When they pursue profits instead by providing athletic entertainment, they almost always fail at their primary mission, and this failure causes them to sacrifice their integrity, which is their most valuable asset.

These two lessons are the foundation of this book, which will argue that colleges should preserve varsity sports and even expand sports opportunities for women students but should replace the current commercial model of college sports with a participation model. The principal beneficiaries of the participation model will be the students who play, not coaches, athletic directors, boosters, sports journalists, or fans. The impetus for change is the colleges' need to comply with Title IX, the federal law that prohibits sex discrimination in education, which the federal courts have recently ordered college athletic departments to do. For most colleges the need to comply with Title IX is an invitation to adopt the participation model because they cannot afford to fund women's sports at the same generous, even lavish, levels at which they fund men's sports. Still, many colleges will be reluctant to accept this invitation because their leaders and their sports fans would prefer to live in hope that athletic fame and fortune are just a season away. That is why this book will show college faculty members how to use Title IX to spur the adoption by their respective colleges of the participation model of college sports.

One must understand the problem, though, in order to solve it. Toward that end, Chapter 1 will describe the current state of college sports in America, and Chapter 2 will recount their history. Chapters 3, 4, and 5 will discuss the negative financial, academic, and social consequences, respectively, of big-time college sports. Chapter 6 will show how Title IX can be a force for change, and Chapter 7 will present that change in the form of the participation model. Chapter 8 will draw a blueprint for college sports reformers, which they can use to construct the participation model and put it into effect.

A New Season, as its title suggests, is a hopeful book. It is based on the belief that there can be fiscal sanity, academic integrity, personal responsibility, and gender equity in college sports. *A New Season* is also a realistic book. It recognizes that (1) reformist tinkering has not solved the deep-seated problems that plague college sports; (2) only the replacement of the commercial model by the participation model can solve these problems; and (3) this change will not occur unless college faculty members lead a movement to reclaim their institutions from the college sports industry. *A New Season* will guide and support this movement so that college sports can become the "integral part of the educational program" that the NCAA advertises them to be, and that they should be.

NOTES

1. NCAA Operating Bylaws, Article 12, Amateurism: General Principles, 12.01.2, Clear Line of Demarcation, reprinted in NCAA, *2002–03 NCAA Division I Manual* (Michael V. Earle, ed., 2002), p. 69.

ACKNOWLEDGMENTS

A corps of thoughtful friends and colleagues helped to make this book possible, and I am indebted to them. Long ago, my high school cross-country coach, Joe Flower, taught me that sports should be fun and that it is possible to have fun while working hard. The first lesson inspired me to conceive of this book and the second lesson enabled me to write it.

More recently, Michael Hermann, my editor at Praeger, believed in the project and saw it through to completion with wise counsel and a wonderful sense of humor. Bill Dowling, Chuck Green, Allen Sack, Ellen Staurowsky, Dave Schultz, Herb Waltzer, and Andy Zimbalist read the prospectus and offered both advice and encouragement as the project began. Gary Jacobsen, Jack Wilde, and Bruce Williams provided useful critiques of the early chapters. Dan Fulks lent his financial expertise in a thoughtful review of Chapter 3. Linda Carpenter shared her vast knowledge of Title IX and of the history of women's college sports in a cogent review of Chapter 6. Nicci Rinaldi recalled in detail her traumatic introduction to big-time college sports at Auburn and her subsequent enjoyment of both college and college basketball at Dartmouth.

Numerous people furnished information that I might otherwise have overlooked. President Linda Bensel-Meyers of The Drake Group and her predecessor, Jon Ericson, identified and provided electronic links to a treasure trove of recent newspaper articles on college sports. Alice Eberhardt flagged articles in *The New York Times*. Janice O'Donnell pointed out several studies documenting the adverse health effects of Americans' penchant for watching sports instead of playing them. John Gerdy sent copies of several of his perceptive articles on the governance of college sports. Journalists Jim Carty of *The Ann Arbor News* (Michigan.) and Welch Suggs of *The Chronicle of*

Higher Education kindly answered requests for information concerning stories that had appeared in their respective newspapers. Attorneys Pat Gloor of Chicago, Mary Kehoe of Burlington, Vermont, Larry Marcucci of West Des Moines, Iowa, Steve Nielsen of Des Moines, Iowa, Aidan Reynolds of Baton Rouge, Louisiana, and Brian Woolf of East Hartford, Connecticut discussed or sent documents concerning college-sports litigation in which they have participated.

Bob Rossi, co-author of the 1987–88 National Study of Intercollegiate Athletes conducted by the American Institutes for Research, furnished the multiple reports that the study produced and responded patiently and promptly to questions about their findings. Ann Vollano of the University of Michigan provided a copy of the study that she had conducted on gambling among college athletes. The National Women's Law Center and the Women's Law Project also supplied useful information. Director Jennifer Cary and Interlibrary Loan Librarian Sara Tufts of the Windsor Public Library in Vermont searched far beyond the Green Mountains in response to a flurry of interlibrary loan requests, and they never failed to find the book or article I sought.

When the manuscript was complete, Linda Carpenter, John Gerdy, Robert Lipsyte, Tom McMillen, Allen Sack, and Ellen Staurowsky took time out of their busy lives to review and comment on it. I am honored to receive their endorsements.

My greatest debt, though, is to my wife, Sherrie Greeley. Her love, support, and keen eye for ponderous prose and typographical errors have enriched *A New Season*, and the experience of writing it, immeasurably. For these reasons and countless others, I dedicate the book to her.

Brian L. Porto
Windsor, VT.
May 8, 2003

CHAPTER 1

THIS SEASON

THE CURRENT STATE OF COLLEGE SPORTS

A TALE OF TWO PHILOSOPHIES

Women's college basketball in the Southeastern Conference (SEC) is big business. Nicci Rinaldi learned that the hard way in the early autumn of 1995, when she enrolled at Auburn University in Alabama, a member of the SEC. In the summer of 1995, Nicci had accepted an athletic scholarship to play basketball for the Tigers. She was one of the top thirty high school girls' basketball players in America, and many colleges had recruited her. Initially, she chose Dartmouth College in New Hampshire, which could not offer her an athletic scholarship. Dartmouth belongs to the Ivy League, which permits its members to give students only need-based financial aid. Two weeks before she was scheduled to leave her home in Pennsylvania for New Hampshire, she changed her mind and accepted Auburn's offer of a basketball scholarship. Today, she calls her change of mind "rash" and "highly illogical," and says: "I really didn't think much about it."[1] Still, she acknowledges that the prospect of a free college education was a great relief to her because she was uncertain that she could pay for her education at Dartmouth, and that the opportunity to play basketball in the SEC was immensely exciting.

Three weeks after her arrival at Auburn, Nicci changed her mind again and transferred to Dartmouth. She disliked her life at Auburn because it consisted largely of playing basketball. She concluded that she had made a terrible mistake when she had accepted the basketball scholarship. "I realized I had sold out to the devil," she told a New Hampshire newspaper reporter after her transfer to Dartmouth. "I had sold my soul. And now I was in hell." Nicci's hell lacked fire, which it more than made up for in fatigue. "I was in bed by 8:30 every night, I was so exhausted," she said. "I spent my week-ends sleeping." The social isolation of the basketball team was hell, too. "I was there for three weeks and didn't have one friend outside of the basketball team," Nicci recalled.[2]

She added that, at Auburn, "I just didn't have the opportunity to grow intellectually," and "I wasn't feeling like I was in college." "There's so much to see and do when you are a college student, and I didn't feel I was getting that opportunity to explore everything in a situation where basketball is the main priority."[3] Her algebra class was similar to one she had taken as a freshman in high school, her English class focused on diagramming sen-tences, and an academic advisor to the athletic department visited the ath-letes' classes to make sure that they attended. The same advisor influenced the players' course selections. "Needless to say," she recalls now, "I was not intellectually stimulated at Auburn." "The last straw" occurred on September 27, 1995, her eighteenth birthday, when she collapsed on the basketball court from heat exhaustion. "I had already decided that I was miserable and had made a huge mistake. . . . it felt like a sign. . . . I knew I had to get out of there."[4]

Shortly thereafter, Nicci left Auburn and enrolled at Dartmouth, which gave her the chance to be a college student first and a basketball player second. She observed as a freshman that her Dartmouth coaches and team-mates "take [basketball] seriously, but keep it in perspective. They've got their priorities right."[5] She feels the same way today. During an interview she recalled that the Dartmouth basketball coaches encouraged their athletes to study abroad and to pursue interests other than basketball. Nicci spent the spring and summer quarters of her sophomore year studying in Germany and Australia, respectively. The coaches scheduled basketball practices around their players' class schedules, and even held practice late at night in order to avoid conflicts with laboratory sessions in science courses. Basketball players studied on buses, in planes, and in hotels, and even took winter-quarter final exams at the site of their first-round game in the NCAA Tour-nament in 1999. In short, the Dartmouth basketball players went to Dartmouth primarily to be college students, and their coaches supported that choice. "That was the big difference between Auburn and Dartmouth," Nicci recalled.[6]

At Dartmouth, Nicci found time to hold a part-time job on campus, to belong to a sorority, and to teach basketball to children, in addition to stud-ying and playing basketball. She graduated in 1999 with a degree in religion after having started for four years on the Big Green women's basketball team, which won the Ivy League championship and earned a bid to the NCAA Tournament in her senior year. Today, she lives in Connecticut, where her first job after college was as a public relations manager in a human resources consulting firm that teaches displaced workers how to market themselves for new careers.

Nicci Rinaldi's experience shows the difference between the commercial and the participation models of college sports. The commercial model governs in the Southeastern Conference, while the participation model governs in the Ivy League. The commercial model views football, men's basketball, and increasingly women's basketball as "revenue" sports that should provide entertainment for the fans and revenue and public support for the colleges that sponsor the teams. The educational needs of the participants are secondary to winning. Thus, Auburn pursued Nicci Rinaldi not because it was a good place for her to be academically or socially, but instead, because it needed a point guard in order to continue its success in women's basketball. Talented players make for successful seasons, which enable colleges to earn revenue, gain visibility, and keep their fans happy and their arenas full.

In contrast, the participation model views college sports as extracurricular activities that should enhance the educational experiences of the participants. Winning seasons, revenue, and visibility are secondary to educational enhancement. One has an opportunity to be a college student, not merely a point guard. That is precisely as it should be because educational enhancement is the only legitimate reason for colleges to sponsor sports teams. Sports teams that exist for commercial reasons have nothing to do with higher education, and they do not belong on college campuses. Moreover, such semiprofessional teams have produced negative financial, academic, and social costs for colleges for more than a hundred years, and unless fundamental reform occurs soon, these costs will increase as the financial incentives to pursue athletic success increase.

Happily, though, Nicci Rinaldi's experience also shows that the participation model already exists in college sports. Indeed, it exists not just in the Ivy League, which is the only conference in NCAA Division I that prohibits athletic scholarships, but also throughout NCAA Division III, which consists of 395 members, including small private colleges and small state universities. This book will argue that the participation model should govern all sports at all colleges in America and that the goal of replacing commerce with participation is achievable at most colleges sooner rather than later. There is a need for realism, but there is cause for optimism, too.

THE HIGH COSTS OF BIG-TIME COLLEGE SPORTS

Colleges incur high financial, academic, and social costs in their pursuit of athletic success. Big-time college sports are expensive, and contrary to popular belief, most colleges in Division I lose money on football and men's basketball. Consequently, college funds and legislative appropriations are necessary to support non-revenue-producing sports and to balance the athletic budget. These dollars are then unavailable to fund academic scholarships for needy students who are nonathletes.

To be sure, the NCAA and a select few colleges earn substantial revenues from football and from men's basketball. The NCAA has an eight-year, $1.725-billion contract with CBS to broadcast the national championship tournament in men's basketball through 2004. Notre Dame has a seven-year, $45-million contract to televise its regular season football games. The major football conferences have a seven-year, $700-million contract with ABC to televise the Bowl Championship Series through 2005–2006.[7]

Most colleges, however, do not reap bountiful financial harvests from sports. For example, in 1996–97, only 43 percent of the 110 colleges that played football in Division I-A, which represents the big time, reported that their athletic departments enjoyed an operating surplus *without* the benefit of a subsidy from the general fund. The average Division I-A college, excluding a subsidy from the general fund, suffered a deficit in its athletic department of $823,000 in 1996–97, a considerable increase from the 1994–95 figure of $237,000.[8] In 1998–99 the fifty-four colleges that play football in Division I-A, but not in one of the six major conferences, spent an average of $3.2 million on football but earned an average of only $3.1 million, which translates to a net loss of about $100,000 per college. The 122 colleges that play football in the less commercialized Division I-AA fared even worse, earning an average of $671,000 in revenues while incurring an average of $1.1 million in expenses.[9]

This evidence casts doubt on the traditional claim by supporters of commercialized college sports that football and men's basketball raise the revenue that is necessary if colleges are to support men's non-revenue sports and an increasing array of women's sports. Most colleges that participate in big time football and men's basketball do not earn revenues from football and men's basketball that are sufficient to support soccer, swimming, and lacrosse. To make matters worse, the gap between rich and poor college athletic departments is growing, as the costs of playing in the big time increase steadily. A survey conducted for the NCAA, which used financial information from 1998–99, revealed that only forty-eight of the 104 Division I-A colleges that responded to the survey earned a profit from sports, but that the average profit was $3.8 million, which represented an increase of 124 percent over the comparable figure for 1996–97. The rest of the colleges in Division I-A lost an average of $3.3 million apiece, an increase of $500,000 since 1996–97.[10] Under these circumstances it is not surprising that twenty-two colleges, including five in Division I, dropped football during the 1990s.[11] The trend has continued in the new millennium. For example, in early 2003, Canisius College, Fairfield University, and St. John's University, which belong to the Division I-AA Metro Atlantic Conference, dropped football.[12]

Still, colleges continue to spend enormous sums of money in their quests for the profits and the publicity that accompany perennial success in college sports. Coaches are among the major beneficiaries of this spending spree. For example, in November of 1998, Auburn University hired football coach

Tommy Tuberville at a salary that ranged from $750,000 to $900,000 per year, depending on the team's performance. Coach Tuberville's salary was four times what Auburn's president earned.[13] Academic values are among the major casualties of this spending spree. For example, Coach Tuberville's contract contained a provision that would award him a $50,000 bonus if his team did not violate NCAA rules for five years, but would award him a $100,000 bonus if his team won the national championship.[14] When academic values suffer, faculty and students suffer. Faculty and students undoubtedly suffered when Tulane University's board of administrators voted to increase the athletics budget by $3.4 million for the 1996–97 academic year, while it cut $8.5 million from the overall budget, raised tuition by 4 percent, and froze the salaries of faculty and staff.[15]

Ironically, such spending is not only ethically questionable but also financially impractical for most colleges. The reasons for this are that lavish spending does not ensure athletic success and that athletic success does not ensure financial success. The bowl games in football illustrate the first point. Many colleges spend lavishly on football, but the same twenty-odd teams dominate the national rankings and play in the bowl games almost every year.[16] The mind boggles when it tries to recall the most recent year in which Nebraska, Michigan, or Florida State failed to earn a bowl bid.

The University of Michigan illustrates the second point. During the 1988–89 fiscal year, Michigan won the Big Ten championship in football, the Rose Bowl, and the NCAA championship in men's basketball. The football team played on national television seven times and played its home games before an average of 105,000 spectators, while the men's basketball team made numerous appearances on national television. Nevertheless, Michigan's athletic department earned a profit of only $1 million dollars that year because its gross revenues were $35 million, while its expenses were $34 million. A decade later, Michigan spent more than it earned on sports, despite the success of its teams. During the 1998–99 fiscal year the Wolverines won the national championship in football, but the athletic department ran an operating deficit of $2.8 million.[17]

If Michigan—with its huge football stadium, considerable financial resources, and storied athletic tradition—cannot earn substantial profits from sports even when its teams succeed, surely Auburn, Tulane, and most Division I colleges are wasting their money in pursuit of the athletic holy grail. This money should be used instead to fund academic scholarships, a visiting professorship, or numerous other legitimate educational programs. In the long run, these expenditures will enable universities to earn more income and prestige than they can earn from athletic success.

The academic costs of big-time college sports are more difficult to measure than the financial costs, but they are just as real. They can also do more damage to a college than almost any amount of red ink can do. Indeed, academic costs can cause a college to sacrifice its most valuable asset, which is its integrity as an educational institution. A financial scandal in the athletic department is unlikely to devalue a college's degrees in the public mind to the extent that an academic scandal in the athletic department will do so. Still, colleges take this risk regularly by engaging in academic misbehavior in the pursuit of athletic success. Academic misbehavior by college athletic departments takes many forms, including the admission of functionally illiterate athletes, the forgery of high school transcripts, the enrollment of athletes in questionable summer courses so that they can obtain the credits necessary for athletic eligibility, the arrangement of athletes' course schedules by athletic department personnel in order to ensure their availability for daily practice and the grades necessary for continued eligibility, and the use of academically ineligible athletes in competition.[18]

Examples abound, and they are nothing new. In 1977, Oklahoma State University admitted football player Dexter Manley even though he was unable to read or write. When he left Stillwater four years later, he was headed for fame and fortune with the Washington Redskins of the National Football League (NFL), but he was still illiterate, having been kept eligible for football with no hope of earning a degree.[19] In 1978, Creighton University admitted basketball player Kevin Ross even though he had scored a 9 (out of a possible 36) on the American College Test (ACT). During his freshman year at Creighton he took courses titled "Squad Participation," "Theory of Basketball," "Theory of Track and Field," and "Introduction to Ceramics," which represented a blatant attempt by the athletic department to preserve his eligibility to play basketball.[20]

In 1985, North Carolina State University, where the average freshman-class SAT score was 1030 (out of a possible 1600), admitted basketball player Chris Washburn, even though his combined score on the SAT was 470. Washburn's score of 200 on the verbal portion of the exam was the minimal score possible; in other words, he did not answer any questions correctly.[21] Chris Washburn left North Carolina State after his sophomore season in order to play professional basketball, but Kevin Ross never played professional basketball. Instead, when his basketball eligibility ended, he left Creighton possessing "the overall language skills of a fourth-grader and the reading skills of a seventh-grader." Before he could pursue a college degree, he had to enroll for a year of remedial education at the Westside Preparatory School in Chicago, where he attended classes with grade-school children.[22] Kevin Ross's sad story became national news when he sued Creighton for negligence and breach of contract because it had failed to educate him.

The practice of "majoring in eligibility," which enabled Kevin Ross to amass 96 credits and to play basketball at Creighton for four years despite his severe academic deficiencies, continues unabated. At the end of the 1997–98 academic year, the grade point average (GPA) of Ohio State football star Andy Katzenmoyer had fallen below 2.0; unless he could raise it above 2.0, he would be ineligible to play football for the Buckeyes during the 1998–99 season. Katzenmoyer regained his eligibility by taking three classes in summer school that improved his GPA; they were golf, music, and AIDS awareness.[23]

Coaches often foster an antiacademic atmosphere in which majoring in eligibility is the norm rather than the exception. Athletic scholarships encourage majoring in eligibility because they make enrollment in classes dependent on participation in sport, which, in turn, gives coaches undue influence over their athletes' academic lives.[24] This influence can cause college athletes to subordinate their intellectual development and their career prospects to their coaches' athletic demands. Such sacrifices, while unfortunate, are nevertheless understandable in light of the following statements made by coaches to their athletes, which the athletes later reported to academic advisors at Division I-A colleges.

1. "If you wanted an education, you should have gone to Harvard."
2. "You came to school to play football. You could have stayed home if you wanted an education."
3. "I know it's finals week and you should be doing that academic stuff, but try to stay focused on basketball."
4. "You're not smart enough to make it in college, so you're going to have to learn how to cheat."[25]

To make matters worse, big-time college football and men's basketball, if not also women's basketball, are virtually year-round sports now, so players who have taken light course loads during their competitive seasons cannot necessarily concentrate on their studies during the "off-season." Preseason football practice begins in late summer, and the regular season lasts until mid or late November. If a team earns a berth in a bowl game, its players may be off-campus, or at least practicing on campus, through the end of the fall term, including during the final exam period.[26] Under these conditions, supposedly voluntary summer workouts may not really be voluntary, even when they conflict with an athlete's class schedule. Author John Gerdy has reported the following conversation between a football player and an assistant coach at a Division I-A college, which illustrates this point.

COACH: "You need to be at those workouts."
ATHLETE: "I have a class."
COACH: "You need to be at those workouts."
ATHLETE: "You telling me to cut class?"
COACH: "Well, do they check?"

ATHLETE: "I thought academics came first?" (a reference to a statement that the head coach had made to the team).

COACH: "You ever say that again, you can pack your bags."[27]

College basketball schedules are even less compatible with serious academic effort than college football schedules are. Preseason practice begins in mid-October, and the regular season lasts through the conclusion of the fall semester and halfway through the spring semester at most colleges. Unlike football schedules, basketball schedules usually include weeknight games, which often occur late in the evening (especially if televised) and far from home. The postseason tournament begins in mid-March and concludes in early April. Its hectic atmosphere, aptly dubbed "March Madness," is fundamentally incompatible with quiet, careful study. Former University of Michigan president James Duderstadt has observed: Too many student-athletes have seen their studies flounder on the rocks of the NCAA Tournament.[28]

Under these conditions, it is extraordinarily difficult for a basketball player at a Division I college to carry a full load of courses during the academic year, which means that enrollment in summer school and even a fifth year of study are often necessary in order for the player to graduate. Isaiah Thomas, who starred in basketball for Indiana University and later the Detroit Pistons of the National Basketball Association (NBA), reflected on the academic consequences of a big-time college basketball schedule in an interview with *Newsweek* in 1989. Thomas said:

> When you go to college, you're not a student-athlete, but an athlete-student. Your main purpose is not to be an Einstein but a ballplayer, to generate some money, put people in the stands. Eight or ten hours of your day are filled with basketball, football. The rest of your time you've got to motivate yourself to make sure you get something back.[29]

Coaches and athletic directors argue that their academic assistance programs enable athletes to keep up with their schoolwork despite the demands of year-round athletic training. Too often, though, such programs are housed in athletic departments, with the result that they promote majoring in eligibility instead of fighting it. Veteran athletic director Doug Single has written that:

> Academic-assistance programs housed in athletic departments have failed because they are driven toward maintaining eligibility rather than fostering education, and toward "protecting" student-athletes from academic standards, faculty, and deans rather than assisting them to take advantage of available resources.[30]

Moreover, even the best academic-assistance programs for athletes are no substitute for sensible admissions policies that reflect an emphasis on academic values and a de-emphasis on commercialized sport. Professor William C. Dowling of Rutgers University has written that

> The machinery of virtue that the Division I-A schools point to in their athletics programs—tutors, study halls, improved graduation rates—are precisely evidence that the scholarship athletes are *not* real students. If they were real students, you wouldn't need all this elaborate and costly machinery to get them to do what students are supposed to do as a matter of course.[31]

Nor would their graduation rates be so low. The most visible academic cost of big-time college sports is the dreadful rate at which football players and men's basketball players at Division I colleges earn degrees. *The Chronicle of Higher Education* reported in December of 2000 that 42 percent of the men's basketball players and 48 percent of the football players in Division I who started college in 1993–94 had earned their degrees *within six years*. These figures compare to graduation rates of 54 percent for all male students and 51 percent for all male athletes, at the same colleges during the same time period. In the year 2000 men's basketball players had the lowest graduation rates of athletes in any sport; only 56 percent of white players and 34 percent of black players earned degrees between 1993–94 and 1999–2000.[32] In other words, football players and men's basketball players were less likely than other male college students to graduate within six years—even though they received both full scholarships and formal academic assistance while in school.

These data reflect an "achievement gap" that exists not only between athletes and nonathletes but also between athletes in "revenue" sports (football and men's basketball) and athletes in "non-revenue" sports (all other sports). A recent social-science study concluded that this gap is the result of two factors, namely, that (1) football players and men's basketball players are disproportionately African Americans whose precollege educations have been inadequate, and (2) the time demands of revenue sports hinder academic success, especially for athletes who are academically underprepared for college.[33] Thus, the academic condition of big-time college sports demands dramatic change just as much as the financial condition does.

The social costs of college sports are high, too, and increasingly, they also cry out for major change. One social cost of college sports is the exploitation of athletes by colleges and universities. A prominent example of athletic exploitation is colleges' history of using the physical talents of athletes for four years, then, when the athletes have exhausted their eligibility, casting them to the four winds without a degree or marketable skills other than athletic talent, which will take only a fortunate few to the NFL or to the

NBA. The principal victims of this type of exploitation have been African-American males, who are frequently the stars of college football and basketball teams, but who are just as frequently casualties of big-time college sports, which their low graduation rates reflect.

Two related examples of athletic exploitation are freshman eligibility to compete in sports and annually renewable athletic scholarships, both of which began in the early 1970s. The NCAA made freshmen eligible for varsity competition in 1972, principally in order to save colleges the considerable expense of maintaining separate freshman teams, which had existed prior to 1972. Evidently, the needs of freshmen to make the often-difficult social, academic, and athletic transition from high school to college as smoothly as possible were not sufficiently compelling to override the needs of athletic directors to reduce the costs of their sports programs. In 1973, only a year after instituting freshman eligibility for varsity competition, the NCAA converted athletic scholarships, which had been four-year grants ever since their establishment in 1956, into one-year, annually renewable grants.[34]

Taken together, freshman eligibility and annually renewable athletic scholarships turn the NCAA's ideal of the "student-athlete" on its head. They force college students who play varsity sports to be athletes first and students second, if at all. Freshman eligibility in this television-driven era results in freshman football players at Division I-A colleges playing in regular-season football games before they have attended college classes. Annually renewable scholarships mean that some of those freshmen will lose their access to a college education before sophomore year begins because they have failed to satisfy their coaches' expectations. If requiring a college student to play a football game before his first class meets and depriving him of access to a college education because of his athletic deficiencies are not exploitation, then the NCAA has redefined that word, and my dictionary is obsolete. My dictionary says that *to exploit* is "to take advantage of" or "to use selfishly for one's own ends," and that is what freshman eligibility and annually renewable scholarships enable colleges to do to their athletes.[35]

Ironically, the NCAA invented the term "student-athlete" in support of its insistence that college football and basketball players are students and amateur athletes, not employees of their colleges who are entitled to workers' compensation when injured on the job. The denial of workers' compensation benefits, or a comparable alternative, to athletes who have suffered serious injuries while playing for their colleges may be the most compelling evidence that the NCAA and its members exploit college athletes. To add insult to injury, annually renewable scholarships permit colleges not only to deny seriously injured athletes workers' compensation benefits but also to rescind their athletic scholarships if they are unable to play or to play up to the coach's expectations.[36]

Under these circumstances it is not surprising that athletes try to exploit their own athletic ability for financial rewards. The behavior of the adults who run college sports signals that the games exist for the purpose of making money, so the athletes conclude that they should share in the profits for which their sweat and talents are responsible. NCAA rules prohibit them from sharing legally, but some do so illegally. In a 1989 survey of professional football players, 31 percent of the respondents admitted to having accepted illegal payments during their college careers, and 48 percent of the respondents said that they knew of other athletes who took such payments during college.[37] Former North Carolina State University basketball player Charles Shackleford, who left school in favor of the NBA after his junior season, admitted to having accepted approximately $65,000 in illegal payments during his three years in Raleigh.[38]

These examples show that college athletes are not always victims; they can be villains, too. Recently, their villainy, which has often been criminal, has become a major social cost of big-time college sports. This is sad and disturbing, but it is no more surprising than athletes' acceptance of under-the-table payments from athletic boosters. If the pressures for institutional fame and fortune through sports can cause colleges to admit athletes who are academically deficient, surely those same pressures can and do cause colleges to admit athletes who are not solid citizens. Evidently, colleges admit such athletes routinely because newspaper sports pages report criminal behavior by college athletes with frightening regularity.

Between May of 1996 and May of 1997, authorities arrested 18 members of the Virginia Tech football team, including 2 for rape. In October 1996 between 35 and 50 members of the University of Rhode Island's football team attacked a fraternity house in retribution for 2 teammates having been asked to leave the house during a party the previous weekend. The football players broke windows and doors, and assaulted members of the fraternity, 3 of whom required hospital treatment.[39] Such incidents are not isolated. In 1995, 220 college athletes were the subjects of criminal prosecutions, for alleged crimes that ranged from illegal gambling to manslaughter. In 1995 and 1996, 112 college athletes were charged with sexual assault or with domestic violence. Most of the victims were female college students.[40]

Gambling by athletes is a growing social cost of big-time college sports. It reflects their conclusion that adults make money from college sports, so they should do so, too. This thinking is especially troublesome when it causes athletes to use their privileged positions in order to make money from gambling. According to a recent University of Michigan study, it is not uncommon for college football and basketball players to try to exploit their athletic status for financial gain through gambling. In January of 1999, *U.S.A. Today* reported the results of the Michigan study, which revealed that more than 5 percent of college football and men's basketball players have either given inside information about their teams to gamblers (usually their classmates), bet on games in which they have played, or shaved points in return for money.[41] One athlete, former Northwestern running back Dennis

Lundy, went so far as to fumble the football intentionally near the goal line during a close game with Iowa in 1994 in order to save his bet.[42]

Ironically, Lundy's bet nullified what *New York Times* columnist Robert Lipsyte referred to as "Northwestern University's bet," during the mid-1990s, that the millions of dollars it had spent to improve its football and men's basketball teams, which were perennial doormats in the Big Ten Conference, "would pay off in national happy news, increased enrollment, and alumni donations."[43] The payoff was brief; applications to Northwestern increased after the Wildcats' trip to the Rose Bowl in 1995 but declined again amidst the revelations of the gambling scandals in both football and men's basketball. The scandals enraged many Northwestern alumni, who are justifiably proud of their alma mater's lofty academic reputation; some alumni vowed not to contribute any money to Northwestern until it adopted a "sane athletics policy."[44]

A sane athletics policy should include subjecting coaches who exhibit abusive or otherwise inappropriate behavior to the same penalties that other college employees would receive for such behavior. When a coach escapes punishment because of an outstanding win-loss record, another social cost of college sports is revealed, namely, a loss of perspective that elevates athletic success above all other values. A clear example of a loss of perspective is Indiana University's tolerance of basketball coach Bob Knight's abusive and boorish behavior toward his players, athletic department colleagues, and the press corps for twenty-nine years, during which his teams won three national championships and Knight became one of the most successful coaches in the history of college basketball.

In May of 2000, IU president Myles Brand declined to fire Knight despite a videotape that showed the coach grabbing a player by the neck during basketball practice and evidence that he had been physically abusive to several athletic department employees, including a female secretary, during his stormy tenure in Bloomington. Instead, Brand announced that there would be a zero-tolerance policy toward such behavior in the future; therefore, if Knight behaved abusively again, he would be punished.[45] This stance begs the question why Coach Knight, who is an intelligent and articulate sixty-three-year-old man, did not intuitively know that pushing an assistant coach into a bookcase and throwing a vase at a secretary are unacceptable forms of behavior in the workplace. Still, if he did not know this before May of 2000, he should have known it by the following September, when, after an undergraduate greeted him by saying, "Hey, Knight," he held the student by the arm and delivered a lecture about the importance of respecting one's elders. By that point, even President Brand and the IU Board of Trustees had lost patience with Knight, and they fired him shortly thereafter.[46]

A professor of art, economics, or chemistry at Indiana University could not have behaved as Bob Knight did and remained employed there for twenty-nine years, no matter how gifted a teacher or how talented and famous a researcher that professor might have been. The Nobel laureate or the National Book Award winner would have been fired for assaulting a colleague, and the Hall of Fame basketball coach should have been fired for such behavior, too. To do otherwise is to permit the athletic tail to wag the academic dog, which defeats the purposes for which a college or university exists.

The athletic tail has wagged the academic dog on American campuses for decades, during which the public has become cynical about the educational value of college sports. A 1991 survey by Louis Harris and Associates revealed that 75 percent of the 1,255 adults polled agreed: "Intercollegiate athletics have got out of control," and "In too many universities with big-time athletics programs the academic mission has not been given proper priority over the athletics program."[47] A 1997 CBS News poll of 1,037 adults found that 47 percent of the respondents agreed that college sports were "overemphasized," as did 62 percent of the college graduates surveyed.[48] Cynicism peaks when a scandal is revealed, and the offending college must bear the brunt of that cynicism. The comments of Rev. John LoSchiavo—who was the president of the University of San Francisco (USF) in 1982, when USF disbanded its basketball team as a result of NCAA violations by players and boosters—illustrate this point. According to Father LoSchiavo, "The price the university has had to pay for those problems has been much greater than the heavy financial price. There is no way of measuring the damage that has been done to the university's most priceless asset, its integrity and its reputation."[49]

There is a way to reduce the high financial, academic, and social costs of college sports, though, and it lies in changing the purpose of those sports from commerce to participation. This is no pipe dream, despite the popularity of the games and the economic power of the college-sports industry. The ray of hope for change is Title IX, the federal law that revolutionized college sports for women.

A RAY OF HOPE

Congress enacted Title IX of the Education Amendments Act on June 23, 1972. Title IX states that "[n]o person in the United States shall, on the basis of sex, be excluded from participation in, be denied the benefits of, or be subjected to discrimination under any education program or activity receiving Federal financial assistance. . . ."[50] In 1975 the Secretary of Health, Education, and Welfare (HEW) put into effect regulations that were designed to enforce Title IX in schools and colleges. Consequently, during the 1970s schools and colleges expanded athletic opportunities for their female students significantly.

The impact of Title IX has been clear and dramatic. In 1972 only one girl in twenty-seven played a sport sponsored by her high school, and colleges spent a total of $100,000 on athletic scholarships for women. By 1996, one girl in three played a sport sponsored by her high school, and colleges spent a total of $180 million on athletic scholarships for women.[51] The participation of women in college sports increased fourfold between 1970 and 1999, from 31,000 to 110,000.[52] The little girls of the 1970s, whom Title IX enabled to hone their athletic skills in high school and in college, became the women of the 1996 Summer Olympic Games who won America's first gold medals in soccer and softball.

Despite such progress, Title IX remains controversial. Advocates for Title IX are dissatisfied because relatively few colleges are in compliance with its requirement of "equal opportunity" for males and females in athletics. Most colleges have enrollments that are about 50 percent male and 50 percent female, but in 1998–99 women were 42 percent of the athletes and accounted for 42 percent of the athletic scholarship funds, 31 percent of the funds spent on recruiting, 34 percent of the funds spent on coaching salaries, and 33 percent of the total athletic operating expenses at 311 Division I colleges surveyed by the *Chronicle of Higher Education*.[53] The advocates argue that in order for colleges to comply with Title IX, the percentages of women students who are athletes must be substantially proportional to the percentages of women in undergraduate student populations. Thus, if women are 51 percent of the undergraduates at a college, they should be at least 46 percent of the athletes at that college. Critics of Title IX are also dissatisfied. They charge that the substantial-proportionality standard has forced colleges to disband men's teams—especially in non-revenue sports such as swimming, wrestling, and gymnastics—in order to add women's teams for purposes of Title IX compliance.[54] The critics note that disbanding men's non-revenue teams defeats the purpose of Title IX, which is to maximize opportunities for both men and women to participate in college sports.

Financial constraints exacerbate this controversy. During the 1970s and the 1980s neither federal courts nor federal agencies enforced Title IX aggressively, and colleges spent lavishly on men's sports, especially football and basketball. Today, federal courts require colleges to meet the substantial-proportionality standard, regardless of the cost. The athletic director's dilemma is how to fund big-time football and men's basketball, plus women's sports, without gutting men's non-revenue sports. The athletic director's dilemma is also the reformer's golden opportunity. Title IX is not to blame for the current dilemma. The colleges are to blame, and they can solve the dilemma by abandoning the "commercial" model of college sports in favor of the "participation" model that this book advocates.

The price tag for the commercial model—which features football rosters of more than one hundred players, massive arenas, nationwide recruiting of athletes, plush training facilities, intersectional travel to play games, and princely salaries for coaches—is so high that when the cost of women's teams is added to it, the total strains most athletic department budgets to the break-

ing point. Large football rosters make it difficult to comply with the proportionality standard because no women's sports have rosters of comparable
size. There is not enough money available at most colleges to comply by
adding women's teams while keeping the number of men's teams constant.
Yet colleges must comply with Title IX, or they will face expensive litigation
and court-ordered compliance. This environment is fertile ground for the
growth of a new model of college sports. Sports scholars Allen Sack and
Ellen Staurowsky recognized this when they wrote, in 1998, that "Title IX
and the struggle for gender equity have a greater potential for restoring the
educational integrity of college sport than any reform passed by the
N.C.A.A. in the past 100 years."[55]

Educational integrity will be one of the positive results of the replacement
of the commercial model of college sports by the participation model. If the
participation model had been in place in 1994, Clemson University would
not have disbanded its twenty-five-man wrestling team in order to add a
women's crew without having first reduced the size of its football roster,
which included more than one hundred men.[56] If the participation model
had been in place in 2000, the University of Miami (FL) would not have
disbanded its men's crew and its men's swimming team in order to comply
with Title IX without having trimmed the size of its football roster first.[57]
If the participation model were in place today, colleges would not be dividing
their men's teams into "tiers" increasingly, giving lavish financial support to
top-tier teams and demoting those in the bottom tier to "glorified club
teams" with little financial support and few coaches.[58] Disbanding or demoting men's non-revenue teams violates the spirit of Title IX, which seeks
to increase, not decrease, athletic opportunities. Disbanding these teams also
defeats the only legitimate purpose for college sports, which is the enhancement of an undergraduate education. Non-revenue sports enhance an undergraduate education because they offer opportunities for athletic
participation of which the primary beneficiaries are the participants themselves.

Colleges will stop disbanding, or assigning second-class status to, men's
non-revenue sports when colleges seize the opportunity that Title IX provides and adopt the participation model, which would reduce roster sizes in
football and would end athletic scholarships and the off-campus recruitment
of high school athletes, among other things. The participation model would
enable colleges to comply with Title IX and to save men's sports such as
wrestling and swimming, thereby providing athletic opportunities for more
students at less cost than is possible under the commercial model. Colleges
would cease to view sports as a source of revenue and their "revenue sports"
as farm teams for professional leagues. College sports would achieve gender
equity, fiscal sanity, academic integrity, and personal responsibility, which
they have not achieved, and cannot achieve, by following the commercial
model. Participation must replace commerce as the primary purpose of col-

lege sports in order to slash the financial, academic, and social costs of the games.

PARTICIPATION, NOT COMMERCE

This book advocates that colleges replace the commercial model of college sports with the participation model, and it shows reformers how to attain this goal. It begins from the premise that college sports are valuable only when they enhance an undergraduate education by teaching skills that a student is unlikely to learn in a classroom or a laboratory. It argues, therefore, that the principal beneficiaries of the college-sports experience should be the students who play the games, not their coaches or the fans, and certainly not sports journalists, television networks, or college-town innkeepers and automobile dealers. The change of beneficiaries will not occur unless college faculty and others who value higher education recognize the exorbitant price that colleges pay for elusive, temporary athletic glory and become advocates for the participation model. Faculty members must lead this fight because they are responsible for ensuring the academic integrity of the courses they teach and the degrees they award. *A New Season* will show them and their allies how the participation model works, how to fight for its adoption, and how to win the fight.

Thus, *A New Season* is part celebration and part call-to-arms. It celebrates the educational potential of college sports but rejects and seeks to end the antieducational practices that ruin college sports when the commercial model governs. Chapter 2 will trace the origins of these practices as it discusses the history of college sports.

NOTES

1. Nicci Rinaldi, Email message to the author, April 4, 2001.
2. Don Mahler, "What a Strange Trip It's Been for Rinaldi," *The Valley News*, October 16, 1995, p. B1.
3. Ibid.
4. Rinaldi, E-mail message.
5. Mahler, "What a Strange Trip It's Been for Rinaldi," *The Valley News*, October 16, 1995, p. B1.
6. Nicci Rinaldi, telephone interview with the author, April 18, 2001.
7. Andrew Zimbalist, *Unpaid Professionals: Commercialism and Conflict in Big-Time College Sports* (Princeton, N.J.: Princeton University Press, 1999), pp. 3–5.
8. Ibid., p. 150.
9. Welch Suggs, "Football's Have-Nots Contemplate Their Place in the N.C.A.A.," *The Chronicle of Higher Education*, June 30, 2000, p. A47.
10. Welch Suggs, "Gap Grows Between the Haves and Have-Nots in College Sports," *The Chronicle of Higher Education*, November 17, 2000, p. A73.
11. Zimbalist, *Unpaid Professionals*, p. 194.

12. Welch Suggs, "More Small Universities Are Getting Rid of Football," *The Chronicle of Higher Education*, February 21, 2003, p. A33.

13. Ted Gup, "Losses Surpass Victories, By Far, in Big-Time College Sports," *The Chronicle of Higher Education*, December 18, 1998, p. A52.

14. Ibid.

15. Zimbalist, *Unpaid Professionals*, p. 166.

16. Roger G. Noll, "The Economics of Intercollegiate Sports," in Judith Andre and David N. James, eds., *Rethinking College Athletics* (Philadelphia: Temple University Press, 1991), p. 202.

17. James J. Duderstadt, *Intercollegiate Athletics and the American University: A University President's Perspective* (Ann Arbor, Mich.: The University of Michigan Press, 2000), pp. 127–128.

18. Brian L. Porto, *Completing the Revolution: Title IX as Catalyst for an Alternative Model of College Sports* 8, no. 2 Seton Hall Journal of Sport Law 351, 389–390 (1998).

19. Murray Sperber, *Beer and Circus: How Big-Time College Sports is Crippling Undergraduate Education* (New York: Henry Holt and Company, 2000), p. 26.

20. Zimbalist, *Unpaid Professionals*, p. 28.

21. Walter Byers, *Unsportsmanlike Conduct: Exploiting College Athletes* (Ann Arbor, Mich.: The University of Michigan Press, 1995), pp. 304–305.

22. *Ross v. Creighton University*, 957 F.2d 410 (7th Cir. 1992).

23. Zimbalist, *Unpaid Professionals*, p. 36.

24. Allen L. Sack and Ellen J. Staurowsky, *College Athletes for Hire: The Evolution and Legacy of the NCAA's Amateur Myth* (Westport, Conn.: Praeger, 1998), p. 95.

25. John R. Gerdy, *The Successful College Athletic Program: The New Standard* (Phoenix: American Council on Education and the Oryx Press, 1997), p. 72.

26. Robert L. Simon, "Intercollegiate Athletics: Do They Belong on Campus?" in Andre and James, eds., *Rethinking College Athletics*, p. 54.

27. Gerdy, *The Successful College Athletic Program*, p. 72.

28. Duderstadt, *Intercollegiate Athletics and the American University*, p. 79.

29. See Sperber, *Beer and Circus*, p. 28.

30. Doug Single, "The Role of Directors of Athletics in Restoring Integrity to Intercollegiate Sport," in Richard E. Lapchick and John Brooks Slaughter, *The Rules of the Game: Ethics in College Sport* (New York: American Council on Education and Macmillan Publishing Company, 1989), pp. 157–158.

31. Jim Naughton, "Athletes on Top-Ranked Teams Lack Grades and Test Scores of Other Students," *The Chronicle of Higher Education*, July 25, 1997, pp. A43–A44.

32. Welch Suggs, "Graduation Rates for Athletes Hold Steady," *The Chronicle of Higher Education*, December 1, 2000, p. A47.

33. Tanya R. Upthegrove, Vincent J. Roscigno, and Camille Zabrinsky Charles, "Big Money Collegiate Sports: Racial Concentration, Contradictory Pressures, and Academic Performance," *Social Science Quarterly* 80, no. 4 (December, 1999): 718–737.

34. Sack and Staurowsky, *College Athletes for Hire*, p. xii.

35. *Random House Webster's Dictionary*, 3d ed., s.v. "exploit."

36. Sack and Staurowsky, *College Athletes for Hire*, p. 6.

37. Zimbalist, *Unpaid Professionals*, p. 25.

38. Ibid., p. 24.

39. Ibid., pp. 48–49.

40. Jeffrey R. Benedict, "Colleges Must Act Decisively When Scholarship Athletes Run Afoul of the Law," *The Chronicle of Higher Education*, May 9, 1997, p. B6.

41. Sperber, *Beer and Circus*, p. 210.

42. John Sayle Watterson, *College Football: History, Spectacle, Controversy* (Baltimore: Johns Hopkins University Press, 2000), p. 378.

43. Sperber, *Beer and Circus*, p. 211.

44. Ibid., pp. 211–212.

45. Alexander Wolff, "General Amnesty," *Sports Illustrated*, May 22, 2000, p. 42: Joe Drape, "Knight Gets 'Last Chance' to Coach at Indiana," *The New York Times*, May 16, 2000, p. A27.

46. Welch Suggs, "Ouster at Indiana," *The Chronicle of Higher Education*, September 22, 2000, p. A49; Alexander Wolff, "Knight Fall," *Sports Illustrated*, September 18, 2000, p. 54; Joe Drape, "Citing His Behavior, Indiana's President Fires Coach Knight," *The New York Times*, September 11, 2000, p. A1.

47. Brian L. Porto, *Completing the Revolution: Title IX as Catalyst for an Alternative Model of College Sports*, 8, no. 2 Seton Hall Journal of Sport Law 351, 394 (1998).

48. Ibid.

49. Donald Chu, *The Character of American Higher Education and Intercollegiate Sport* (Albany, N.Y.: State University of New York Press, 1989), p. 206.

50. This language appears in Title 20 of the United States Code at section 1681(a).

51. Mary Leonard, "Sporting Chance," *Boston Sunday Globe*, June 1, 1997, p. C1.

52. Jackie Koszczuk, "Gender Equity in Sports: Will Hastert Go to the Mat?" *Congressional Quarterly Weekly Report*, March 27, 1999, p. 745.

53. Welch Suggs, "Uneven Progress for Women's Sports," *The Chronicle of Higher Education*, April 7, 2000, p. A52.

54. Brian L. Porto, *Completing the Revolution: Title IX as Catalyst for an Alternative Model of College Sports*, 8, no. 2 Seton Hall Journal of Sport Law 351, 355 (1998).

55. Sack and Staurowsky, *College Athletes for Hire*, p. xiii.

56. Jackie Koszczuk, "Gender Equity in Sports: Will Hastert Go to the Mat?" *Congressional Quarterly Weekly Report*, March 27, 1999, p. 745.

57. Welch Suggs, "U of Miami Drops 2 Men's Sports," *The Chronicle of Higher Education*, March 24, 2000, p. A56.

58. Welch Suggs, "Female Athletes Thrive, but Budget Pressures Loom," *The Chronicle of Higher Education*, May 18, 2001, p. A45.

CHAPTER 2

SEASONS PAST

A BRIEF HISTORY OF COLLEGE SPORTS

A BOAT RACE IN NEW HAMPSHIRE

The old French saying: The more things change, the more they stay the same, usually describes politics, but it describes college sports, too. Almost all of the financial, academic, and social problems that plague college sports today existed in 1900. They were the offspring of a fateful marriage between athletic commerce and higher education that was well established by that date.

Athletic commerce and higher education began courting on August 3, 1852, a "perfect summer day, cloudless, moderately warm, with a light zephyr from the northwest," when Harvard and Yale competed in America's first college-sports contest, a boat race on Lake Winnipesaukee in New Hampshire.[1] The race drew an estimated one thousand spectators, and corporate support made it possible.[2] James Elkins, the superintendent of the Boston, Concord, and Montreal Railroad, paid for the athletes to travel to, and to stay at, the lakeside resort village of Center Harbor.[3] Elkins's support for the race was the first "date" in a long, but troubled relationship between athletic commerce and American higher education that would change the latter in ways that nobody could have imagined in 1852.

AN UNLIKELY MARRIAGE

The first date began a courtship that spanned the last four decades of the nineteenth century. During this period students organized and participated in intercollegiate athletic competitions with increasing seriousness. In 1858 student representatives from four colleges formed the College Union Regatta Association, which sponsored popular intercollegiate boat races in 1859 and 1860.[4] In 1869, Harvard competed in a boat race against Oxford University on the Thames River in London. This event spurred American undergraduates, in 1870, to form the Rowing Association of America, which sponsored regattas in which up to sixteen northeastern colleges competed.[5] The students' eagerness to win induced them to endure rigorous, twice-daily workouts, to follow a strict dietary regimen, and to hire professional coaches and trainers in order to gain a potential advantage over their rivals from other colleges.

Such actions reflected a uniquely American attitude toward sport, which stood in stark contrast to the "amateurism" that British undergraduates practiced. The British "gentleman-amateur" opposed systematic training that threatened to transform sport from a pastime into an occupation. Sport existed at British universities at the turn of the twentieth century only to provide recreation for the participants. It was an integral part of the liberal-arts education of a gentleman, but it was not a form of public entertainment.[6] An American observer of British sport during this time captured the difference between British and American attitudes toward sport when he referred to American oarsmen who trained year-round by using indoor tanks for stationary rowing. He noted: "Englishmen would never dream of taking such pains. They have a vague feeling that such action is unsportsmanlike."[7]

It is not surprising that most Americans rejected the British view of sport, because the rejection of British institutions and traditions was a prominent organizing principle in the development of the United States. Americans had previously rejected such hallmarks of British society as the monarchy, a government-supported church, the parliamentary system of government, and titles of nobility, so it was easy for them to reject amateurism in sport, too. Amateurism, like the monarchy and titles of nobility, conflicted with Americans' preference for an open society that rewarded success achieved through talent and effort, regardless of one's social station. Amateurism rewarded heredity instead of achievement, thereby preserving England's class structure because it restricted participation in sport to members of the upper class, who enjoyed the wealth and the leisure that amateurism required. Moreover, there was no hereditary aristocracy in America, as there was in England, to uphold the amateur ideal in sport.[8] Consequently, American undergraduates developed games that reflected American values, including organizational efficiency, an emphasis on winning, and a penchant for the measurement of results and the achievement of records.[9]

Rowing was not the only sport that inspired the devotion and the industry of nineteenth-century undergraduates. Indeed, baseball was the most widely played sport on college campuses throughout the nineteenth century. Amherst College and Williams College played the first intercollegiate baseball game in Pittsfield, Massachusetts, on July 1, 1859.[10] Ten years later colleges throughout America were fielding baseball teams in response to a student demand for intercollegiate baseball. Students began to link the prestige of their college to the success of its baseball team. In 1870, when the Massachusetts Agricultural College (now the University of Massachusetts at Amherst) defeated Harvard in baseball, the students at the Agricultural College were ecstatic because they thought that the victory gave their school "standing as a real college." Evidently, the Massachusetts Legislature thought so, too, because it increased the annual appropriation to the Agricultural College shortly thereafter.[11]

Despite the popularity of rowing and baseball, no sport won the hearts or inflamed the passions of nineteenth-century undergraduates as much as football did. Princeton and Rutgers played the first intercollegiate football game at New Brunswick, New Jersey, in 1869.[12] Modern college football fans would not recognize that game as football, though. It was actually a game of soccer, or what was known then as "association football," the rules of which prohibited running with the ball.[13] Soccer might have become the dominant sport on campus in the late nineteenth century had Harvard, then the preeminent athletic power among American colleges, not rejected it in 1874 in favor of its own version of football, which grew out of rugby and permitted running with the ball.[14] Two years after Harvard adopted "rugby football" as its own, the game became popular at elite eastern colleges, and college football as we know it was born. Harvard, Yale, Princeton, and Columbia formed the student-run Intercollegiate Football Association, and Yale beat Princeton for the first championship of college football on Thanksgiving Day in 1876.[15]

Unlike rowing and baseball, football was popular not only with the undergraduates on campus but with the public off campus, too. Indeed, college presidents of the late nineteenth century discovered that football was much more effective in attracting public attention, even devotion, to their institutions than was a reputation for rigorous course work, religiosity, or inspired teaching.[16] Therefore, they tried to use football as a means of attracting public support, which they hoped would yield both students and dollars. In short, colleges married athletic commerce to higher education in hopes that the popularity of the former would give them the resources necessary to achieve their goals for the latter.

The pressure on colleges during the nineteenth century to attract students and dollars to their campuses influenced the commercialization of college sports far more than the popularity of football did. Indeed, without the pressure on colleges to increase enrollments and to generate revenue, it is unlikely that college football would have become a commercial enterprise despite its popularity with the public. In more favorable financial circumstances, colleges would not have felt a need to make the monetary commitments and the ethical compromises that commercial success in sports required.

The sheer number of colleges in America contributed to their fierce competition for students and dollars. There were nine colleges in America in 1775, when the Revolutionary War began; by 1861, when the Civil War began, there were 250.[17] At the end of the nineteenth century, England had four universities for a population of 23 million people, while Ohio had thirty-seven colleges and universities for a population of just 3 million people.[18] One reason for the proliferation of colleges in the United States during the nineteenth century was federalism, which divided political power between a national government and state governments and caused states to compete with each other in numerous ways, including the creation of colleges and universities. Natural rivalries between neighboring states made each state reluctant to lose its capable young residents to a neighbor's college or university, so it created its own institutions in order to encourage its best and brightest to stay at home.[19]

The size of the United States and the difficulties of travel, especially early in the nineteenth century, also encouraged the founding of numerous colleges, which gave students access to higher education close to home.[20] The most important reason, though, for the establishment of many colleges in America was that after 1800 the Protestant religious denominations devoted considerable energy to founding colleges in the new territories of the "West," now the states of the Midwest. The Protestants' desire to spread the faith is the major reason why, for example, eleven colleges were founded in Kentucky before 1865, twenty-one colleges were founded in Illinois before 1868, and thirteen colleges were founded in Iowa before 1869.[21]

These sectarian colleges, like their state-supported counterparts, struggled to attract students and dollars because most Americans did not see value in higher education beyond the training of young men for the ministry. By and large, Americans were not impressed with men who were formally educated; instead, they were impressed with self-taught, self-made men who had achieved wealth, political power, and/or social prominence without formal education. This mind-set made it difficult for colleges to convince the public of the worth of higher education as an opportunity for rigorous intellectual training.[22] Moreover, their European counterparts could cater to an intellectual and socioeconomic elite, thanks to generous governmental subsidies, but American colleges had to attract the children of farmers and merchants in order to survive.[23] Consequently, American colleges needed to be engines of social mobility; they could not afford to be cloisters of intellectual inquiry.

Colleges therefore encouraged, even adopted, a measure of anti-intellectualism in order to make higher education attractive to young people and their parents. One prominent example was the argument that higher education rewarded students with higher incomes after graduation than they could have attained had they not gone to college.[24] Another example was the arrival on campus during the 1870s, of what are commonly known today as "extracurricular activities." To be sure, these activities were not entirely anti-intellectual. Indeed, they included literary societies, clubs, journals, and organizations that enhanced the curriculum—which emphasized Latin, Greek, mathematics, and religion—by increasing students' awareness of science, English literature, history, music, and art, which the curriculum usually neglected.[25]

The two most prominent extracurricular activities in the late nineteenth century, though, were Greek-letter fraternities and organized sports, which, arguably, remain the two most prominent extracurricular activities on American campuses today. Fraternities existed at most of the colleges of New York State and New England by 1840, and they spread to colleges in Ohio, Indiana, Michigan, and Kentucky before 1850.[26] They spread quickly because they offered an escape from the dreariness of the classical curriculum and of long winters in small, isolated communities and from the regimented collegiate routine, which began each day with required prayers before dawn, followed by monotonous recitation periods, and ended with required prayers after dark.[27]

Organized sports became popular on college campuses soon after the establishment of fraternities. Both fraternities and sports satisfied undergraduates' need for diversions from their academic tasks at a time when Americans' traditional distrust of play and amusement, inherited from Puritan ancestors, was gradually dissolving. Many college administrators welcomed the popularity of sports on campus, at least initially, because sports promised to exhaust the undergraduates' abundant physical energy, thereby leaving them with less zeal for hazing and other excesses.[28]

Football quickly became the most popular extracurricular activity after 1880, both for participants and spectators, and college football games became major social events in the Northeast by the 1890s. In 1893 the annual Thanksgiving Day game between Yale and Princeton in New York City presented a cornucopia of social opportunities for the members of New York society, and a similar abundance of commercial opportunities for the city's merchants. Hotels were filled with guests who had tickets for the game. On Fifth Avenue, blue-and-white Yale banners hung from the mansions of the Vanderbilt and the Whitney families, respectively. The mansions of the Sloanes, the Alexanders, and the Scribners displayed the orange-and-black of Princeton. Clergymen shortened their Thanksgiving services so that they and their congregations could get to the game in time.[29] College football was already big business in America.

Many college presidents saw football as an unparalleled promotional tool with which they could build their institutions, both academically and financially. Football's greatest promise was that it would improve the public's image of higher education generally and of "college men" in particular. During the nineteenth century newspapers and other popular media depicted the "typical" male undergraduate as a "dyspeptic, shriveled up, and cowering scholar" whose only interests lay in acquiring useless knowledge and in cultivating an effeminate and ineffective spirituality.[30] This critique reflected

anti-intellectualism born of evangelical Christianity, democratic values, and
a passion for business. It assumed that intellectuals were "pretentious, con-
ceited, effeminate, and snobbish," if not also "immoral, dangerous, and sub-
versive."[31] Football, which embodied action and quick thinking, had much
in common with America's business ethic, and college presidents hoped that
it would transform the image of higher education by depicting the college
man as rugged, fearless, and capable of holding his own in the rough-and-
tumble world outside academe.[32] The presidents also hoped that football
would attract to their institutions the financial support of the pragmatic business leaders who were prevalent on college boards of trustees by the turn of
the twentieth century.[33]

Furthermore, college presidents saw football as a democratic antidote to
the increasing number of rich men's sons on campus, especially at the elite
institutions in the East. In 1906, for example, President Hadley of Yale
remarked that football had taken "hold of the emotions of the student body
in such a way as to make class distinctions relatively unimportant," and that
it had made "the students get together in the old-fashioned democratic
way."[34] Indeed, football was an engine of social mobility that enabled the
athletically talented sons of Irish, Italian, and eastern European immigrants
to attend college and to enter the middle class after graduation. In western
Pennsylvania, football liberated thousands of immigrants' sons from the coal
mines in which their fathers toiled.[35]

Football's masculine image and its preference for talent over pedigree
inspired numerous colleges to embrace the game as a means of improving
their public standing in the short run and of ensuring their survival in the
long run. Fortunately for these colleges, several social forces converged in
America at the turn of the twentieth century to enable college football to
become a popular form of public entertainment and a major source of revenue on some campuses. Urbanization produced rising wages and increased
leisure time, which gave more people than ever before the wherewithal to
attend sporting events. Mass-circulation daily newspapers created and maintained fan loyalty. Locked in circulation wars in major cities, rival newspapers, such as the *Herald*, the *World*, and the *Journal* in New York City,
sought to expand their readership by adding coverage of sports, including
college football. Their football stories in October and November filled a
void in the sports calendar created by the conclusion of the baseball and
horse-racing seasons.[36] These stories gradually became a permanent feature
of the "sporting page" of newspapers, which aided colleges' efforts to appeal
to ordinary Americans because coverage of football on the sports pages replaced coverage on the society page as part of the social elite's leisure news.[37]
On the new sports pages, journalists celebrated college football players and
coaches and created the "football hero," whose physical prowess and quick
wits appealed to Americans' passion for action and distrust of intellectual-
ism.[38] The early sportswriters were rabid fans who shared their readers' love

of the local teams, players, and coaches, and this bond helped to spread the love of college football among Americans whose only link to higher education was their favorite college football team.[39]

Improvements in technology also helped to make college football popular and a commercial success. Trains made intersectional rivalries possible, and the telegraph enabled fans to root for the home team even when it played far away from home.[40] Newspaper accounts of these far-flung contests built college sports heroes into national heroes and made previously obscure colleges prominent.[41] For example, the University of Chicago achieved national recognition for its football prowess long before it earned a reputation as one of America's preeminent research universities.

The marriage between athletic commerce and higher education brought professionalism to college athletics, including the transfer of authority to govern college sports, principally football, from undergraduates to adults. The financial and public relations benefits of football made it too important for undergraduates to manage, so students yielded to adults the responsibility for hiring, firing, and paying coaches, scheduling and financing games and travel, building stadiums, and promoting the home team.[42] At most colleges, the faculty created an athletic committee, which was a buffer between the students, who usually wanted the faculty to keep its hands off sports, and faculty members, many of whom wished to restrict sports severely or even to eliminate them.[43] Gradually, alumni power increased, and faculty power decreased, on these athletic committees as alumni financial support for athletics translated into alumni governance of athletics.[44] Undergraduates lost control over the games in which they participated to administrators and alumni, who made athletic policy with precious little resistance from largely impotent or indifferent faculties. When faculties offered resistance, they rarely prevailed because presidents, trustees, coaches, and alumni usually outvoted them. More frequently, faculty representatives on athletic committees either supported professionalism in college sports or surrendered to it for fear of alienating their friends, neighbors, and colleagues by fighting it.[45]

Another hallmark of professionalism in college sports was the hiring of football coaches, often at salaries that exceeded even those paid to the most senior and celebrated faculty members. A case in point occurred at Harvard in December of 1904. The Crimson's football supporters were frustrated because for three consecutive years Yale had not only defeated Harvard in football but had held it scoreless. The Harvard boosters responded by hiring football coach Bill Reid, a twenty-six-year-old alumnus, at a salary of $7,000 a year. This salary, which made Reid the highest-paid collegiate coach in America, was 30 percent higher than the salary of the highest-paid Harvard professor, and it nearly equaled the salary of Charles Eliot, who had been Harvard's president since 1869.[46]

The clearest hallmark of professionalism, though, was the connection that college officials perceived between the prestige and the financial health of their institution, on the one hand, and the success of its football team, on the other. This connection was not only perceived but real at several colleges early in the twentieth century. For example, Yale earned a profit of more than $105,000 from football in 1903.[47] At the University of Chicago, revenue from football had so outpaced football expenses by 1905 that the surplus funded the other activities sponsored by the University's Department of Physical Culture and Athletics, which football coach Amos Alonzo Stagg chaired.[48]

The connection, real or imagined, between institutional wealth and football success put considerable pressure on coaches to win football games, with adverse consequences for players and their colleges. The most immediate consequence of this pressure was that for the players, football was transformed from recreation to occupation. As early as 1897, a University of Chicago player said: "I have no more fun in practice games. It isn't amusement or recreation anymore. It is nothing less than hard work."[49] In a 1904 magazine article, Frank Butterworth, a former All-American football player at Yale, noted the reason for this change. "Players like to win," Butterworth observed, "but head coaches, and especially paid coaches, ha[ve] to win."[50] The pressure to win restricted opportunities to play football to the most athletically talented students and relegated their less-physically-gifted classmates to watching the games. One University of California student lamented this situation, stating in 1904 that "Athletics as conducted now in our larger universities is for the few picked teams while the very students who most need physical development become stoop-shouldered rooting from backless bleachers."[51]

The pressure to win also spawned unethical practices. Chief among these was the enrollment of athletes with little or no regard for their academic qualifications. Colleges commonly hired "tramp athletes" to represent them on the football field, knowing full well that these athletes had no intention of matriculating as students, or even of playing a full season. An egregious example occurred in 1896 and featured Fielding H. Yost, who later became famous as the football coach at the University of Michigan. Yost, a "hefty, six-foot tall, 195-pound tackle for West Virginia University," "transferred" to Lafayette College in Pennsylvania in the autumn of 1896, just in time to play in the most important football game in Lafayette's history, against the University of Pennsylvania. Penn brought a 36-game winning streak into its game with Lafayette, but Lafayette ended the streak with a 6–4 win, aided by Yost. Shortly after the game, Yost transferred back to West Virginia University, where he completed work for a law degree six months later.[52]

Unlike Yost, Walter Eckersall, the University of Chicago's star quarterback, never earned a degree. Indeed, he compiled a notoriously weak academic record, but university authorities permitted him to remain enrolled until his football eligibility ended.[53] Undoubtedly, the university would have preferred that Eckersall's academic shortcomings remain an in-house secret, but that was not to be. Instead, they received national exposure in 1905, when *Collier's* magazine dubbed Eckersall "simply an athletic ward" of the university whose academic qualifications were substantially less than those of the "most poorly prepared freshman."[54]

Freedom from academic responsibilities was not always sufficient to keep a star athlete on campus at the turn of the century. Therefore, being an "athletic ward" of a university proved to be lucrative for some football players, especially Yale tackle James Hogan. Yale lured Hogan to New Haven with free tuition, a suite in Vanderbilt Hall, free meals, a trip to Cuba, the exclusive right to sell scorecards at football games, and a job as a cigarette agent for the American Tobacco Company.[55]

Thus, by 1905, when Bill Reid began his coaching duties at Harvard, Walter Eckersall was helping Amos Alonzo Stagg to build a football dynasty at Chicago, and Fielding Yost was building a dynasty of his own at Michigan, athletic commerce and higher education were an old married couple. Ironically, the marriage thrived because of social forces that had little to do with sport, including demographic changes, technological developments, colleges' pressing need to attract public support, and a growing acceptance by Americans of play and amusement. Sports fans revered this marriage, and college presidents blessed it, notwithstanding the attendant abuses, because it promised to yield students and dollars. The marriage survives—despite more than a century of stresses and strains—because colleges still pursue students and dollars through sports and fans still love "their" Hokies, Trojans, or Fighting Irish.

GROWING PAINS

Time tested the marriage between athletic commerce and higher education. The first test resulted from the brutality of college football, which reached a crisis level in 1905. At the conclusion of the 1905 season, the *Chicago Tribune* reported that 18 college and high school students had died and that 159 had been injured while playing football that season.[56] The principal culprit in these tragedies was the "mass play," wherein offensive players linked arms in order to protect the ballcarrier while pushing and pulling him toward the opponent's goal line. In college football the carnage began on the first Saturday of the season when during a game between Columbia and Wesleyan, a Wesleyan player kicked a downed Columbia ballcarrier in the stomach. A bench-clearing brawl followed, in which even the Columbia coach participated, and mayhem reigned until police officers restored order.[57] Late in the season, on November 25, Union College end Harold Moore died when he received a blow to the head from another player's knee while making a tackle during a game with New York University (NYU).[58]

Ironically, this tragedy, and most of the violence of the 1905 season, occurred *after* a meeting at the White House between President Theodore

Roosevelt and representatives of Harvard, Yale, and Princeton that aimed to end brutality in college football. President Roosevelt loved the game, but he believed that it had become unnecessarily violent. He was eager to preserve it by eliminating extreme and intentional acts of violence that went beyond aggressive blocking and hard tackling. Therefore, on October 9, 1905, two days after the first Saturday of the season, he summoned to the White House the head football coaches and the chairs of the alumni committees from Harvard, Yale, and Princeton, respectively, to meet with him and Secretary of State Elihu Root.[59] The president asked the alumni leaders to draft an agreement on the train ride home that included their pledges to abide by the rules of fair play on the gridiron, and they complied.[60]

The violence of the 1905 season, therefore, reflects the failure of the White House meeting to end brutality in college football. Still, tragedy is the birthplace of reform. The death of Harold Moore spurred Columbia and MIT to abolish football, and it convinced Stanford and the University of California to replace football with rugby.[61] More importantly, though, Moore's death prompted Henry B. McCracken, the chancellor of NYU, to organize a meeting in New York City aimed at ending brutality in college football. On December 5, 1905, the presidents of thirteen colleges attended this meeting, during which they voted against the abolition of football but in favor of reform, and in favor of a general meeting of all football-playing institutions.[62] The second, larger meeting, which occurred on December 28, also in New York City, and which attracted representatives from sixty-eight colleges, produced two important results: namely, the creation of the Inter Collegiate Athletic Association, which later became the National Collegiate Athletic Association (NCAA), and the establishment of a new football rules committee, which the reformers dominated.[63]

Coach Bill Reid of Harvard led the reformers on the new rules committee because he was certain that Harvard would drop football unless the committee adopted a package of rules changes that a Harvard alumni committee had devised.[64] In eight meetings during a four-month period in 1906, the rules committee adopted the changes that had originated at Harvard. They included: (1) a prohibition on runners hurdling the line; (2) the creation of a ball-length "neutral zone" between the offensive team and the defensive team; (3) the requirement that six men be on the line of scrimmage to prevent players "massing" in the backfield; (4) a prohibition on tackling below the knees; (5) an increase in the number of game officials to four, along with greater penalties for rule infractions; (6) the requirement that the offensive team gain 10 yards (instead of the existing 5 yards) in three downs in order to retain possession of the ball; and (7) the legalization of the forward pass.[65] The committee limited the impact of the forward pass though; it stipulated that if no player on either team touched the thrown ball, the team that threw the pass would lose possession of the ball and the opposing team would take possession at the spot where the ball was thrown.[66]

Additional rules changes followed in 1908 and in 1912. In 1908, the rules committee gave the offensive team four downs in which to gain 10 yards or lose possession of the ball, and it increased the value of a touchdown from five points to six points.[67] In 1912, the committee reduced the circumference of the football from 27 inches to 23 inches,[68] thereby making it easier to throw, and eliminated the automatic change of possession after an incomplete pass that neither side had touched.[69]

These rules changes accomplished what the president of the United States could not accomplish—namely, the preservation of college football through reform. They reduced incidents of brutality by strengthening the enforcement of existing rules and by shifting the game's reward structure toward speed and skill, and away from brute strength. They could not prevent NYU, Union College, the University of Rochester, Stevens Institute of Technology, and Northwestern from joining the ranks of the colleges that had already dropped football, but they convinced Harvard's trustees to retain the game.[70] This undoubtedly influenced many other colleges to follow suit because Harvard was both an athletic powerhouse and the preeminent institution in American higher education early in the twentieth century.[71] Moreover, not only did college football survive, but most of the colleges that abolished it after the 1905 season resumed playing it after the 1912 reforms took effect.[72]

It was easier to end brutality on the field than financial and academic shenanigans off the field. Journalist Henry Beach Needham chronicled these shenanigans in two articles that appeared in *McClure's* magazine during the spring and summer of 1905. Needham charged that the prestigious eastern colleges had prostituted themselves to athletic commerce by providing illegal inducements to athletes, hiring tramp athletes, tolerating classroom cheating by athletes, and squandering large sums on the construction of football stadiums, all in pursuit of lucrative gate receipts.[73]

In November of 1905, Edward Jordan published an article in *Collier's* magazine, which he titled "Buying Football Victories." Jordan reported that University of Chicago authorities permitted football coach Amos Alonzo Stagg to use an eighty-thousand-dollar trust fund to subsidize talented athletes, even though the original purpose of the fund was to assist needy students.[74] Jordan also reported that athletes at Chicago received a remission of tuition in return for campus jobs that required no work. He noted that colleges often defended this practice on the ground that it was unreasonable to expect an undergraduate to attend classes, play big-time football, and work at a campus job.[75]

Chicago was not alone in finding imaginative means of subsidizing athletes. Colleges commonly assigned athletes to light-duty jobs in the athletic department, such as dispensing towels, giving rubdowns, supervising intramural athletics, or sweeping floors. Alternatively, athletes obtained off-campus jobs arranged by their coaches. Some colleges, especially those in the South and Southwest, subsidized athletes directly by awarding them athletic scholarships.[76]

To be sure, not all college leaders condoned such practices. Indeed, in 1898 seven members of the Ivy Group (all except Yale) had sent faculty, student, and alumni representatives to a conference at Brown University on the subject of college athletic reform. The agenda included athletic scholarships, the athletic eligibility of undergraduates and of graduate students, summer baseball leagues that paid college players to participate, commercialism, and the role of faculty in the governance of college sports.[77] After the conference concluded, a subcommittee of seven faculty members produced a report that expressed a clear preference for amateurism in college sports. The report condemned athletic scholarships as "degrading to amateur sport" and said that students must be in good academic standing in order to participate in sports. It recommended limiting the number of years of athletic eligibility and prohibiting undergraduates from receiving payment for playing summer baseball. These recommendations reflected the view of the report's authors that intercollegiate athletics must be secondary to the educational missions of the institutions that sponsor them. The authors expressed this view unequivocally in the report, stating that: "No student should be permitted to make athletics the principal occupation of his college life. We are not engaged in making athletes."[78]

The Brown Conference Report did not become the basis for governance in any athletic conference during the early years of the twentieth century, but that does not mean that it is merely a footnote in the history of college sports. On the contrary, its philosophy is closely akin to those of the contemporary Ivy League and of the NCAA's Division III.[79] It is also akin to the participation model of college sports that is the focus of this book.

The athletic conference that came closest to governing its members according to the principles of the Brown Conference Report was the Big Ten. In 1906 the Big Ten adopted several reforms that sought to combat commercialism and professionalism in college sports. They included: (1) the imposition of a price ceiling on game tickets; (2) restrictions on the length of the football season, which would include no more than five games and would end before Thanksgiving; (3) the abolition of training tables and training quarters for athletes; (4) the establishment of common preseason practice dates; and (5) the requirement that coaches have regular academic appointments at moderate salaries.[80] Still, the response of the University of Michigan to these reforms illustrates how difficult it was to tame the college sports beast, even in the first decade of the twentieth century.

The president of the University of Michigan, James Angell, had persuaded his counterparts at several universities in the Midwest to form the Western Athletic Conference, which later became the Big Ten. President Angell and the Michigan faculty supported the Big Ten's rules changes, but students and alumni objected for fear of losing their football dynasty.[81] Football coach

Fielding Yost also objected to the new rules, particularly the rule that required coaches to have "regular academic appointments," that is, to be full-
time employees of the institutions where they coached.[82] This requirement
would have forced Yost to choose between coaching and his substantial business interests outside of football, which he did not wish to do. Yost took
advantage of student and alumni opposition to the rules changes, and helped
himself in the process, when he bypassed President Angell, to whom he was
supposed to report. He convinced the university's Board of Regents to withdraw Michigan from the Big Ten in protest against the new rules.[83] The
regents also abolished the existing faculty committee on athletics, which had
favored the rules changes, and replaced it with a board of athletics that
reported directly to them.[84] Michigan did not rejoin the Big Ten until
1917.[85]

The young NCAA also favored amateurism in college sports. At its founding in 1906, the NCAA believed that coaches should select their athletes
from the student body instead of recruiting them to campus with offers of
financial assistance. It prohibited its members from providing financial inducements to athletes from any source, including the faculty and financial
aid committees.[86] In 1922 at its annual convention, the NCAA issued a statement that endorsed amateurism. The statement said: "An amateur sportsman
is one who engages in sport solely for the physical, mental, or social benefits
he derives therefrom, and to whom the sport is nothing more than an avocation."[87]

The NCAA could not enforce amateurism, though, because until 1948 it
lacked enforcement power, which meant that it had to rely on colleges and
athletic conferences to police themselves, and this self-policing was uneven
at best. Foxes routinely guarded henhouses in college sports. Persons who
were supposed to enforce rules against the recruitment and the subsidization
of athletes often supported these practices, instead of preventing them, out
of loyalty to the home team. Presidents complained publicly about commercialism and professionalism but gloated privately about the students, dollars, and public recognition that big-time sports brought to their institutions.
While gloating, they often turned a blind eye to under-the-table subsidization of athletes by alumni, boosters, townspeople, and college officials.[88]

The subsidization of athletes reflects the importance that Americans at-
tached to college football by the second decade of the twentieth century.
The most visible examples of this attachment were the massive stadiums that
sprang up on college campuses throughout the United States during the
1920s. In the Big Ten, Michigan, Ohio State, and Illinois built stadiums
with seating capacities of 101,001, 81,109, and 71,227, respectively, and by
1929 seven members of the conference had stadiums with more than 55,000
seats.[89] In Los Angeles, private businesses raised the funds necessary to build
the famed Coliseum, and in neighboring Pasadena, they did the same in
order to build the Rose Bowl; both stadiums could accommodate enormous

crowds.[90] Like medieval cathedrals, these gargantuan brick-and-concrete structures welcomed throngs of the faithful to participate in public rituals of worship, albeit worship of what writer John R. Tunis called "the Great God Football."[91]

As Tunis's characterization suggests, not everybody was happy about the college football boom of the 1920s. Indeed, as early as 1916, the NCAA had become concerned about the growing commercialism and professionalism in college football and had adopted a resolution that called for an independent foundation to study conditions in college sports and to make recommendations for reform. The Carnegie Foundation for the Advancement of Teaching agreed to conduct the study, after several other foundations had declined the NCAA's invitation. The Foundation issued its now-famous report "American College Athletics," in 1929.[92]

The Carnegie Report indicated that the financial and academic shenanigans in college sports that Henry Beach Needham and Edward Jordan had chronicled in 1905 were more rampant than ever in the late 1920s. The section of the report that received the greatest attention was titled "The Recruiting and Subsidization of Athletes." It defined a *subsidy* as "any assistance, favor, gift, award, scholarship, or concession, direct or indirect, which advantages an athlete because of his athletic ability or reputation, and which sets him apart from his fellows in the undergraduate [student] body."[93] Athletes received one form of subsidy or another at 81 of the 112 colleges and universities that the authors investigated.[94] Subsidies came in the form of jobs, loans, scholarships, and "miscellaneous assistance";[95] the latter included cash gifts and more imaginative arrangements, such as providing football players with complimentary game tickets that they sold for cash.[96] The jobs often entailed little or no work for comparatively high wages, and they were not available to students who were not athletes. Loans to athletes often went unpaid, and some colleges maintained alumni-controlled slush funds to provide financial assistance to athletes. Many colleges used academic scholarship funds to recruit athletes.[97]

The report failed to prescribe a viable alternative, though, to the commercial model of college sports that produced the subsidization that the report criticized. Instead of "reaching for a new and realistic standard," in John Sayle Watterson's words, the report advocated returning the control of college sports to undergraduates, who ran sports at many colleges during the late nineteenth century.[98] This was a dubious recommendation because undergraduates, assisted by alumni, initiated the hiring of professional trainers and paid coaches in football, which fostered the commercial model of college sports that the report rejected. Consequently, a return to undergraduate control was more likely to perpetuate than to end commercialism and professionalism in college sports.[99]

Its weak prescription for reform helps to explain why the Carnegie Report was not the catalyst for a successful reform movement in college sports. It received considerable publicity and got the attention of the NCAA, but it produced no specific NCAA action that was designed to combat violations of the association's rules.[100] This result was especially unfortunate because the revelations in the report, in conjunction with the financial restraints that the Great Depression imposed on colleges, gave reformers their best opportunity in a generation to change the governance of college sports in a fundamental way.

Several factors other than its call for a return to undergraduate control contributed to the report's failure to foster reform. Its release in late October 1929 coincided with the crash of the stock market and forced it to compete for attention with matters of greater public concern.[101] The onset of the Great Depression, which followed the stock market crash, may have prevented the Carnegie Corporation, the funding arm of the Carnegie philanthropies, from supporting continued efforts to reform college sports.[102] It is unclear, though, whether the Carnegie Foundation's continued participation would have ensured the success of the reform movement in college sports. The report triggered an array of reactions, including refutations and denials by many college presidents, so there was not a consensus among educators about the direction that college sports should take in the future.[103] In any event, whatever opportunity for reform existed after the publication of the Carnegie Report passed quickly as radio made college sports even more popular in the 1930s and the 1940s than they were in the 1920s.

RADIO, TELEVISION, AND THE GROWTH OF THE NCAA

During the 1930s radio expanded the audience for college football far beyond the stadium. "Radio parties" in living rooms throughout the country linked Americans to distant campuses, giving college sports an increasingly secure place in American culture. The National Broadcasting Company (NBC) began network radio coverage of college football in 1926, and on January 1, 1927, NBC broadcast the first Rose Bowl game.[104] By 1929 there were more than ten million radios in the United States, which many colleges saw as partners in their continuing quests for revenue and publicity through sports.[105] The University of Michigan evidently saw radio as a partner when it signed a twenty-thousand-dollar-per-year radio contract in 1935, as did Yale when it signed a radio contract for the same sum in 1936.[106]

The NCAA, however, feared that the broadcasts would reduce the profitability of college football by inducing fans to listen to games at home for free instead of paying to watch them at the stadium. This fear prompted the association to establish a three-member committee in 1935 to study the likely effects of radio on attendance at college football games. In 1936, after conducting a yearlong study, the committee announced that it could not determine whether radio broadcasting affected game attendance adversely.

Consequently, the NCAA chose not to set a national policy on radio broadcasting, thereby allowing each college to decide independently whether or not to broadcast its football games.[107]

By 1940 it was clear that the NCAA's fear that radio broadcasts would reduce attendance at college football games was unfounded. On the contrary, radio broadcasts enhanced the popularity of college football by broadening the audience for the game, and they proved to be an unexpected source of income and publicity for the colleges.[108] The greatest beneficiaries of this trend were the large public universities of the Midwest and the West, which came of age at approximately the same time as radio did. By 1937, as radio broadcasts of college football games mushroomed, many of these universities had enrollments that were three times the size that they had been thirty years earlier. Ohio State, for example, had 15,600 students, while the University of Minnesota had 15,000 students, and 25,000 students attended the University of California.[109] Radio enabled these universities and their counterparts in other states to use sports for the same purpose for which they had long used their agricultural extension services, namely, to create links, real or imagined, between themselves and the far-flung citizens of their respective states.[110]

Television strengthened the links between Americans and distant college campuses greatly. Television was uniquely able to convey the festive spirit of a college game to an enormous audience, to connect a Vermont teenager to the Michigan Wolverines or the Alabama Crimson Tide, and to build lifelong loyalties to college teams and to college sports. Many such loyalties occurred among Americans who were skeptical about, even hostile to, the intellectual missions and the perceived snobbery of colleges.

Initially, each college negotiated its own television contracts with stations or networks, as it had done previously with radio stations.[111] In 1949, for example, the University of Southern California (USC) and the University of California at Los Angeles (UCLA) signed television contracts worth $34,500 apiece, and in 1950, Penn signed a contract worth $75,000 for telecasts of its home games.[112] Unlike radio, though, television appeared to affect game attendance adversely, as 1,403,000 fewer fans attended college football games in 1950 than had attended in 1948.[113] Consequently, the NCAA banned live telecasts of college football games.[114]

The NCAA did not forego television, though. Instead, in 1951 it signed a contract with the Westinghouse Corporation in which Westinghouse paid the association $679,800 in rights fees to televise a limited schedule of college football games on Westinghouse's network of fifty-two stations, which served approximately 58 percent of the American population. This arrangement, which the NCAA viewed as an experiment, enabled fans in each region to see three nationally telecast games and four regionally telecast games during the 1951 season. There would be no telecasts of any games on two Saturdays, and the regions would be blacked out on a rotating basis during the season in order to provide a "control" variable in the experiment so the NCAA could assess the impact of television on game attendance.[115] The 1951 experiment convinced the NCAA that college football would benefit from limited television exposure, so the association signed a television contract with NBC for the 1952 season that was worth $1.14 million.[116]

For the next three decades the NCAA's television plan for college football provided for one game to be telecast nationally and for several games to be telecast regionally each Saturday. No college could make more than two appearances on television during the regular season, and the only colleges that received television revenue directly were colleges whose teams appeared on television.[117] The NCAA received 12 percent of the proceeds of the television contract in 1952, its first year, but considerably less thereafter, typically 4 or 5 percent.[118] It distributed the remainder among the colleges whose teams had appeared on television; teams that had appeared in national telecasts earned approximately 30 percent more money than teams that had appeared only in regional telecasts.[119]

The television plan had a major economic impact on college football and an even greater institutional impact on the NCAA. It restricted the access of viewers to televised college football, which, in turn, increased the colleges' revenues from ticket and concession sales. Limited access to televised games also raised the prices of the rights fees that television networks paid the NCAA to televise college football, thereby increasing the NCAA's revenues from college football and the colleges' revenues from television appearances by their teams.[120] Thus, the television plan made college football a more expensive product for the television networks to provide and for fans to consume than it would have been had the colleges been free to negotiate their own contracts. It was profitable for the NCAA, but it pleased neither the powerhouse teams, which could earn more money if allowed to appear on television more than twice per season, nor the weaker teams, which wanted more sharing of the revenues from televised college games.[121]

The television plan changed the NCAA even more than it changed college football. It transformed the NCAA from a relatively weak advisory body into a regulatory body that wielded enormous economic power. Specifically, the NCAA became a "cartel," which is a combination of producers of a product joined together to control its production, sale, and price. A cartel seeks to maximize the price of its product by limiting that product's availability to consumers, which the cartel achieves by restricting competition among producers.[122] This was precisely what the television plan for college football sought to do and did for more than thirty years.

As a cartel, the NCAA was a commercial association and a regulator, instead of the educational association that it professed to be. Ironically, this newfound commercial significance limited the NCAA's moral authority to punish colleges that broke its rules in order to achieve the commercial ends that it trumpeted. Under these circumstances it is not surprising that the association's critics, especially advocates of amateurism, began to view the NCAA as part of the problem, rather than as part of the solution, in college sports.

During the late 1940s and the early 1950s the limits of the NCAA's power were evident in its attempt to establish and to enforce nationwide rules concerning the subsidization of college athletes. As the 1950s approached, financial aid policies for athletes varied considerably between conferences and between regions of the country. Northeastern colleges and the members of the Big Ten refused to award athletic scholarships because they agreed with the NCAA that financial aid based on athletic ability violated the principle of amateurism. Still, many colleges, especially those located in the South, rejected this view and awarded athletic scholarships.[123] The NCAA sought to address the variation in financial aid to athletes in 1946, when a meeting of association and conference officials produced a document titled "Principles for the Conduct of Intercollegiate Athletics," better known as the "Sanity Code."[124]

The Sanity Code was a compromise between colleges that favored athletic scholarships and colleges that opposed them. It provided that an athlete could receive a tuition remission and a waiver of student fees by demonstrating a financial need and meeting the college's entrance requirements. An athlete could also receive financial assistance beyond tuition and fees, regardless of need, if he ranked in the upper 25 percent of his high school graduating class or maintained a B average in college courses.[125] The college could not revoke a financial aid award if the recipient decided not to participate in sports.[126]

The enforcement mechanism in the Sanity Code represented the first attempt by the NCAA to punish violators of its rules. A three-member compliance committee, aided by an investigative fact-finding committee, would determine whether a violation had occurred.[127] Any athlete who received impermissible aid would be ineligible to participate in college sports, and any college that awarded such aid was subject to dismissal from the association, pursuant to a two third's vote of the delegates at the annual convention.[128]

No sooner was the ink dry on the Sanity Code than critics began to charge that it was unenforceable, and that by limiting financial aid to the cost of tuition, it virtually guaranteed that athletes would violate NCAA rules in search of creative ways to pay their room and board.[129] The most vehement criticisms came from members of the Southern, Southeastern, and Southwest conferences, which had awarded athletic scholarships since the 1930s and did not wish to end that practice.[130] Under these circumstances it is not surprising that seven colleges called the NCAA's bluff by violating the Sanity Code and gambling that their fellow members would not banish them from the NCAA. Presumably, the so-called Sinful Seven reasoned that their fellow members lived in glass houses, hence, would hesitate to throw stones.[131] In any event, at the 1950 NCAA Convention, a proposal to expel the miscreants failed to garner the two-thirds vote necessary for expulsion, which indicated the membership's lack of confidence in the Sanity Code.[132] The vote emboldened the Sanity Code's opponents, who, at the 1951 convention, eliminated the section of the association's constitution that contained it. In 1952 the convention rewrote Article III, Section 4, of the NCAA Constitution to give each college the freedom to establish its own financial aid policies for athletes, so long as the college itself was the source of the aid.[133] This change effectively ratified the athletic scholarship awards that the southern colleges had established two decades earlier.

In 1956 the last barrier to athletic scholarships fell when the NCAA membership voted to extend financial aid for athletes to cover "commonly accepted educational expenses" in addition to tuition and fees, and to award it on the basis of athletic ability, independent of financial need. In 1957 the NCAA defined "commonly accepted educational expenses" to include room and board, books, and $15 per month for nine months for laundry.[134] The association was careful to avoid the appearance of paying players to perform, which could have triggered workers' compensation claims and an end to the tax-exempt status of college sports. It insisted that it only reimbursed players for their expenses, and it prohibited the reduction or the cancellation of financial aid to an athlete who performed below expectations or who quit the team.[135] Nevertheless, by 1957 the NCAA had written into its constitution practices that, for the first half-century of its existence, it had opposed as indicative of professionalism. They were still indicative of professionalism fifty years later; but by then they were the cornerstones of the college-sports enterprise over which the NCAA presided.

This enterprise, as of the early 1950s, included college basketball, the geographical hub of which was Madison Square Garden in New York City. Unfortunately, Madison Square Garden was home to as many professional gamblers as college basketball teams, and the gamblers were eager to exploit their recent invention, the "point spread." This device changed sports gambling because it did not require one to pick the winning team or to "give odds" of a win by the favorite. Instead, it required a wager on the number of points by which a particular team would win a game. It also induced gamblers to solicit players to "fix" games, not by losing intentionally, because that was not necessary in order to "beat the point spread," but instead, by "shaving points," or winning by fewer points than the quoted point spread, in return for a share of the gambler's profits.[136]

In 1951 the point spread sent college basketball reeling as a result of revelations that players at seven colleges, most of which were located in the New York City area, were guilty of shaving points. The first athletes arrested were students at colleges in New York, including the City College of New York (CCNY), which was the NCAA champion in 1950.[137] Later, Manhattan District Attorney Frank Hogan's investigation revealed that point shaving was widespread in college basketball and that players from the University of Kentucky, Bradley University in Peoria, Illinois, and the University of Toledo—which were among the best teams in the nation—had participated, too.[138]

The gambling scandal illuminated the dark corners of college basketball and revealed that the players' ethics were no worse than their coaches' ethics. In other words, gambling was hardly the only problem that plagued big-time college basketball. The New York City Board of Education, which governed CCNY, learned this firsthand when it investigated the basketball program there in the wake of the gambling scandal. The board discovered that between 1945 and 1951, the basketball office at CCNY had altered "the high school transcripts of fourteen [players]" in order "to establish their eligibility for admission."[139] A player commented later that "forging transcripts was a widely accepted practice at City."[140] Another player recalled that "[a]ll [coach] Nat [Holman] wanted was ballplayers. He didn't care how he got them."[141] Thus, gambling was merely the most visible symptom of the corruption that plagued college sports, which colleges' greed and coaches' ambition had created and persistent enabling by the NCAA had perpetuated.

Still, neither college basketball nor the NCAA suffered in the long term because of the gambling scandal of 1951. Attendance declined temporarily, and the geographical hub of college basketball moved from the New York–area colleges to the public universities of the Midwest, many of which built field houses during the 1950s and the 1960s so that their basketball teams could play before large crowds.[142] Yet, both college football and college basketball remained popular during the 1950s and afterward, despite periodic scandals. This is because they seem less tainted than their professional counterparts, thanks to an affiliation with higher education; an absence of salaried, unionized players; and their depiction by the NCAA as wholesome, healthy, and All-American.

MODERN TIMES, MODERN PROBLEMS

The problems in college sports during the past generation might have occurred without television, but television has surely made them worse. In the 1980s changes in the television industry, the demise of the NCAA Football Television Plan, and the growing popularity of college basketball touched off a fierce battle between the networks, and between the colleges, for dollars and visibility. As a result, big-time college sports became more commercial and more professional than ever before.

Cable television fired the first shot in this battle when it entered the televised sports market at the dawn of the 1980s. Cable's most significant entry in the sports market was ESPN, the twenty-four-hour all-sports network, which began life in 1979 as a small, low-budget operation but grew dramatically in size, scope, and popularity during the 1980s.[143] ESPN increased significantly Americans' exposure to college sports, especially football and basketball, as its all-sports menu caused colleges to schedule games on all days of the week and at all times of the day and night.[144] Thursday night college football games and Sunday afternoon college basketball games became standard fare.

These developments occurred after 1984, the year in which the United States Supreme Court invalidated the NCAA's Football Television Plan. The plan's restrictions on viewers' access to televised college football were its undoing, as the Court concluded that they violated the Sherman Antitrust Act.[145] In the Court's view, the plan was "inconsistent with the Sherman Act's command that price and supply be responsive to consumer preference" because it limited the number of games that could be telecast, which made the games less accessible to viewers and more expensive to televise than they would have been in a competitive marketplace.[146] Moreover, the goals that the plan supposedly furthered—namely, full stadiums and a competitive balance among teams—were achievable by means that did not violate antitrust law.[147]

The Supreme Court's decision caused a dramatic increase in the number of college football games telecast, from eighty-nine during the 1983 season to almost two hundred during the 1984 season.[148] This change shrank the rights fees that the networks paid to colleges to telecast their games because the increased supply of televised college football games reduced their market value.[149] The lower rights fees heightened the importance of success on the field because televised football was profitable only for teams that appeared on television often, namely, the powerhouses. The pursuit of multiple television appearances, in turn, increased the incentive for colleges to cheat in order to build successful teams whose games the networks would televise.[150] Thus, the Supreme Court's decision, in tandem with the arrival of cable television, propelled commercialism and professionalism in college sports to new heights during the 1980s and the 1990s.

Conferences reorganized their memberships as colleges tried to make their football teams more attractive to the television networks. Penn State and the University of Miami surrendered their independence to the Big Ten and the Big East, respectively.[151] Florida State did the same to the Atlantic Coast Conference (ACC), and in 1994 the Southwest Conference disbanded. Four of its members—Texas, Texas A & M, Baylor, and Texas Tech—joined the former members of the Big Eight to form the Big Twelve Conference.[152] Both the joiners and the revamped conferences were more attractive to the television networks as a result of these moves. Perhaps the biggest winner was the Big Twelve Conference, which, as the Big Eight, had lacked for television appearances because its members were located in small media markets between Missouri and Colorado.[153] When the Texas colleges joined, the Big Twelve signed a lucrative contract for football telecasts.[154] By the late

1990s it had also joined the other five major football conferences (Big East, ACC, Southeastern, Big Ten, and Pacific Ten) in signing a seven-year, $700 million contract with ABC to televise the Bowl Championship Series.[155]

College basketball also reaped a windfall during the 1980s and the 1990s, thanks in part to the growth of ESPN, which offered fans a steady diet of games from November to March. Between 1987 and 1994 the annual revenue from college basketball telecasts jumped from $49 million to more than $150 million.[156] In 1994, CBS and the NCAA signed the biggest sports contract in the history of television, whereby CBS agreed to pay $1.7 billion for the rights to televise the Men's College Basketball Championship tournament through 2002.[157] In 1999 they renegotiated their contract to extend through 2013 and to include a rights fee of almost $6 billion.[158] This amount reflects the commercial success during the past generation of the men's basketball tournament, which, by the early 1990s, produced approximately 75 percent of the NCAA's annual operating income. According to former executive director Walter Byers, "Tournament income, for practical purposes, finances the entire organization."[159]

Consequently, the NCAA must share the blame for the heightened professionalism that television-driven commercialism imposed on college sports during this period, often at great cost to colleges and to individuals. Among the casualties of this commercialism were several relatively small private universities that tarnished their excellent academic reputations by trying to compete with the big boys in sports. In 1982 the University of San Francisco (USF) disbanded its basketball team after authorities there discovered that boosters had made illegal payments to a team member and to a recruit.[160] In 1986, Tulane University did the same thing after its authorities learned that members of the basketball team had shaved points in return for drugs.[161]

The greatest institutional casualty in this era, though, was Southern Methodist University (SMU). In 1987 the NCAA forced SMU to disband its football team in the wake of revelations that approximately sixty boosters had contributed to a $400,000 slush fund, which they had used to lure players to SMU and pay them monthly stipends while they played for the Mustangs.[162] SMU received the "death penalty" from the NCAA because the Mustangs' boosters had apparently not learned from the probation that SMU had suffered two years earlier for the same offense. The NCAA's enforcement code states that any member institution that incurs two major violations of association rules within five years risks losing the right to compete for up to two years.[163] SMU lost its gamble. The NCAA prohibited it from practicing and from competing in football in 1987, and limited it to seven games in 1988, "none of which may be considered a home game."[164] The SMU administration then decided that the Mustangs would not play football in 1988.[165] Instead, the university tried to polish its tarnished reputation, while the boosters pondered whether the going up (three consecutive conference championships and a top-ten ranking for four consecutive years) was worth the coming down.[166]

Individuals were also casualties of big-time college sports during the 1980s. Athletes, such as Dexter Manley and Kevin Ross, whom colleges admitted for their athletic skills and failed to educate (see Chapter 1), are obvious examples, but nonathletes suffered, too. One such person was Jan Kemp, a tutor in remedial English at the University of Georgia. In 1982, Kemp protested a decision by the university's vice president for academic affairs to permit nine football players to exit the remedial studies program and enter the regular undergraduate track even though each one had received a D in English during his fourth quarter in the remedial program instead of the necessary C.[167] The vice president for academic affairs, acting on the recommendation of Kemp's supervisor, fired Kemp for having challenged these academic shenanigans.[168] The university rationalized its retaliation by claiming that Kemp had been "insubordinate" and that she had failed to publish.[169] Kemp sued the university for having deprived her of employment because she had exercised her freedom of speech.[170]

In court, it became clear that if Kemp was insubordinate, then the University of Georgia needed more insubordinate employees in order to end academic corruption by, and for, its athletes. Similarly, the university's claim that Kemp had failed to publish, while literally true, did not warrant her termination because she was a tutor, and tutors at Georgia were not required to publish in order to keep their jobs. Thus, the jury awarded Kemp $79,680.95 in back pay, $200,000 for her "pain and suffering," $1.00 for loss of professional reputation, and $2.3 million in punitive damages to punish Georgia for firing a whistle-blower and to dissuade it from doing so again.[171] The size of the damages indicated the extent to which Jan Kemp was a casualty of the commercial priorities of college sports in the television era.

She was also an agent of change because her lawsuit unearthed embarrassing academic revelations that spurred the NCAA to require freshmen to achieve minimum high-school grade point averages and minimum standardized test scores in order to compete in sports.[172] In 1983 the NCAA adopted Proposition 48, which took effect on August 1, 1986,[173] and which required freshmen to have achieved a minimum GPA of 2.0 on a 4.0 scale in eleven core courses in a college-preparatory curriculum in order to compete in sports.[174] It also required them to have attained a combined minimum score of 700 (out of a possible 1600) on the Scholastic Aptitude Test (SAT) or of 17 (out of 36) on the American College Test (ACT).[175] Freshmen who did not satisfy both requirements could not compete in sports in Division I or Division II, but "partial qualifiers," who had the requisite grades yet lacked a sufficient test score, could still receive athletic scholarships.[176]

In 1989 the NCAA adopted Proposition 42, which prohibited colleges from awarding athletic scholarships to freshmen who had not satisfied both the GPA and the test-score requirements, yet allowed these students to receive financial aid that was available to their nonathlete classmates, too.[177] Proposition 42 angered black coaches and the presidents of historically black colleges even more than Proposition 48 had done, and Proposition 48 had indeed made them angry because a disproportionately high percentage of the athletes whom its test-score requirement had disqualified were black. Proposition 42 made matters worse, according to the coaches and presidents, by forcing partial qualifiers, who were also disproportionately black and poor, to pay their own college costs as freshmen.[178]

In 1992 the NCAA adopted Proposition 16, which became effective on August 1, 1995,[179] and which required freshmen to achieve a high-school GPA of at least 2.5 on a 4.0 scale in thirteen core academic courses and to score at least 820 on the SAT or 68 on the ACT in order to receive an athletic scholarship and to participate in sports.[180] Yet it reduced the impact of the test-score requirement by creating a sliding scale of grades and test scores that determined eligibility. Consequently, a freshman who had a GPA of only 2.0, but an SAT score of 1010 or an ACT score of 86, could compete in sports, and a classmate who had a GPA of 2.5 or above was eligible to compete despite having scored only 820 on the SAT or 68 on the ACT.[181] The change in the minimum ACT score from 17 under Propositions 48 and 42, respectively, to 68 under Proposition 16 reflected a new method of computing the minimum score, not a dramatic increase in the stringency of eligibility standards. The current minimum score of 68 is based on the *sum* of one's scores on the four parts of the ACT. Each part is worth 36 points, so the highest sum possible is 144. The previous minimum score of 17 was based on the highest *composite* score possible (the average of the four scores, rounded to the nearest whole number), which was (and is) 36.[182]

Despite the sliding scale, four disqualified black athletes alleged in a lawsuit against the NCAA that the test-score requirement violated Title VI of the Civil Rights Act of 1964, which prohibits racial discrimination in programs or activities that receive federal funds.[183] In March 1999 a federal district court in Philadelphia agreed with the athletes that the minimum test-score requirement violates Title VI by disqualifying black students from sports disproportionately, and concluded that the test-score requirement was unnecessary to achieve the NCAA's goal of increasing the graduation rates of college athletes. Thus, the court prohibited the NCAA from using test scores to determine freshman eligibility for sports.[184]

The athletes' victory was short-lived, though. In December 1999 a federal appellate court reversed the district court's decision on the procedural ground that the athletes could not sue the NCAA pursuant to Title VI, because the NCAA is not a recipient of federal financial assistance within the meaning of Title VI.[185] The appellate court did not address the merits of the minimum test-score requirement for freshman eligibility for sports, but its reversal of the district court's decision nevertheless preserved this requirement for freshmen athletes. Thus, mandatory minimum test scores survived, but they remained controversial. Recognizing this, in October of 2002 the NCAA Board of Directors reduced the impact of the sliding scale even further, permitting a freshman who enters college beginning in August of 2003 with an SAT score of 400 (no correct answers) to play sports if (s)he has a high school GPA of 3.55 or higher in fourteen core courses (see Chapter 4).[186]

Whether or not test scores continue to be a challenge for the NCAA, it surely will face other challenges in the future. One is whether colleges can continue to earn revenue from sports without risking a ruling by the Internal Revenue Service (IRS) that college sports, as they are played in Division I, are commercial enterprises, not educational programs. This conclusion would subject the profits that colleges earn from sports to the Unrelated Business Income Tax (UBIT), which would mean that (1) the profit margins on sports for athletically successful colleges would shrink considerably, and (2) colleges that currently break even or lose money on sports might have to leave Division I.[187]

Another challenge is whether colleges can pay athletes who earn revenue for them a stipend in addition to their athletic scholarships without triggering the legal conclusion that athletic scholarship recipients are employees of the colleges for which they compete, hence, eligible to unionize, bargain collectively, and receive workers' compensation benefits when injured on the job. Still another challenge is whether the NCAA can continue to regulate commercial aspects of college sports without facing antitrust lawsuits against the limitations it imposes on the number of athletic scholarships that colleges can award, the income that athletes can earn from employment during the school year, the size of coaching staffs, and the expenses that an athletic scholarship can cover.

The most immediate challenge to college sports, though, is to satisfy the requirements of Title IX—the federal law that prohibits sex discrimination in educational programs that receive federal funds—to provide equal athletic opportunities for their male and female students without overextending themselves financially.[188] This is difficult to achieve because for too long, colleges offered only males the opportunity to play sports, and they spent lavishly on men's sports, especially football and basketball. Therefore, many colleges have responded to recent federal court orders that have mandated compliance with Title IX by disbanding men's non-revenue teams (e.g., wrestling, swimming, and gymnastics) in order to add women's teams.[189] Title IX does not require colleges to cut men's teams in order to add women's teams, but this has occurred because colleges have refused to de-emphasize their football and basketball programs, whether or not those programs earn revenues.

Title IX can be a catalyst for change in college sports. It can spur most Division I colleges that do not earn a profit from sports to stop trying and, instead, to reduce their football and basketball costs in order to offer a wide array of truly amateur sports for men and women. Colleges could reduce football and basketball costs by shrinking the size of football rosters, replacing athletic scholarships with need-based financial aid, and channeling athletic gate receipts and donations into the general fund for campuswide distribution.

Therein lies the answer to the legal and the financial challenges that college sports face and the solution to a century-long ethical lapse in the pursuit of institutional fame and fortune. The history of college sports shows that unless colleges divorce athletic commerce from higher education, they will pay high financial, academic, and social costs on their way to the Rose Bowl and March Madness. Later chapters will discuss the terms of the divorce. First, though, Chapter 3 will explain the financial costs of big-time college sports.

NOTES

1. James M. Whiton, "The First Harvard-Yale Regatta (1852)," *Outlook* 68 (June 1901), p. 286, quoted in Ronald A. Smith, *Sports and Freedom: The Rise of Big-Time College Athletics* (New York: Oxford University Press, 1988), p. 4.

2. Benjamin G. Rader, *American Sports: From the Age of Folk Games to the Age of Televised Sports*, 4th ed. (Upper Saddle River, N.J.: Prentice-Hall, 1999), p. 82.

3. Smith, *Sports and Freedom*, p. 3.

4. Rader, *American Sports*, p. 82.

5. Ibid.

6. Allen L. Sack and Ellen J. Staurowsky, *College Athletes for Hire: The Evolution and Legacy of the N.C.A.A.'s Amateur Myth* (Westport, Conn.: Praeger, 1998), p. 14.

7. Ibid.

8. Wilford S. Bailey and Taylor D. Littleton, *Athletics and Academe: An Anatomy of Abuses and a Prescription for Reform* (New York: American Council on Education and Macmillan Publishing Co., 1991), p. 2.

9. Ibid., p. 3. *See also* Smith, *Sports and Freedom*, pp. 173–174.

10. Frederick Rudolph, *The American College and University: A History* (Athens, Ga.: The University of Georgia Press, 1962, 1990), p. 154.

11. Ibid.

12. Ronald A. Smith, ed., *Big-Time Football at Harvard, 1905: The Diary of Coach Bill Reid* (Urbana, Ill.: The University of Illinois Press, 1994), p. xvi.

13. Ibid.

14. Ibid.

15. Ibid.

16. Rader, *American Sports*, p. 90.

17. Rudolph, *The American College and University*, p. 47.

18. Ibid.

19. Ibid., p. 51.

20. Ibid.

21. Ibid., p. 55.

22. Ibid., p. 64.

23. Donald Chu, *The Character of American Higher Education and Intercollegiate Sport* (Albany, N.Y.: State University of New York Press, 1989), p. 159.

24. Rudolph, *The American College and University*, p. 65.

25. Ibid., p. 144.

26. Ibid.

27. Ibid., pp. 146–147.

28. Robin Lester, *Stagg's University: The Rise, Decline, and Fall of Big-Time Football at Chicago* (Urbana, Ill.: The University of Illinois Press, 1995), p. 12.

29. Rudolph, *The American College and University*, p. 375.

30. Rader, *American Sports*, pp. 90–91.

31. Richard Hofstadter, *Anti-Intellectualism in American Life* (New York: Vintage Books, 1963), pp. 18–19.

32. Rader, *American Sports*, pp. 90–91.

33. Sack and Staurowsky, *College Athletes for Hire*, p. 20.

34. Rudolph, *The American College and University*, p. 378.

35. Ibid.

36. Rader, *American Sports*, pp. 92–93.

37. Lester, *Stagg's University*, p. 33.

38. Rudolph, *The American College and University*, p. 390.

39. Murray Sperber, *Onward to Victory: The Crises That Shaped College Sports* (New York: Henry Holt and Company, 1998), pp. 53–54.

40. Sack and Staurowsky, *College Athletes for Hire*, p. 19.

41. Ibid., p. 31.

42. Chu, *The Character of American Higher Education and Intercollegiate Sport*, p. 57.

43. Smith, *Sports and Freedom*, p. 131.

44. Ibid.; *See also* Rudolph, *The American College and University*, pp. 382–383.

45. Rader, *American Sports*, p. 178.

46. Smith, *Sports and Freedom*, p. 156.

47. Charles Farrell, "Historical Overview," in Richard E. Lapchick and John Brooks Slaughter, *The Rules of the Game: Ethics in College Sport* (New York: American Council on Education and Macmillan Publishing Co., 1989), p. 6.

48. Lester, *Stagg's University*, p. 40.

49. Ibid., p. 45.

50. Frank S. Butterworth, "Honesty in Football," *Outing* 45 (Nov. 1904), p. 141, quoted in Smith, *Sports and Freedom*, p. 147.

51. Rudolph, *The American College and University*, p. 387.

52. Smith, *Sports and Freedom*, p. 139.

53. Lester, *Stagg's University*, p. 57.

54. Ibid.

55. Edwin H. Cady, *The Big Game: College Sports and American Life* (Knoxville, Tenn.: The University of Tennessee Press, 1978), p. 170.

56. Rader, *American Sports*, p. 181.

57. Smith, *Sports and Freedom*, pp. 199–200. *See also* John Sayle Watterson, *College Football: History, Spectacle, Controversy* (Baltimore: The Johns Hopkins University Press, 2000), p. 70.

58. Watterson, *College Football*, p. 72.

59. Ibid., p. 69.

60. The agreement that the alumni leaders reached acknowledged that "an honorable obligation exists to carry out in *letter* and in *spirit* the rules of the game of football, relating to roughness, holding and foul play, and the active coaches of our universities being present with us, pledge themselves to so regard it and to do their utmost to carry out that obligation." *See* Smith, *Sports and Freedom*, p. 194.

61. Rader, *American Sports*, p. 181.

62. Ibid. *See also* Smith, *Sports and Freedom*, p. 200.

63. Smith, *Sports and Freedom*, p. 202; Watterson, *College Football*, p. 78.

64. Smith, *Sports and Freedom*, pp. 203–204; Watterson, *College Football*, p. 78.

65. Smith, *Sports and Freedom*, p. 202.

66. Ibid., p. 205.

67. Rader, *American Sports*, p. 182.

68. Ibid., p. 184. In 1934 rule-makers reduced the circumference of the ball further, to 21½ inches.

69. Smith, *Sports and Freedom*, p. 206.

70. Ibid. *See also* p. 200.

71. Smith, *Sports and Freedom*, p. 206.

72. Lester, *Stagg's University*, p. 77.

73. Smith, *Sports and Freedom*, pp. 192–193.

74. Edward S. Jordan, "Buying Football Victories," *Collier's*, November 18, 1905, pp. 19–20, quoted in Sack and Staurowsky, *College Athletes for Hire*, pp. 19–20.

75. Ibid.

76. Rader, *American Sports*, p. 187.

77. Sack and Staurowsky, *College Athletes for Hire*, p. 27.

78. Ibid., p. 28.

79. Ibid.

80. Lester, *Stagg's University*, pp. 79–80.

81. Sack and Staurowsky, *College Athletes for Hire*, p. 26.

82. James J. Duderstadt, *Intercollegiate Athletics and the American University: A University President's Perspective* (Ann Arbor, Mich.: The University of Michigan Press, 2000), p. 232.

83. Ibid.

84. Sack and Staurowsky, *College Athletes for Hire*, p. 26.

85. Duderstadt, *Intercollegiate Athletics and the American University*, p. 233.

86. Sack and Staurowsky, *College Athletes for Hire*, p. 34.

87. NCAA, *Proceedings of the Seventeenth Annual Convention, 1922*, quoted in Sack and Staurowsky, *College Athletes for Hire*, p. 35.

88. Ibid., pp. 35–36.

89. Murray Sperber, *Shake Down the Thunder: The Creation of Notre Dame Football* (New York: Henry Holt and Company, 1993), p. 184.

90. Rudolph, *The American College and University*, p. 388.

91. Quoted in Watterson, *College Football*, p. 352.

92. Howard J. Savage, Harold W. Bentley, John T. McGovern, and Dean F. Smiley, *American College Athletics*, Bulletin no. 23 (New York: The Carnegie Foundation for the Advancement of Teaching, 1929).

93. Ibid., p. 240.

94. Ibid., p. 241.

95. Ibid., p. 242.

96. Ibid., p. 263.

97. Sack and Staurowsky, *College Athletes for Hire*, p. 37.

98. Watterson, *College Football*, p. 175.

99. John R. Thelin, *Games Colleges Play: Scandal and Reform in Intercollegiate Athletics* (Baltimore: The Johns Hopkins University Press, 1996), p. 33. When undergraduates ran college sports, professionalism often took the form of permitting ineligible athletes to represent colleges in competition. For example, in the second intercollegiate sports event on record, a boat race between Harvard and Yale in 1855, the Harvard coxswain was not a student, but an alumnus. Similarly, seven members of the 1893 University of Michigan football team were not students at the university. The discovery of the Michigan players' ineligibility spurred the establishment of the "Presidents' Rules," which later became the Intercollegiate Conference of Faculty Representatives, more commonly known as the Big Ten. *See* Hal D. Sears, "The Moral Threat of Intercollegiate Sports: An 1893 Poll of Ten College Presidents, and the End of the Champion Football Team of the Great West," *Journal of Sport History* 19, no. 5 (Winter 1992): 211–226.

100. Paul R. Lawrence, *Unsportsmanlike Conduct: The National Collegiate Athletic Association and the Business of College Football* (Westport, Conn.: Praeger, 1987), p. 27.

101. Watterson, *College Football*, p. 172.

102. Ibid., p. 175.

103. Thelin, *Games Colleges Play*, pp. 38–39.

104. Andrew Zimbalist, *Unpaid Professionals: Commercialism and Conflict in Big-Time College Sports* (Princeton, N.J.: Princeton University Press, 1999), p. 91.

105. Ibid.

106. Ibid., pp. 91–92.

107. Lawrence, *Unsportsmanlike Conduct*, p. 29.

108. Thelin, *Games Colleges Play*, p. 60.

109. Ibid., pp. 68–69.

110. Ibid., p. 70.

111. Rader, *American Sports*, p. 263.

112. Zimbalist, *Unpaid Professionals*, p. 93.

113. Rader, *American Sports*, p. 263.

114. Thelin, *Games Colleges Play*, p. 125.

115. Zimbalist, *Unpaid Professionals*, p. 94.

116. Ibid.

117. Ibid.

118. Ibid., p. 96. *See also* Walter Byers and Charles Hammer, *Unsportsmanlike Conduct: Exploiting College Athletes* (Ann Arbor, Mich.: The University of Michigan Press, 1995), p. 90.

119. Zimbalist, *Unpaid Professionals*, p. 96.

120. Lawrence, *Unsportsmanlike Conduct*, p. 78.

121. Zimbalist, *Unpaid Professionals*, p. 96.

122. Lawrence, *Unsportsmanlike Conduct*, p. 78.

123. Sack and Staurowsky, *College Athletes for Hire*, p. 43.

124. Ibid.

125. Byers, *Unsportsmanlike Conduct*, p. 67. The use of the male pronouns "he"

and "his" reflects the reality that during the 1950s, men received athletic scholarships and women ordinarily did not.

126. Ibid. *See also* Sack and Staurowsky, *College Athletes for Hire*, p. 44.

127. Arthur H. Fleischer, III; Brian L. Goff; and Robert D. Tollison, *The National Collegiate Athletic Association: A Study in Cartel Behavior* (Chicago: The University of Chicago Press, 1992), p. 47.

128. Lawrence, *Unsportsmanlike Conduct*, p. 42.

129. Sack and Staurowsky, *College Athletes for Hire*, p. 45.

130. Ibid.

131. The "Sinful Seven" included Maryland, Virginia, Boston College, Villanova, the Citadel, Virginia Military Institute (VMI), and Virginia Polytechnic Institute (VPI), which is better known today as Virginia Tech. *See* Watterson, *College Football*, p. 214.

132. Sack and Staurowsky, *College Athletes for Hire*, p. 46. *See also* Rader, *American Sports*, p. 262.

133. Sack and Staurowsky, *College Athletes for Hire*, pp. 46–47.

134. Ibid., p. 47. *See also* Byers, *Unsportsmanlike Conduct*, p. 72.

135. Sack and Staurowsky, *College Athletes for Hire*, p. 47; Byers, *Unsportsmanlike Conduct*, p. 72.

136. Rader, *American Sports*, p. 271.

137. Thelin, *Games Colleges Play*, p. 104.

138. Ibid., p. 106. Ultimately, District Attorney Hogan arrested more than thirty players. Besides CCNY, the New York–area arrestees represented Long Island University (LIU), Manhattan College, and New York University (NYU), respectively. Most of the players who were arrested avoided serving jail sentences, but the NBA barred all of the arrestees from playing for any of its teams. *See* Charles Rosen, *Scandals of '51: How the Gamblers Almost Killed College Basketball* (New York: Holt, Rinehart and Winston, 1978) and Randy Roberts and James S. Olson, *Winning Is the Only Thing: Sports in America Since 1945* (Baltimore: The Johns Hopkins University Press, 1989).

139. Murray Sperber, *Onward to Victory: The Crises That Shaped College Sports*, N.Y.: Henry Holt and Company, 1998) p. 306.

140. Ibid.

141. Ibid.

142. Rader, *American Sports*, p. 271.

143. Murray Sperber, *Beer and Circus: How Big-Time College Sports is Crippling Higher Education* (New York: Henry Holt and Company, 2000), p. 40.

144. Duderstadt, *Intercollegiate Athletics and the American University*, p. 75.

145. *National Collegiate Athletic Association v. Board of Regents of the University of Oklahoma*, 468 U.S. 85 (1984).

146. Ibid.

147. Ibid.

148. Watterson, *College Football*, p. 348.

149. Ibid.

150. Roger G. Noll, "The Economics of Intercollegiate Sports," in Judith Andre and David N. James, eds., *Rethinking College Athletics* (Philadelphia: The Temple University Press, 1991), p. 202.

151. Rader, *American Sports*, p. 266.

152. Ibid.

153. Welch Suggs, "Players Off the Field," *The Chronicle of Higher Education*, November 24, 2000, pp. A59–A61.

154. Ibid.

155. Zimbalist, *Unpaid Professionals*, pp. 3–4.

156. Rader, *American Sports*, p. 273.

157. Sperber, *Beer and Circus*, p. 37.

158. Ibid.

159. Byers, *Unsportsmanlike Conduct*, p. 261.

160. Paul Desruisseaux, "A Big Basketball Power Drops the Sport, Blaming Abuses by Alumni 'Boosters,'" *The Chronicle of Higher Education*, August 11, 1982, p. 1. *See also* Chu, *The Character of American Higher Education and Intercollegiate Sport*, p. 206.

161. Murray Sperber, *College Sports Inc.: The Athletic Department vs The University* (N.Y.: Henry Holt and Company, 1990), p. 119. *See also* Brian L. Porto, "Completing the Revolution: Title IX as Catalyst for an Alternative Model of College Sports," *Seton Hall Journal of Sport Law* 8, no. 2 (1998): 351–418.

162. David Whitford, *A Payroll to Meet: A Story of Greed, Corruption and Football at SMU* (New York: Macmillan Publishing Co., 1989), p. 130.

163. NCAA Operating Bylaws, Article 19.6.2.3.2(a), reprinted in NCAA, *2002–03 NCAA Division I Manual* (Michael V. Earle, editor, 2002), p. 319.

164. Whitford, *A Payroll to Meet*, p. 200.

165. Ibid.

166. Ibid., p. 60.

167. *Kemp v. Ervin*, 651 F. Supp. 495 (N.D. Ga. 1986).

168. Ibid.

169. Ibid.

170. Ibid.

171. Ibid.

172. Michael R. Lufrano, "The NCAA's Involvement in Setting Academic Standards: Legality and Desirability," *Seton Hall Journal of Sport Law* 4, no. 1 (1994): 97–141.

173. Ibid., pp. 100–101.

174. Ibid., p. 101 n. 17.

175. Ibid.

176. Ibid., p. 102.

177. Ibid.

178. Ibid., pp. 102–103.

179. NCAA Operating Bylaws, Article 14.3.1.1(a) and (b), reprinted in NCAA, *2002–03 NCAA Division I Manual* (Michael V. Earle, editor, 2002), pp. 38–39.

180. NCAA Operating Bylaws, Article 14.3.1.1.1, reprinted in NCAA, *2002–03 NCAA Division I Manual* (Michael V. Earle, editor, 2002), pp. 139–140.

181. Ibid.

182. *See* http://www.act.org/aap/scores/under.html.

183. *Cureton v. National Collegiate Athletic Association*, 37 F. Supp. 2d 687 (E.D. Pa. 1999). Title VI of the Civil Rights Act of 1964 is located in volume 42 of the United States Code at section 2000d.

184. *Cureton v. National Collegiate Athletic Association*, 37 F. Supp. 2d 687 (E.D. Pa. 1999).

185. *Cureton v. National Collegiate Athletic Association*, 198 F.3d 107 (3d Cir. 1999).

186. Welch Suggs, "NCAA Approves New Academic Standards for Athletes," *The Chronicle of Higher Education*, November 1, 2002 [available at http://chronicle. Com/daily/2002/11/2002110103n.htm].

187. Brian L. Porto, *The Legal Challenges to 'Big-Time' College Sports: Are They Threats or Opportunities for Reform?* 27, no. 2, The Vermont Bar Journal (June 2001).

188. Title IX is located in volume 20 of the United States Code at sections 1681–1688.

189. Brian L. Porto, *The Legal Challenges to 'Big-Time' College Sports: Are They Threats or Opportunities for Reform?* 27, no. 2, The Vermont Bar Journal (June 2001).

CHAPTER 3

SEASONS OF DEBT

FINANCIAL CONSEQUENCES OF COLLEGE SPORTS

THE BONANZA MYTH

In 1936 University of Chicago president Robert Maynard Hutchins, who would lead his college's withdrawal from intercollegiate football in 1939 and its departure from the Big Ten in 1946, observed that "it is sad but true that when an [academic] institution determines to do something in order to get money, it must lose its soul and frequently does not get the money."[1] This observation is as accurate today as it was in 1936. It forms a backdrop for this chapter, which will explain why colleges frequently do not get the money that they seek from sports.

To be sure, the evidence indicates that most colleges, most of the time, do not "get the money" that spurred their entry into big-time sports. A 1997 investigation by the *Kansas City Star* revealed that the costs to Division I colleges of maintaining their sports programs increased by 90 percent between 1992 and 1997, and that taken together, these colleges amassed a total athletic deficit of $245 million in 1995–96.[2] Nobody is more familiar with such grim statistics than Cedric Dempsey, who retired in 2002 as the president of the NCAA, and who offered one of his own at the association's annual meeting in January of 2001. Dempsey noted that the more than 970 NCAA member colleges earn slightly more than 3 billion dollars annually from sports but spend $4.1 billion annually to maintain their sports programs, which means that many athletic departments, and colleges, incur substantial debt in their quests for athletic fame and fortune.[3]

Still, a myth persists that big-time sports deliver a financial bonanza to the colleges that sponsor them, as is evidenced by the results of a 1996 Gallup Poll, wherein 50 percent of the respondents expressed their belief

that all or most colleges make money on sports.[4] The endurance of the
bonanza myth does not mean that colleges do not earn substantial *gross*
revenues, because they do. Yet economists have shown that the revenue
figures for college sports that sports journalists tout repeatedly in print and
on the air are usually gross, *not net* figures. In other words, the published
numbers do not represent profits, because they have not taken expenses into
account.

It would be foolhardy to fail to take expenses into account in any business,
and the business of big-time college sports is no exception, especially since
expenses are rising faster than revenues at 149 of the 321 colleges in Division
I.[5] There is precious little room for growth in revenues from televised games
or from ticket sales, yet the costs of maintaining college teams continue to
grow.[6] Consequently, of the 114 Division I-A colleges (those that field big-
time football teams) that replied to the NCAA's biennial survey of revenues
and expenses in college sports published in 2002 only forty-eight, or 35
percent, reported that their earnings from sports exceeded their expenses in
2000–2001.[7] The profitable colleges are more profitable than ever before,
but their less fortunate rivals are struggling to tread water in stormy seas.
The average profit earned by the 40 "winners" was $5.3 million dollars,
which represents an increase of $1.5 million from their 1998–99 earnings;
the average loss incurred by the 74 "also-rans" (65 percent) was $3.8 million,
an increase of $500,000 from the comparable figure for 1998-99.[8]

Even the winners have cause for concern, though, when they read the
NCAA survey, which was the work of accountant Daniel J. Fulks. One cause
for concern is the fragile financial health of the college sports industry. The
data show that in 2001 the members of Division I-A, which is the NCAA's
most profitable division, earned, on average, total revenues of $25.1 million
from sports and incurred average total expenses of $23.2 million in pursuit
of that revenue.[9] At first blush, these numbers are encouraging, albeit hardly
indicative of great profitability. The numbers become downright discour-
aging, though, when Dr. Fulks deducts "institutional support" (i.e., subsidies
from the general fund, student activities fees, and so forth) from revenues,
which yields a figure of $2.6 million or $100,000 less, on average, than Division I-A colleges spend on sports. In other words, absent institutional support, the revenues (i.e., ticket sales, leases of stadium boxes, athletic licensing
income, proceeds from television and radio broadcasts, and so forth) that
the average college in Division I-A earns from sports falls short of the expenses that it incurs to maintain its teams by $600,000.[10]

Another cause for concern is that the total expenses the colleges have
reported do not include debt service or capital expenditures, such as stadium
or arena expansions or construction of training rooms.[11] Therefore, it is safe
to assume that the full cost of competition in sports in Division I-A is considerably higher than the figures in the NCAA survey suggest. Had debt

service and capital expenditures been included in the survey, they may well have turned more than one winner into an also-ran.

If the news from the NCAA survey is mixed for members of Division I-A, the news for members of Divisions I-AA, I-AAA (no football teams), and II—most of which offer athletic scholarships—is unquestionably bleak. In 2001, on average, members of Division I-AA earned total revenues of $5.6 million from sports, and incurred total expenses of $6.8 million, which resulted in an average loss of $1.2 million.[12] Absent institutional support, the revenue figure declined to $3.4 million and the deficit ballooned to $2.2 million.[13] Members of Division I-AAA, on average, earned total revenues of $5.1 million from sports and incurred total expenses of $5.5 million resulting in a deficit of $400,000,[14] which increases to $2.82 million absent institutional support.[15]

Members of Division II that do not field football teams earned, on average, total revenues of $1.2 million and incurred total expenses of $1.6 million resulting in a deficit of $400,000, which would have increased to $1.1 million absent institutional support. Members of Division II that field football teams earned, on average, total revenues of $1.9 million and incurred total expenses of $2.3 million leaving them a deficit of $400,000 which would have climbed to $1.3 million absent institutional support.[16] Unlike in Division I-A, then, where institutional support may be the difference between a surplus and a deficit in the athletic department at the end of the fiscal year, in Divisions I-AA, I-AAA, and II, institutional support is more likely to be the difference between a deficit of less than or more than $1 million at the end of the fiscal year.

The results of the NCAA survey coincide with the conclusions that economist Richard Sheehan reached in his study of the economics of big-time college sports that used data from 1994. Sheehan's general conclusions were that (1) relatively few colleges earn large profits from sports; (2) great disparities in profitability exist between member colleges within each athletic conference, and between conferences; and (3) some colleges are "losing a bundle" on big-time football and basketball even though the most frequently stated justification for these activities is that they are "revenue-producers."[17] Sheehan's data show that in most conferences, there is a pronounced financial gap between "rich" and "poor" members, which reflects the win-loss records of their respective football and men's basketball teams.[18] These data also show that although most so-called revenue-producing college teams earn gross revenues, absent donations and institutional funds, their expenses would exceed their revenues, which would cause even some athletically successful colleges to lose money on sports.[19]

Like the more recent NCAA survey, Sheehan's study indicates that most athletic departments at Division I colleges cannot balance their budgets without voluntary contributions from on-campus and off-campus sources because they do not earn enough money from football and basketball to cover their expenses. According to Sheehan, assuming that (1) a college athletic department must show an annual surplus (in 1994–95 dollars) of at least $1 million to be considered financially healthy; (2) the estimated combined cost of administrative overhead and maintenance (also in 1994–95 dollars) is $2.5 million and (3) athletic departments received no voluntary contributions, only 31 of the 103 Division I-A colleges in his study had football and men's basketball programs that were financially healthy.[20] In Sheehan's words: "The Michigans, Notre Dames, and Floridas do very well and compare favorably with most professional franchises. The next tier of 25–30 schools does relatively well, but the remaining Division I-A programs either barely cover or do not cover all [their] costs."[21]

To make matters worse, "the Michigans, Notre Dames, and Floridas" are less profitable than they appear to be. Late in 1999 the athletic director at Michigan, which has a storied sports history and always fills its 110,000-seat football stadium and 20,000-seat basketball arena, reported that his department had incurred a deficit of more than $2 million during 1998–99.[22] This news prompted Professor Murray Sperber of Indiana University, the author of several books about college sports, to ask: "If Big Blue loses money in college sports, what hope is there for smaller programs?"[23] The answer is "little or none" so long as the financial arms race to build bigger and better facilities, and to offer athletes more and better amenities, continues. Between 1994 and 2001 capital expenditures on athletic facilities and equipment, which generally do not appear as expenses on athletic department financial statements, increased by 250 percent at Division I-A colleges.[24] In order to help cover these costs, institutional support, legislative appropriations (to public colleges only), and student activities fees increased from 14 percent of athletic-department revenues in Division I-A in 1993 to 16 percent in 1997.[25]

Under these circumstances, instead of being a financial bonanza for the colleges that sponsor them, big-time sports are likely to drain financial resources from faculty salaries, classroom and laboratory construction, research budgets, and student organizations. Late in the 1990s the chancellor of Vanderbilt University, which was then spending $4,000 per-student per-year on sports, acknowledged this problem when he observed that the "long-term effect [of the athletic arms race] may be to seriously impair [the university's] ability to invest in some critical educational and research programs."[26] In June 2001, shortly before his retirement, University of Virginia athletic director Terry Holland suggested a solution when he said: "At some point, there's got to be a change in the way we do business at the national level. If we're not going to drop sports, maybe we all need to drop the competitive level."[27] Indeed, they do; otherwise, athletic departments will be awash in red ink, and colleges will continue to divert scarce resources from teaching, research, and student organizations in order to feed the sports monster.

THE HIGH COST OF THE BIG-TIME

The bonanza myth persists because the public fails to realize how expensive it is to keep the sports monster fed, that is, to field big-time teams, even if only in football and basketball. To be sure, colleges earn revenue from sports via ticket sales, "guarantees" (the home team guarantees the visitor a sum certain for playing in the home team's stadium or arena), proceeds from football bowl games and basketball tournaments, television appearances, corporate sponsorships and advertising, and licensing agreements for use of collegiate logos on apparel and other merchandise.[28] Colleges also benefit from sports-related "unearned" revenues, including donations from boosters, student activities fees, legislative appropriations, and institutional support (i.e., monies from the general fund).[29] Yet colleges incur substantial expenses in pursuit of revenue from sports, which expenses include salaries for athletic-department personnel, athletic scholarships, travel, recruiting, equipment and supplies, medicine, insurance, legal services, public relations, administration, debt service, and the construction and maintenance of sports facilities.[30]

The budget figures of Division I colleges reflect the high cost of maintaining big-time sports programs. In 1999–2000, according to *The Chronicle of Higher Education*, the average athletic-department budget in Division I was $11.2 million which represented an increase of more than $1 million from 1997–1998.[31] The sixty-three Division I-A colleges that participate in the Bowl Championship Series (BCS) in football had an average athletic-department budget of $28.7 million in 1999–2000, which represented an increase of more than $2 million from 1997–98. Football is a moneymaker for some of the BCS colleges, but it is also the most expensive sport that they offer. Consequently, it is an enormous drain on the financial resources of Division I-A colleges that either belong to conferences that are not a part of the BCS or are athletically marginal members of BCS conferences. In 1999–2000 the average football budget for members of BCS conferences was $6.4 million, whereas the comparable figure for Division I-A colleges that did not belong to a BCS conference was $2.9 million. Only fifteen members of Division I-A spent a larger total sum on their women's sports teams than they spent on football during that year.

Football is expensive in part because its personnel costs are high. A Division I-A college football team usually has more than one hundred players, eighty-five of whom are recipients of full athletic scholarships,[32] plus up to twelve coaches (one head coach, nine assistant coaches, and two graduate assistants)[33] and support staff (e.g., strength coach, trainers, equipment manager, and so forth). Equipment costs are also high; it costs on average $900 per year to equip one college football player, which is substantially higher than the comparable cost for any other college sport.[34] The capital costs of constructing and maintaining football facilities, such as stadiums, practice fields, weight rooms, and training rooms, are extremely high. Finally, football usually makes more demands on athletic department services, such as marketing and media relations, than any other sport. Thus, according to former University of Michigan president James Duderstadt, "football is a cost-driver rather than a revenue center."[35] Duderstadt's successor, Lee Bollinger, undoubtedly understood that when he announced during 2000 that Michigan's athletic department would finish fiscal year 2000 with a deficit of between $2.5 million and $3 million in its $48 million budget. President Bollinger authorized a transfer of $3 million from Michigan's general fund to the athletic department in order to cover the projected deficit.[36]

NCAA rules increase financial pressures, especially on the athletically marginal members of Division I-A. The NCAA distinguishes between two types of sports for purposes of awarding athletic scholarships, namely, "head-count" sports and "equivalency" sports. Each athletic scholarship in a head-count sport must provide what is colloquially referred to as a "full ride," which means a scholarship that covers the full cost of tuition, fees, room and board, and books.[37] In Division I the head-count sports for men are football, with a limit of 85 scholarships,[38] and basketball, where the limit is 13 scholarships.[39] The head-count sports for women are basketball, gymnastics, tennis, and volleyball, for which the scholarship limits are 15, 12, 8, and 12, respectively.[40] Each athletic scholarship in an equivalency sport, however, is divisible into partial scholarships. For example, a college in Division I may award the equivalent of 11.78 scholarships in baseball and 12 scholarships in field hockey, which it may divide into partial awards.[41]

The head-count rule, especially as it pertains to football, increases the cost of college sports because it prevents a college from dividing one scholarship among several athletes in order to save money. The head-count rule may also result in the denial of an athletic scholarship to a skier, swimmer, or pole-vaulter who contributes to the success of his or her team, while the third-string offensive tackle who rarely plays in games receives a full ride. This is because it is prohibitively expensive for many colleges to support eighty-five football players on full athletic scholarships, offer a varied menu of women's sports, *and* offer a comparable menu of men's non-revenue sports. The usual casualties in this battle for dollars are men's non-revenue sports. The cultural primacy, if not the revenue potential, of football protects it from cutbacks or elimination, and the gender-equity requirements of federal law do the same for women's sports, which leaves men's sports such as swimming, wrestling, and gymnastics vulnerable to the budget-cutter's ax.

NCAA rules also raise the price of admission to the big time, namely, football's Division I-A. In 1978, at the urging of the major football-playing colleges, the NCAA reorganized its Division I into Division I-A, which includes the major football powers, and Division I-AA, which includes colleges that offer football scholarships but do not play big-time football.[42] In order to qualify for membership in Division I-A, a college must (1) sponsor at least fourteen varsity sports, (2) schedule at least 60 percent of its football games against opponents who belong to Division I-A; (3) average a "paid atten-dance" (i.e., tickets sold) of at least seventeen thousand at its home football games, and (4) play its home football games in a stadium that contains at least thirty thousand permanent seats.[43]

Six of the ten members of the Mid-American Conference (MAC), whose stadiums contained less than thirty thousand permanent seats, undertook expensive renovations during the early 1980s in order to add the seating capacity necessary to remain in Division I-A. These renovations were ex-pensive not only because of the customary costs of construction but also because football is a money-losing proposition in the MAC. Thus, the col-leges that upgraded their stadiums not only failed to recoup their construc-tion costs by means of increased football revenues but also added to their debt-service burdens.[44]

Despite such sacrifices, members of the MAC and other financially mar-ginal conferences are not secure in Division I-A. In 2001 the NCAA con-vened a committee that considered toughening the criteria for membership in Division I-A and enforcing the existing criteria more strictly than the NCAA had done in the past. The committee proposed to require a college that wished to maintain its membership or to qualify for membership in Division I-A to (1) play at least five home football games per season against Division I-A colleges; (2) average at least fifteen thousand *persons* (not tickets sold) at its home football games; (3) sponsor at least sixteen varsity sports, including eight women's sports; (4) award at least two hundred athletic scholarships in all sports annually; and (5) award at least 90 percent of the maximum number of football scholarships (eighty-five) that NCAA rules permit.[45] The board of directors of Division I, which consists of college presidents and chancellors, approved these proposals in April of 2002.[46] As a result, the NCAA will place colleges that fail to meet the new criteria by 2004 on "restricted membership" status within Division I-A for three years, and it may demote them to Division I-AA in 2008 if they have not met the criteria by the end of the period of restricted membership.[47] According to a study that *The Chronicle of Higher Education* conducted before the adoption of the new criteria, they could force up to 36 colleges out of Division I-A, which has 114 members currently.[48]

The greatest impact will occur in the conferences that are marginal finan-cially, such as the MAC, the Sun Belt, and the Western Athletic (WAC). The members of these conferences lose money on football even though they belong to Division I-A, and they fear losing even more money if demoted to Division I-AA, where they could not benefit from "guarantee" games because the I-A colleges that host these games play against I-A opponents only. If the NCAA enforces the new criteria, members of the MAC, the WAC, the Sun Belt, and similar conferences will face a Hobson's choice between (1) joining Division I-AA, where they are certain to wallow in ob-

scurity and red ink and (2) spending themselves silly in order to keep "playing with the big kids" in Division I-A. If history is any guide, more than a
few colleges will choose the second option, regardless of whether it "busts"
their budgets, because membership in Division I-A coincides with their unrealistic, even misguided, institutional aspirations.

The State University of New York at Buffalo is a case in point. Buffalo
is an academically prestigious public institution with an enrollment of
twenty-four thousand undergraduates. The freshmen who entered in the fall
of 1999 had an average SAT score of 1137, and most of them were ranked
in the top one third of their high-school graduating classes.[49] Buffalo played
football in Division I until 1971, when it dropped the sport for financial
reasons. In 1977 it reinstated football, but at the Division III level, where
athletic scholarships are prohibited. Buffalo continued to play football in
Division III until 1993, when it joined Division I-AA. In the fall of 1999,
the Bulls moved up to Division I-A, where they joined the MAC.

A prime mover behind Buffalo's ascension to Division I in all sports except
football in 1991–92—and later, in football—was Steven B. Sample, its president from 1982 until 1991. Sample argued that membership in Division I
fit Buffalo's institutional profile and aspirations. "We looked around," he
recalled in 1999, "and saw that there was not a flagship public institution
anywhere in the United States that wasn't playing on the Division I level.
To me it was obvious that [membership in Division I] was something that
we needed, and I think it was absolutely the right thing to do."[50]

Both points are debatable. First, it is unclear why a large, academically
prestigious institution, such as Buffalo, needs to participate in big-time sports
in order to raise its profile when its profile is already high enough to attract
more than twenty thousand undergraduates who have strong academic credentials. Second, it is all too clear that the principal consequences for Buffalo
of membership in Division I-A are losing seasons and mounting expenses.
The athletic budget grew by more than four times between 1992–93 and
1999–2000, having increased from $2.2 million to $10.1 million annually
during that time period. In 1999–2000, gate receipts, concession sales, and
donations together covered only one quarter of Buffalo's athletic budget;
student activities fees in the amount of $3.2 million and a legislative appro-
priation of $4.3 million made up the difference.

The legislative appropriation was part of the $19 million that the New
York State Legislature contributed to the operating costs of Buffalo's athletic
department between 1992 and 2000. Apparently the legislators prefer football to French or philosophy because they cut appropriations to Buffalo's
academic operations by $44 million during the 1990s, which resulted in
budget cuts for many academic departments and a freeze on hiring new
faculty members. To add insult to injury, in 1999–2000 the university as-
sessed its students, who had suffered from the budget cuts during the 1990s,
an athletics fee of $280 in order to help defray the athletic department's

ever-increasing expenses. This fee will undoubtedly continue to rise if Buffalo and its MAC cohorts decide to pay the increased price of admission to membership in Division I-A.

If inherent athletic costs and NCAA rules do not deter Buffalo and other athletically marginal colleges from pursuing the athletic Holy Grail in Division I-A, perhaps the financial implications of Title IX will do so. Title IX is a law that the United States Congress enacted in 1972, which states that "[n]o person in the United States shall, on the basis of sex, be denied the benefits of, or be subjected to discrimination under any education program or activity receiving Federal financial assistance. . . ."[51] Title IX requires colleges to provide equal athletic opportunities for their male and female athletes. The Office for Civil Rights (OCR) in the federal Department of Education, which is responsible for enforcing Title IX, interprets "equal opportunity" to mean that the percentage of women students at a college who are athletes is "substantially proportional" to (i.e., within 5 percent of) the percentage of women in the undergraduate student body, and that the percentage of athletic-scholarship funds that women athletes at a college receive is directly proportional to (i.e., within 1 percent of) the percentage of female undergraduates at that college who are athletes.[52] Therefore, a college complies with Title IX if women are 52 percent of its undergraduates and at least 47 percent of its athletes, and if the women athletes receive no less than 46 percent and no more than 48 percent of the athletic-scholarship funds that the college awards annually.

Financial constraints make it difficult for colleges to comply with Title IX. During the 1970s and the 1980s neither OCR nor the federal courts enforced Title IX aggressively, which enabled colleges to spend lavishly on men's sports, especially football and men's basketball.[53] Today, as a result of several successful lawsuits by female college athletes during the 1990s, colleges are required to meet the proportionality standards noted above, regardless of the cost.[54] Despite this incentive for compliance, Division I colleges have found substantial proportionality between their percentages of female undergraduates and female athletes, respectively, to be an elusive goal. For example, data from the 1999–2000 academic year indicate that women were 53 percent of the undergraduates but only 42.3 percent of the athletes at Division I colleges during that year.[55] The latter figure represents considerable progress relative to even the recent past, but the growing percentage of female undergraduates and the high cost of adding sports programs still prevent most Division I colleges from achieving the substantial proportionality that Title IX requires.

Many colleges have responded to this dilemma by disbanding men's non-revenue teams (e.g., wrestling, swimming, and gymnastics) in order to free up funds with which to establish additional women's teams. This strategy usually angers athletes and coaches in the discontinued men's sports and breeds hostility toward Title IX without solving the proportionality dilemma. On average, the thirty-one colleges that lost a team's worth of male athletes in 1999–2000 got only 3 percent closer to substantial proportionality, while the colleges that dropped fewer male athletes got 1.2 percent closer to that goal, and the colleges that did not drop any male athletes moved just 0.7 percent farther away from it.[56] In such cases, the remedy may be more problematical than the malady it treats.

The best remedy for the proportionality dilemma is money, which is why at least some of the members of wealthy, highly visible conferences—such as the ACC, Big Ten, Big 12, Big East, PAC 10, and SEC—can afford to field big-time football and men's basketball teams, other men's teams, and a wide array of women's teams. Athletically successful colleges that earn revenue from football and men's basketball are better able than their less successful rivals to solve the proportionality dilemma. In 1998–99, for example, the members of these so-called equity conferences had an average gap of only 8.6 percent between the percentage of women in the undergraduate student body (just over 50 percent) and the percentage of women who played a varsity sport.

In contrast, at the fifty-three Division I-A colleges that do not belong to one of these conferences, women were 51 percent of the undergraduates but only 39 percent of the athletes, and at the Division I-AA colleges the gap between women undergraduates and women athletes was 14.1 percent.[57] This is because the high cost of football at colleges that field big-time, but unprofitable, football teams leaves the athletic department with insufficient funds to support either a wide array of women's teams or large rosters per team. The best evidence of this may come from the state of Arkansas. In 1998–99 Arkansas State University, which has a football team, spent only 23 percent of its $4.8 million athletic budget on women's sports, and the University of Arkansas–Pine Bluff, which plays football in Division I-AA, spent just 29 percent of its $2 million athletic budget on women's sports, whereas the University of Arkansas-Little Rock, which does not offer football, spent nearly 45 percent of its $2.2 million athletic budget on women's sports, a figure that approximates the average for colleges in Division I-AAA.[58]

Thus, the cost of compliance with Title IX, like the price of admission to Division I-A, is especially high for colleges that aspire to membership in the big time but that lack a profitable football team. Walter Byers, who was the executive director of the NCAA from 1951 until 1987, has observed that "[m]oney begets money, but in college athletics there never seems to be enough of it."[59] As a result, colleges that play football on the margins of Division I-A or in Division I-AA often deny equal athletic opportunities to their female undergraduates and still face annual deficits in their athletic department budgets.

Nevertheless, Walter Byers counsels: "The costs of Title IX and the entry of women into the big time should not be blamed for today's highly publicized financial problems for college sports. At the heart of the problem is an addiction to lavish spending."[60] Therefore, absent costly NCAA rules and Title IX, and even assuming high gross revenues, many college athletic departments would still incur deficits because they spend money irresponsibly. For example, reporters for the *Kansas City Star* discovered during their 1997 investigation of the NCAA that the University of Kansas football team spent the night before each *home* game at a local hotel. During the 1996 season the team's five overnight stays at a hotel in Overland Park, Kansas, cost approximately $47,000. Athletic director Bob Frederick defended this practice on the ground that it focused the players' attention on the upcoming game. This was a weak defense because Kansas won only one of its five home games in 1996.[61]

Bowl games in football frequently trigger lavish spending by college athletic departments. For example, in 1999 the University of Wisconsin received $1.8 million for its appearance in the Rose Bowl, but it lost money on the game because it amassed nearly $2.1 million in expenses on the trip to Pasadena. The expenses included $831,400 for airfare, housing, and meals for an entourage of 832 people, which included the coaches' families, six baby-sitters for the coaches' children, the marching band, the cheerleaders, and *three* "Bucky Badger" mascots.[62] A university-sponsored New Year's Eve party cost $34,400.[63] Thus, instead of using profits from the Rose Bowl to shrink the $1.1 million deficit it had incurred in 1998, the Wisconsin athletic department transformed a much-anticipated "payday" into an additional $286,700 of debt to be absorbed by institutional funds.[64]

Perhaps the best evidence of lavish spending by athletic departments is their high personnel costs. Economist Andrew Zimbalist has noted that athletic departments at Division I-A colleges resemble large corporations in that they employ one hundred to two hundred staff members full-time and their top executives earn hundreds of thousands of dollars annually, besides enjoying generous perquisites.[65] The top wage earners are usually the coaches of football and men's basketball, whose salaries reflect the celebrity status that they often enjoy. As of June 2001 thirty Division I-A football and men's basketball coaches earned $1 million or more annually.[66] Steve Spurrier, the University of Florida's former head football coach, is a case in point. In 1997, Coach Spurrier signed a contract with Florida in which the university agreed to pay him a base salary of $168,850. The compensation package also provided that he would receive $430,000 from his radio and television shows, $525,000 from contracts with athletic apparel and equipment companies, $300,000 in forgiven loans, $125,000 in speaking fees, and more than $500,000 in bonuses and other compensation, for a total of more than $2 million excluding perquisites.[67]

When a big-time college coach signs a lucrative contract at College A, pressure mounts at A's rival, College B, to increase the compensation of its coach for fear that without such an increase, he will leave for College C, which will meet his demands gladly in return for the prospect of its first

winning season in five years. For example, at the conclusion of the 2000
college football season, the University of North Carolina at Chapel Hill
offered Virginia Tech coach Frank Beamer a reported $1.4 million per year
to coach the Tar Heels, beginning in 2001. Virginia Tech responded by
raising Coach Beamer's salary by one third, increasing the salaries of his
assistant coaches, and promising to upgrade its football facilities, whereupon
he decided to remain in Blacksburg.[68] Similarly, Oregon State University
held on to Coach Dennis Erickson by rewarding him with a seven-year
contract worth $7 million. On the other hand, Texas Christian University
lost Coach Dennis Franchione to the University of Alabama, which signed
him to a seven-year contract worth more than $1.2 million per year.

The salaries of athletic directors and coaches do not reflect market forces;
instead, they reflect the autonomy of big-time college athletic departments
and the inclination of the "old boy" network that runs these departments to
reward its members. These factors plus the players' amateur status, which
bars them from earning money from sports, account for the inflated salaries
of athletic-department personnel, especially coaches of football and men's
basketball.[69] The lack of market pressure on athletic directors also accounts
for their tendency to list as assets on their financial statements hoped-for
revenues from unpredictable sources such as gate receipts, postseason bowl
game or tournament appearances, licensing income, and private gifts, which
often fail to meet expectations.[70] Thus, athletic directors are not the hard-
nosed corporate executives that they think they are, because unlike corporate
executives, athletic directors are not necessarily held accountable for failing
to control costs. According to Andrew Zimbalist: "If there were true economic competition [in college sports], athletic directors would have to make
wise decisions and spend wisely or they would go out of business. But these
programs don't go out of business."[71]

Thus, lavish spending will continue in football and basketball, as will the
tendency of athletically profitable colleges to, in the words of Walter Byers,
"set higher expenditure levels that destroy the balance sheets of most of the
other Division I-A colleges that are trying to keep up."[72] Under these circumstances, Northwestern University's athletic director, Rick Taylor, undoubtedly spoke for many of his colleagues when he raised the following
questions and expressed the following concern. "What happens when people
can't pay the ticket prices? What happens when all that disposable income
dries up? Who's going to pay these salaries? I worry about that and the
long-term future of college athletics."[73] The long-term financial future of
college sports is the subject of the remainder of this chapter.

DECLARE VICTORY AND GET OUT

Walter Byers might have had the University of Kansas in mind when he
referred to Division I-A colleges that struggle to keep up with their profit-

able rivals within that division. In the spring of 2001, the Kansas athletic department announced that it faced a projected deficit of $789,545 for the year and that it would eliminate its men's swimming and tennis teams in order to cut costs.[74] This announcement reflects the marginal position that Kansas occupies in the Big Twelve Conference, even though its men's basketball team is frequently ranked among the top teams in the nation.

One reason why Kansas is financially marginal in the Big Twelve is that it is disadvantaged with respect to football revenues. The disadvantage flows from the conference's practice of distributing half of the revenues that its members earn from television appearances among the members and the other half according to the number of appearances that each member's football team makes on television. This arrangement hurts Kansas because the state's relatively small population limits the Jayhawks' fan base and, in turn, their appeal to the television networks. Consequently, Kansas struggles to keep pace with conference rivals such as Texas and Texas A&M, which have large numbers of fans and, hence, appear on television often and earn substantially higher revenues from football than Kansas earns. For example, between 1997 and 1999, Kansas spent $26 million to improve its football stadium by broadening the concourses, renovating the restrooms, and adding a new press box and thirty-six suites to the grandstand. During the same time period Texas spent $90 million to upgrade its athletic facilities, primarily its football stadium, where it increased the seating capacity to eighty thousand and installed sixty-six suites and a luxurious private club.

The other reason why Kansas is financially marginal is that it is more expensive for the Jayhawks to compete in the Big Twelve than it was for them to compete in their former conference, the Big Eight. A comparison of revenue and expense figures for 1995–96 and 2000–2001 illustrates this point. In 1995–96, its last year in the Big Eight, Kansas earned a modest profit of $545,886 on sports; in 2000–2001, as a member of the Big Twelve, Kansas lost $789,544 on sports. Travel costs are much higher in the Big Twelve than they were in the Big Eight because Kansas teams must now travel to Texas regularly for games against the University of Texas, Texas A&M, Baylor, and Texas Tech. On the subject of travel costs, assistant athletic director Richard Konzem observed: "In the Big Eight [which included Kansas, Kansas State, Missouri, Nebraska, Iowa State, Oklahoma, Oklahoma State, and Colorado], we were [located] in the middle of the league and we could bus anywhere except Colorado. Now, it's chartering planes to Lubbock, Waco, Austin, and College Station."[75] Indeed, the Kansas football team spent $95,000 on chartered planes in 2000.

The relative wealth of the Texas colleges, especially the University of Texas and Texas A&M, also makes it more expensive for Kansas to compete in the Big Twelve than it was to compete in the Big Eight. In the spring of 2001, then athletic director Robert Frederick illustrated this problem when he observed: "Texas is paying its women's soccer coach $180,000 a year and the rest of us [are paying our women's soccer coaches] $40,000 to $50,000. Then, all of a sudden, the soccer coaches are moving up [in salary], and its tough [for Kansas to compete financially.]"[76] Frederick worried aloud about how Kansas would be able to compete in the big time in the future. "In 10 years" he said, "I just don't know where the revenues are going to come from. It's just like the pros for the big-market teams versus the small-market teams."[77]

If Kansas is a small-market team, Rutgers, the State University of New Jersey, is surely a big-market team. Rutgers, an academically prestigious institution, is a member of the Big East Conference, where it plays football against Boston College, Virginia Tech, Syracuse, West Virginia, the University of Pittsburgh, the University of Miami, and Temple. Rutgers also plays basketball in the Big East, against all of its football rivals except Temple, plus Providence, Connecticut, Villanova, St. John's, Georgetown, Seton Hall, and Notre Dame. Unlike Kansas, Rutgers is located in a populous state within the New York media market; like Kansas, though, its fan base is small. In Rutgers's case, this is because (1) there are many entertainment alternatives in the New York area; (2) the Scarlet Knights lack a tradition of success in the big time in any sport; and (3) traditionally, star football and basketball players who have graduated from high schools in New Jersey have spurned Rutgers and chosen to attend colleges in other states.

These factors have made Rutgers, which joined the Big East in 1990 in order to raise its profile among potential applicants and donors, a perennial conference doormat in football and an also-ran in basketball. Still, university and state officials believe that Rutgers will enhance its "brand name" by playing big-time football and basketball, and they have backed their aspirations with generous financial support. Between 1997 and 2001, the New Jersey Legislature gave Rutgers $12.5 million with which to renovate its athletic facilities. The Rutgers athletic budget in the 2001–02 academic year is 45 percent larger than it was in the 1997–98 academic year.[78] Thus far, though, Rutgers has spent much more money on sports than it has earned, as the athletic department's $13 million deficit at the end of 2001–02 indicates. Even the so-called revenue sports of football and men's basketball do not come close to breaking even, and their shortfall of $2.5 million has doubled since 1998.[79] Institutional support will be necessary to erase the current deficit. Unless the Scarlet Knights beat the odds and become an athletic powerhouse, such support will be necessary to balance future athletic budgets too, undoubtedly to the detriment of academic programs. This is why, several years ago, faculty members, students, and alumni organized Rutgers 1000, a group that urges Rutgers to leave the Big East Conference, to stop awarding athletic scholarships, and to reduce its spending on sports dramatically.[80]

Despite their problems, both Kansas and Rutgers benefit from membership in one of the so-called equity conferences (Big East, ACC, Big Ten,

Big Twelve, SEC, and Pac-10) because they share in the proceeds that their fellow members earn from television appearances during the regular season and from participation in postseason competition. The fifty-four colleges in Division I-A that do not belong to an equity conference do not appear on television regularly, so their athletic success may not translate into financial success. Between 1996 and 1999, for example, these colleges averaged a paid attendance of only 24,335 per game for their home football games.[81] In 1998–99, they lost, on average, $100,000 apiece on football. The financial picture is even bleaker for colleges that play football in Division I-AA, which averaged a paid attendance of only 9,059 per home game between 1996 and 1999 and lost, on average, $429,000 on football in 1998–99. Perhaps the clearest example of the bleak financial picture in Division I-AA is the experience of the University of Massachusetts at Amherst, which lost more money on football ($2.1 million) in 1998, when it won the I-AA national championship, than it had lost in less successful years (usually, about $1.9 million) because the Minutemen spent approximately $200,000 to participate in the I-AA playoffs.

The principal financial advantage that the equity conferences enjoy is their participation in the Orange Bowl, Sugar Bowl, Fiesta Bowl, and Rose Bowl football games of the Bowl Championship Series. In 1994 the ACC, Big East, SEC, and Big Twelve conferences, along with the University of Notre Dame, formed the "Bowl Alliance," which reached an agreement with the Orange, Sugar, and Fiesta Bowls, respectively, that would enable each bowl to host a postseason showdown between the nation's two top teams every three years. The respective champions of the four conferences, Notre Dame (unless it had a losing season), and one other highly ranked team, which may or may not belong to the alliance, would play in the three bowl games each year, and the game that featured the two top teams would rotate among the three bowls annually. Consequently, each bowl could expect to enjoy an advertising windfall every third year.[82]

In 1996 the Bowl Alliance added to its fold the Big Ten and the Pac-10 conferences, the Rose Bowl game, and ABC, which owned the rights to televise the Rose Bowl. Their agreement provided that, beginning in the 1998–99 college football season, the mythical national championship game would rotate among the four bowls, and ABC would own the rights to televise all four games during a seven-year period. A computer-driven formula that accounted for a team's win-loss record, the difficulty of its regular-season schedule, and its rankings in various polls would choose the teams that would participate in the "championship" game.[83] Renamed the "Bowl Championship Series," this arrangement is a compromise that aims to crown a credible "national champion" without instituting a playoff system that would render the bowl games irrelevant, causing them to fold, and would likely extend the college football season well into January. These prospects have caused both bowl executives and college presidents to regard the BCS as an acceptable, albeit imperfect, alternative to a playoff system.[84] Its major imperfection is a persistent failure to pit the best two teams in the nation against each other in the "championship" game. The most recent example is the 2002 Rose Bowl, in which the University of Miami routed Nebraska by a score of 37–14.

The BCS is a valuable Christmas gift to the members of the equity conferences because it guarantees that their top teams will appear in the most lucrative bowl games, sometimes in favor of more talented teams that do not belong to an equity conference. For example, under the BCS the Big Twelve is guaranteed an appearance in an "Alliance" bowl (Rose, Sugar, Orange, or Fiesta) plus five other bowls, the SEC and the Big Ten are guaranteed an appearance in an Alliance bowl plus four other bowls, and the ACC, Big East, and Pac-10 are each guaranteed an appearance in an Alliance bowl plus three other bowls. In contrast, the Mountain West, Western Athletic, Big West, Sun Belt, and Mid-American Conferences, along with Conference USA, all of which belong to Division I-A, have no right to participate in any of the Alliance bowls and, hence, are usually represented only in the so-called minor bowls, where the proceeds are substantially less than they are in an Alliance bowl.

For example, the 2002 Fiesta, Sugar, Orange, and Rose Bowls, respectively, paid the participating teams, which belong to equity conferences, between $11 million and $13 million each.[85] In contrast, at the New Orleans Bowl, where Colorado State of the Mountain West Conference beat the University of North Texas, a member of the Sun Belt Conference; at the Motor City Bowl, where the University of Toledo, a member of the Mid-American Conference beat the University of Cincinnati, which belongs to Conference USA; and at the GMAC Bowl, in which Marshall University of the Mid-American Conference beat East Carolina University of Conference USA, the participating teams each received proceeds of just $750,000, which revenue sharing among conference members and the costs of a bowl-game trip can consume quickly.[86] Marshall learned this lesson in 1998, after participating in the Motor City Bowl, where its "payout" was $750,000, of which it kept just $62,500.[87] The only teams from outside the equity conferences that participated in a bowl game after the 2001 season that paid out more than $1 million were Brigham Young University of the Mountain West Conference and the University of Louisville of Conference USA, which each received $1.3 million at the Liberty Bowl.[88] The Liberty Bowl was one of twenty-five bowl games played between December 18, 2001, and January 3, 2002.

Virtually barred from the major bowl games, marginal Division I-A colleges must look elsewhere for their big paydays. Typically, those paydays result from "guarantee" games, in which a marginal team agrees to play against a Division I-A powerhouse at the latter's stadium, where the former typically endures a humiliating defeat but receives a much-needed infusion of cash for its athletic department. Cash-starved Mid-American Conference teams have long endured such defeats in return for their attendant financial benefits, as Bowling Green did in 1997, when it lost to Ohio State 44–13 but earned $350,000 and lost to Kansas State 58–0, but earned $175,000. In the same year the University of Akron lost to Nebraska 59–14 but earned $450,000 for its lumps and bruises. Said Akron coach Lee Owens, in justifying the scheduling of this mismatch: "Obviously, the money was something we needed to consider. We have struggled, as do most have-nots in the Mid-American Conference."[89]

Akron, Bowling Green, and other colleges that inhabit the margins of Division I-A may lose their membership in that division, along with their occasional paydays, now that the NCAA has adopted tougher criteria for I-A membership. A study that the *Chronicle of Higher Education* conducted before the adoption of these criteria concluded that if the NCAA adopted them, eleven of the thirteen football-playing members of the MAC, all seven football-playing members of the Sun Belt Conference, seven members of the WAC, and three members of Conference USA would have difficulty meeting them by the target date, 2004.[90] Failure to meet the new criteria could lead to demotion to Division I-AA and, as noted earlier, an end to "guarantee" games.

No conference is more threatened by this prospect than the Western Athletic Conference, or WAC, which includes Fresno State, the University of Texas-El Paso, Tulsa, Hawaii, SMU, Louisiana Tech, Boise State, San Jose State, the University of Nevado-Reno, and Rice University. The WAC suffers from high travel costs, limited opportunities to appear on television due to its lack of "marquee" teams, and, because of the BCS, almost no chance to participate in a lucrative bowl game.[91] Indeed, these factors caused eight former members of the WAC, including Brigham Young University, Colorado State, San Diego State, the University of Nevada-Las Vegas, New Mexico, Utah, Wyoming, and the Air Force Academy, to leave in 1999 and to form the Mountain West Conference, which they hope will eventually become an equity conference.[92]

San Jose State, a member of the WAC, offers a case study in the problems that marginal Division I-A colleges face. Perennially under-financed, the Spartans must play several "guarantee" games in football each year in order to obtain needed cash. During the 2001 season they played at the University of Southern California (USC), where they lost 21–10; at Colorado, where they lost 51–15; and at Arizona State, where they lost 53–15—but collected a check for several hundred thousand dollars at each stop.[93] These contests, plus their WAC schedule, left the Spartans with only four home games in 2001, one better than their three home games in 2000. Perhaps it is just as well that the Spartans play most of their games away from home because their 30,456-seat stadium held an average of just over ten thousand fans per home game in 2001. This results partly from the proximity of Stanford and the University of California at Berkeley, which play in the more competitive Pac-10, and partly from the ethnic diversity of San Jose, where many residents are immigrants who lack a cultural attachment to football.

Low attendance figures at home games, a record of 39 wins and 74 losses since 1992, and the high travel costs in the far-flung WAC make football (and the athletic department) a perennial money-loser at San Jose State. To add insult to injury, the low home-attendance figures and the small number of home games threaten to demote San Jose State to Division I-AA in football if the NCAA enforces the new standards for membership in Division I-A.

Thus, in Division I college sports there is a wide gap between the rich and the poor, and it is getting wider. Kansas struggles to retain its traditional big-time status despite demographic disadvantages; Rutgers tries, at great cost and apparently in vain, to build a big-time athletic tradition; and Akron, Bowling Green, and San Jose State scramble to maintain their shaky hold on I-A membership. Meanwhile, the traditional powerhouses of college football fill the prestigious and lucrative bowl-game slots on and around New Year's Day.[94] In 2002, for example, perennial powers Ohio State, Oklahoma, Arkansas, Florida State, Virginia Tech, Tennessee, Michigan, Colorado, Louisiana State, Florida, Miami (FL.), and Nebraska played in the most lucrative bowl games that occurred between January 1 and January 3. The "newcomers" in those games were South Carolina, Oregon, and Maryland, which, as flagship public universities in equity conferences, are far better positioned than Akron, Bowling Green, or San Jose State to reach for the brass ring on New Year's Day, if only occasionally.[95]

In light of the gap between the rich and the poor in Division I, the poor ought to do what former senator George Aiken of Vermont supposedly said that the United States should have done during the Vietnam War, namely, "declare victory and get out."[96] Colleges that struggle to compete athletically and financially in Division I ought to abandon the commercial model of college sports. No big paydays are in the offing for Akron, Bowling Green, San Jose State, or other members of marginal conferences in Division I-A. Big paydays are highly unlikely for Rutgers, despite its membership in the Big East, and they will become rare for Kansas, as the cost of competition in the Big Twelve escalates. The time has come for members of marginal conferences and for marginal members of the equity conferences to lay down their checkbooks, salute fiscal sanity, make peace with their boosters, and call in the helicopters to evacuate the disappointed.

THE GOOSE THAT LAID THE GOLDEN EGG?

Perhaps the first step toward fiscal sanity is to recognize that, contrary to myth, football is not the "goose that laid the golden egg" for college athletic departments.[97] In other words, football proceeds are not sufficient at most

Division I-A colleges, or at any Division I-AA college, to cover the costs of the non-revenue sports that the athletic department sponsors. Consequently, institutional support is necessary to balance the athletic budget at most colleges that play big-time sports.

The data reported in the NCAA's biennial survey of revenues and expenses in college sports illustrate the limited reach of football revenues. In 2001, on average, Division I-A colleges earned $10.92 million from football, but spent $10.95 million on men's sports alone; therefore, football proceeds did not even cover the cost of the men's sports at the average Division I-A college.[98] Women's sports, on average, earned revenues of $1.4 million, but incurred expenses of $4.6 million. Thus, revenues from football ($10.92 million) did not come close to matching the $15.55 million in expenses that Division I-A colleges incurred, on average, in 2001.

The financial statement improves only slightly by adding revenues from men's basketball to the calculation. In 2001, on average, Division I-A colleges earned gross revenues of $3.64 million from men's basketball, for which they incurred expenses of $1.97 million, resulting in a profit of $1.67 million. When one adds the $10.92 million that the average Division I-A football team earned to the $1.67 million that the average men's basketball team at a I-A college earned, the total is $12.59 million which means that the proceeds from football and men's basketball fell $2.96 million short of paying for all sports at a Division I-A college in 2001. Football and men's basketball were the only profitable sports, so the athletic department needed donations and institutional support to cover its expenses.

In Division I-AA, football and men's basketball programs were not even able to pay for themselves in 2001, so they surely could not pay for other sports. Football teams in Division I-AA lost, on average, $500,000, while men's basketball teams lost $100,000. No other teams were profitable either.[99] To make matters worse, the expenses for both I-A and I-AA colleges are understated here because the NCAA survey from which they come did not include debt service or capital expenditures in its calculations.[100]

At most Division I colleges, then, football is not the "goose that laid the golden egg" because its revenues do not support men's soccer, women's field hockey, or any other sport. Even when football is profitable, its revenues are usually insufficient to cover its own expenses *and* the expenses of the other sports that the athletic department sponsors. Thus, most Division I colleges cannot justify high expenditures on football as investments that produce the income that supports the rest of the athletic department.

Neither can colleges justify big-time sports on the ground that athletic success improves institutional financial health by boosting enrollments. To be sure, some colleges have experienced noteworthy increases in undergraduate applications in an apparent response to success in sports. For example, Boston College saw a 12.3 percent surge in applications after its successful football season in 1984, which included a dramatic, last-second upset victory

over the University of Miami via a Hail Mary pass.[101] Indeed, this phenomenon, the so-called Flutie factor, is named for Doug Flutie, the quarterback
who threw the fabled pass.[102] More recently, applications to Northwestern
increased by 20.9 percent in 1996, after the Wildcats' 1995 trip to the Rose
Bowl.[103]

These examples are misleading, though, as Andrew Zimbalist found when
he analyzed admissions data from eighty-six Division I-A colleges for the
years between 1980 and 1995. Zimbalist's quantitative analysis revealed that
there was an association between athletic success and increased applications,
but not between athletic success (i.e., winning percentages in football and
basketball, appearances in postseason bowl games or tournaments, poll rankings, number of All-Americans produced, and so forth) and average SAT
scores. Nor did athletic success increase the number of applicants who were
admitted to and who enrolled at the colleges in the survey.[104] In other words,
athletic success may increase the applicant pool at a college, but it will not
improve the academic quality of the applicants or increase the likelihood
that admitted applicants will enroll. Thus, success in sports is hardly the
boon to selective admissions or large freshman classes that it is reputed to
be.[105]

Moreover, even when the Flutie factor occurs, it is usually short-lived. In
1986, the year after Boston College enjoyed a double-digit increase in applications, it suffered a 7.3 percent decline in applications.[106] Indeed, in five
of the six years following the 1985 increase, the numbers of applications to
Boston College declined, so that by 1991 they were back to where they had
been in 1977, which was several years before Doug Flutie enrolled.[107] Similarly, applications to Northwestern have declined since 1996 to a number
that is comparable to the number of applications received in the years just
prior to the Rose Bowl season. Northwestern is the only member of the Big
Ten that received fewer applications in 2000 (14,725) than it received in
1996 (15,620).[108]

Success in sports does not necessarily spur alumni generosity toward colleges, either. The evidence concerning the assumed connection between success in sports and alumni generosity is mixed. Murray Sperber has noted
that data from the annual college issue of *U.S. News and World Report* for
2000 show that Duke and Notre Dame are the only two Division I-A colleges that rank among the top ten recipients of alumni donations. The top
ten were Princeton, Dartmouth, Yale, Notre Dame, Harvard, Cal Tech,
Duke, MIT, Penn, and Brown.[109] Numbers eleven through nineteen included three Division I-A colleges—Rice, Wake Forest, and Stanford—
among which only Stanford has been successful in football recently. This
group also included Lehigh, Emory, the University of Chicago, Cornell,
Washington University of St. Louis, and Brandeis. In contrast, Wisconsin,
Michigan, UCLA, Texas, and Washington, which have been highly suc-

cessful in football recently, received rankings number 126, 128, 134, 136, and 144, respectively, for alumni giving.

The assumption that success in sports spurs alumni giving fails to recognize that the college that thrives on athletic visibility when its teams are winning and free of scandal suffers from that same visibility when its teams are losing or are plagued by scandal. Alumni who are prone to donate to Alma Mater in good athletic times often become angry at, or embarrassed by, her during losing streaks or scandals, and they stop writing her checks, at least temporarily.[110] Besides, as the data in *U.S. News and World Report* suggest, alumni generosity flows more from a mature conclusion that one received a high-quality education than from fond memories of the "Big Game" and its attendant parties and celebrations. Professor William Dowling of Rutgers captured this reality when he told an interviewer: "At schools where genuine school spirit exists, it exists because students are proud of going to the school. It has absolutely nothing to do with sports."[111] Professor Dowling added: "If God waived a wand tomorrow and made college athletics vanish, for instance, kids who go to Harvard would have just as much 'school spirit' as they did before. That's because 'school spirit' at Harvard consists simply in pride in Harvard as an institution."[112] Consequently, colleges ought not to assume or to fear that alumni generosity depends on success in sports. Former Michigan State University president John DiBiaggio made this point when he wrote:

> No data support the oft-heard claim that wins on the field or on the court bring in more private dollars or more state and federal funding. Losses do not result in decreased financial support either. To be sure, wins can and do often bring in more support for athletic programs. But the myth of institutional dependency on athletic revenues—therefore on athletic victories—needs to be aggressively refuted.[113]

The recent experiences of the University of Oklahoma and Virginia Tech may help to refute this myth. The Oklahoma Sooners lost only ten football games between 1979 and 1989, but they lost fifty football games between 1989 and 1999, before returning to gridiron prominence in 2000.[114] The decline in the football team's fortunes during the 1990s did not cause reductions in enrollment or donations, though. On the contrary, Oklahoma's enrollment increased from 19,250 in 1989 to 21,339 in 1999, a twenty-year high. Donations increased from $21.4 million in 1988–89 to $62.3 million in 1998–99. In the fall of 1999, Vice President for Development David L. Maloney observed: "We just experienced, in the last four years, the four largest fund-raising years in the institution's history. We couldn't say lack of success in winning football games has had an impact."[115] Indeed, President David Boren stated: "From my perspective, the time we've gone through, of difficulty and struggle in football, has been good over all. It's been good for our national image in academic circles."[116]

Just as Oklahoma's lack of success in football during the 1990s did not hinder its fund-raising, Virginia Tech's success in football during the late 1990s, which culminated with an appearance in the Sugar Bowl (the "national-championship" game) at the end of the 1999 season, did not spur a flood of donations to the university's general fund. Fund-raisers at Virginia Tech noted that the Hokies' success in football did not affect donations in a significant way, either positively or negatively.[117] They also pointed out that between 1997 and 2000, despite the success of the football team, donors contributed an average of $42 million annually to academic programs and $5.5 million to sports programs.[118]

It is customary, even at athletically prestigious colleges, for donations to academic programs to dwarf donations to sports programs. This is additional evidence that colleges are incorrect when they assume or fear that their financial health depends on their success in sports. For example, the University of Michigan's sports programs receive approximately $5 million in donations annually, but its general fund receives approximately $180 million in donations annually.[119] In 1997, Michigan completed a fund-raising campaign that yielded $1.4 billion dollars in donations, of which less than $10 million was donated to sports programs. According to James Duderstadt, these numbers reflect donors' substantially greater interest in the quality of academic programs than the win-loss records of sports teams.

> University fundraisers know that the most valuable support for a university generally comes from alumni and friends who identify with the academic programs of a university, not its athletic prowess. Many of the most generous donors care little about athletic success and are sometimes alienated by the attention given to winning athletics programs.[120]

Moreover, these donors—and even others who care about, and ordinarily donate to, sports programs—are especially likely to be alienated by revelations of scandal in the athletic department, which may well cause a suspension or a cessation of their generosity. Data from recent social science studies support this proposition. For example, a study of the relationship between success in sports and alumni giving at Mississippi State University found that for each 1 percent increase in the overall winning percentages of the Bulldogs' football, men's basketball, and baseball teams, respectively, donations to academic programs increased by $286,702.00.[121] Still, the authors cautioned: "There is evidence that NCAA sanctions for rules violations may have a negative influence on alumni donations, especially for alumni who follow the team that has been punished by the NCAA."[122]

Another, larger study reached similar conclusions. It examined data concerning athletic success and donations by alumni and friends for eighty-seven

Division I colleges between 1985 and 1996.[123] For any college in the sample, alumni contributions per student increased by 7.3 percent when the football team won a bowl game but declined by 13.6 percent if the NCAA placed the men's basketball team on probation. Therefore, a college of 24,132 students (the mean size in the sample), on average, would receive increased alumni contributions of $858,000 as a result of a bowl-game victory but would suffer a decline in alumni contributions of $1.6 million as a result of probation. Moreover, although participation in bowl games and in the NCAA Men's Basketball Tournament spurred both alumni and friends to donate to academic programs, the effect of athletic success on donations was "relatively weak compared to the effect of student and faculty quality."[124] In other words, the "Carnegie Research I" colleges in the sample, which have selective admissions processes, tended to receive the highest volume of donations from both alumni and friends regardless of their success in sports.

A third study also explained with caution the relationship that it found between success in sports and alumni giving. The authors collected data from 48 private, doctorate-granting universities, 94 public, doctorate-granting universities, and 167 private liberal arts colleges for the period from 1973 to 1990.[125] They calculated that, at a private, doctorate-granting university, participation by the football team in a bowl game generates additional alumni donations of approximately $40.00 per graduate, or a total of more than $2 million for a university of average size. They found no correlation, though, between participation in the NCAA Men's Basketball Tournament and increased donations at this type of university.

At a public, doctorate-granting university, participation by the football team in a bowl game generates additional alumni donations of approximately $6.50 per graduate, or a total of just over $500,000 for a university of average size. An appearance in the NCAA Men's Basketball Tournament generates additional alumni donations of just over $450,000 at this type of university. At a liberal arts college, success in football (a 50 percent increase in winning percentage) generates an average increase in donations of approximately $26,000.

Despite these generally positive results, the authors cautioned that success in sports is not necessarily a boon to alumni giving. They acknowledged that "[a]thletic success has an immediate impact on alumni generosity."[126] Still, they noted that it is risky for colleges to invest heavily in sports because (1) the investment will not necessarily yield more successful teams or additional postseason appearances, and (2) variations in levels of alumni giving result primarily from perceptions of the quality of the education that a college provides, so an investment in sports threatens to reduce alumni giving if academic programs suffer while sports thrive.

This chapter shows, though, that an investment in sports will surely discourage alumni giving if academic programs suffer while sports struggle. Frequently, sports do not earn enough revenue to support themselves; hence they drain resources from academic programs. Football is not the "goose that laid the golden egg," so institutional funds must balance athletic budgets. Moreover, the high cost of football reduces participation opportunities for women and causes the elimination of other men's sports. These colleges, the "Marginal Majority," should inaugurate the "new season" by abandoning commercialized football and basketball, increasing support for women's sports, and preserving other men's sports. Based on the evidence presented here, if they take these actions, they will discover that participation, not commerce, is the preferred path to a balanced athletic-department budget, a sustainable enrollment, and generous alumni support.

NOTES

1. Donald Chu, *The Character of American Higher Education* and *Intercollegiate Sport* (Albany, N.Y.: State University of New York Press, 1989), pp. 58–59. *See also* Brian L. Porto, *Completing the Revolution: Title IX as Catalyst for an Alternative Model of College Sports* 8, no. 2 *Seton Hall Journal of Sport Law* 351, 393 (1998).

2. Mike McGraw, Steven Rock, and Karen Dillon, "Revenues Dominate the College Sports World," *Kansas City Star*, October 5, 1997 [available at www.kcstar.com/ncaa/part1.html].

3. Welch Suggs, "NCAA President Proposes Broad Plan for Reforms," *The Chronicle of Higher Education*, January 19, 2001, pp. A37–A38.

4. Mike McGraw, Steven Rock, and Karen Dillon, "Revenues Dominate the College Sports World," *Kansas City Star*, October 5, 1997 [available at www.kcstar.com/ncaa/part1.html].

5. Welch Suggs, "Female Athletes Thrive, but Budget Pressures Loom," *The Chronicle of Higher Education*, May 18, 2001, pp. A45–A47.

6. Ibid.

7. Daniel L. Fulks, *Revenues and Expenses of Divisions I and II Intercollegiate Athletics Programs: Financial Trends and Relationships—2001* (Indianapolis: NCAA, 2002), p. 28.

8. Ibid.

9. Ibid., p. 20.

10. Ibid., p. 14.

11. Ibid. Fulks defines "Capital Expenditures" on p. 111 of his report.

12. Ibid., p. 38.

13. Ibid., p. 14.

14. Ibid., p. 14.

15. Ibid., p. 14.

16. Ibid.

17. Richard G. Sheehan, *Keeping Score: The Economics of Big-Time Sports* (South Bend, Ind.: Diamond Communications, Inc., 1996), p. 265.

18. Ibid., p. 267.

19. Ibid., p. 274.

20. Ibid., pp. 276–277.

21. Ibid., p. 284.

22. Murray Sperber, *Beer and Circus: How Big-time College Sports Is Crippling Undergraduate Education* (New York: Henry Holt and Company, 2000), p. 220.

23. Ibid.

24. Knight Foundation Commission on Intercollegiate Athletics, *A Call to Action: Reconnecting College Sports and Higher Education* (June 2001), p. 17.

25. Ibid., p. 39.

26. Quoted in Chester E. Finn, Jr., "The Cost of College Sports," *Commentary* (October 2001): 53–57.

27. Welch Suggs, "Female Athletes Thrive, but Budget Pressures Loom," *The Chronicle of Higher Education*, May 18, 2001, pp. A45–A47.

28. James J. Duderstadt, *Intercollegiate Athletics and the American University: A University President's Perspective* (Ann Arbor, Mich.: The University of Michigan Press, 2000), p. 134.

29. Ibid.

30. Ibid., p. 135.

31. Welch Suggs, "Female Athletes Thrive, but Budget Pressures Loom," *The Chronicle of Higher Education*, May 18, 2001, pp. A45–A47.

32. Operating Bylaws, Article 15.5.5.1, reprinted in NCAA, *2002–03 NCAA Division I Manual* (Indianapolis: NCAA, 2002), p. 192.

33. Operating Bylaws, Article 11.7.2, reprinted in NCAA, *2002–03 NCAA Division I Manual* (Indianapolis: NCAA, 2001), p. 60.

34. Lee Sigelman and Paul J. Wahlbeck, "Gender Proportionality in Intercollegiate Athletics: The Mathematics of Title IX Compliance," *Social Science Quarterly* 80, no. 3 (September 1999): 518–538.

35. Duderstadt, *Intercollegiate Athletics and the American University*, p. 134.

36. Welch Suggs, "Abandoning Major Sponsorship Deal, Nike Plays Hardball Over Sweatshops," *The Chronicle of Higher Education*, May 12, 2000, pp. A53–A54.

37. Andrew Zimbalist, *Unpaid Professionals: Commercialism and Conflict in Big-Time College Sports* (Princeton, N.J.: Princeton University Press, 1999), pp. 68–69.

38. Operating Bylaws, Article 15.5.5.1, reprinted in NCAA, *2002–03 NCAA Division I Manual* (Indianapolis: NCAA, 2001), p. 192.

39. Operating Bylaws, Article 15.5.4.1, reprinted in NCAA, *2002–03 NCAA Division I Manual* (Indianapolis: NCAA, 2001), p. 190.

40. Operating Bylaws, Article 15.5.2.1, reprinted in NCAA, *2002–03 NCAA Division I Manual* (Indianapolis: NCAA, 2001), p. 188.

41. Operating Bylaws, Article 15.5.3.1, reprinted in NCAA, *2002–03 NCAA Division I Manual* (Indianapolis: NCAA, 2001), p. 189.

42. Paul R. Lawrence, *Unsportsmanlike Conduct: The National Collegiate Athletic Association and the Business of College Football* (Westport, Conn.: Praeger, 1987), p. 101.

43. Ibid.

44. Murray Sperber, *Beer and Circus*, p. 34.

45. Dana Mulhauser and Welch Suggs, "NCAA Edges Closer to Forcing Teams Out of Its Top Division," *The Chronicle of Higher Education*, November 2, 2001, p. A59.

46. Welch Suggs, "NCAA Board Calls for Stronger Academic Standards," *The Chronicle of Higher Education*, April 20, 2002 [available at http://chronicle.com/daily/2002/04/2002042602n.htm].

47. Welch Suggs, "Football's Have-Nots Contemplate Their Place in the NCAA," *The Chronicle of Higher Education*, June 30, 2000, pp. A47–A48.

48. Ibid.

49. Erik Lords, "Move to the Big Time Yields Losses and Second Guessing," *The Chronicle of Higher Education*, December 10, 1999, pp. A55–A56.

50. Ibid.

51. Title IX, which is a part of the Education Amendments Act of 1972, can be found in volume 20 of the United States Code, at sections 1681 through 1688.

52. Welch Suggs, "More Women Participate in Intercollegiate Athletics," *The Chronicle of Higher Education*, May 21, 1999, pp. A44–A49.

53. Brian L. Porto, *The Legal Challenges to Big-Time College Sports: Are They Threats or Opportunities for Reform?* 27, no. 2 The Vermont Bar Journal 41, 43 (June 2001).

54. *See Favia v. Indiana University of Pennsylvania*, 7 F.3d 332 (3d Cir. 1993); *Roberts v. Colorado State Board of Agriculture*, 998 F.2d 824 (10th Cir.), *cert. denied*, 510 U.S. 1004 (1993); and *Cohen v. Brown University*, 101 F.3d 155 (1st Cir. 1996), *cert. denied*, 520 U.S. 1186 (1997).

55. Welch Suggs, "Female Athletes Thrive, but Budget Pressures Loom," *The Chronicle of Higher Education*, May 18, 2001, pp. A45–A47. On the other hand, Division I colleges were generally able to achieve proportionality between the percentages of women athletes on campus and the percentages of athletic-scholarship funds that the women athletes received. Indeed, in 1999–2000, Division I colleges awarded women athletes slightly more scholarship money than Title IX requires. Women athletes were 41.5 percent of the athletes in Division I that year, and they received 43 percent of the scholarship dollars awarded. Welch Suggs, "Scholarships for Women Exceed Federal Guidelines," *The Chronicle of Higher Education*, May 18, 2001, p. A47.

56. Welch Suggs, "Female Athletes Thrive, but Budget Pressures Loom," *The Chronicle of Higher Education*, May 18, 2001, pp. A45–A47.

57. Welch Suggs, "Uneven Progress for Women's Sports," *The Chronicle of Higher Education*, April 7, 2000, pp. A52–A57.

58. Ibid.

59. Walter Byers, *Unsportsmanlike Conduct: Exploiting College Athletes* (Ann Arbor, Mich.: The University of Michigan Press, 1995), p. 340.

60. Ibid., p. 247.

61. Mike McGraw, Steven Rock, and Karen Dillon, "Revenues Dominate the College Sports World," *The Kansas City Star*, October 5, 1997 [available at www.kcstar.com/ncaa/part1.html].

62. Sperber, *Beer and Circus*, pp. 222–223. *See also* Welch Suggs, "A Look at the Future Bottom Line of Big-Time Sports," *The Chronicle of Higher Education*, November 12, 1999, pp. A57–A58.

63. Sperber, *Beer and Circus*, p. 223.

64. Welch Suggs, "A Look at the Future Bottom Line of Big-Time Sports," *The Chronicle of Higher Education*, November 12, 1999, pp. A57–A58.

65. Zimbalist, *Unpaid Professionals*, p. 127.

66. Knight Commission, *A Call To Action*, p. 18.

67. Zimbalist, *Unpaid Professionals*, p. 81.

68. Andrew Bagnato, "Clipboard Economy: It's a Simple Matter of Supply

and Demand," *The Chicago Tribune*, December 3, 2000. [available at www.chicagotribune.com/sports/printedition/article/0,2669,SAV-0012030554,FF.html].

69. Zimbalist, *Unpaid Professionals*, p. 83.

70. Duderstadt, *Intercollegiate Athletics and the American University*, p. 129.

71. Andrew Bagnato, "Clipboard Economy: It's a Simple Matter of Supply and Demand," *The Chicago Tribune*, December 3, 2000, p. 1.

72. Byers, *Unsportsmanlike Conduct*, p. 340.

73. Andrew Bagnato, "Clipboard Economy: It's a Simple Matter of Supply and Demand," *The Chicago Tribune*, December 3, 2000, p. 1.

74. Welch Suggs, "The Struggle to Stay Competitive in a Big-Time Conference," *The Chronicle of Higher Education*, June 22, 2001, pp. A37–A39.

75. Ibid.

76. Ibid.

77. Ibid.

78. Matthew Futterman, "Rutgers: Price Tag For Athletics Has Reached $30 Million Per Year," *The Newark Star-Ledger*, December 16, 2001.

79. Ibid.

80. Jim Naughton, "A Financial and Moral Battle Over the Role of Athletics," *The Chronicle of Higher Education*, August 14, 1998, pp. A37–A38.

81. Welch Suggs, "Football's Have-Nots Contemplate Their Place in the NCAA," *The Chronicle of Higher Education*, June 30, 2000, pp. A47–A48.

82. Zimbalist, *Unpaid Professionals*, pp. 104–105.

83. Ibid., p. 105.

84. Duderstadt, *Intercollegiate Athletics and the American University*, p. 186.

85. *The Valley News* (West Lebanon, N.H.), January 4, 2002, p. B6. This appears to be a much bigger payday than it actually is, though. The conference to which each participating team belongs allotted the team a percentage of the proceeds to cover expenses and then distributed the balance among the members of the conference, thereby reducing the bowl participant's booty considerably. The 1998 Sugar Bowl illustrates this phenomenon; Ohio State kept only $3,673,818 of its $12,000,000 payout, and Texas A&M kept just $2,136,336 of its $12,800,000 payout. Zimbalist, *Unpaid Professionals*, p. 121.

86. *The Valley News*, January 4, 2002, p. B6.

87. Zimbalist, *Unpaid Professionals*, p. 122.

88. Ibid.

89. Mike McGraw, Steven Rock, and Karen Dillon, "Revenues Dominate the College Sports World," *The Kansas City Star*, October 5, 1997 [available at www.kcstar.com/ncaa/part1.html].

90. Welch Suggs, "Some Colleges May Be Forced Out of NCAA's Top Division in Football," *The Chronicle of Higher Education*, July 27, 2001, pp. A35–A36

91. Welch Suggs, "Breakup of a League Raises Issues of Prestige and Money in Sports," *The Chronicle of Higher Education*, February 12, 1999, pp. A45–A46.

92. Ibid.

93. Welch Suggs, "The Shepherd of San Jose," *The Chronicle of Higher Education*, December 21, 2001, pp. A31–A32.

94. Roger G. Noll, "The Economics of Intercollegiate Sports," in Judith Andre and David N. James, eds., *Rethinking College Athletics* (Philadelphia: Temple University Press, 1991), pp. 197–209.

95. *The Valley News*, January 4, 2002, p. B6.

96. Michael Sherman, ed., *The Political Legacy of George D. Aiken: Wise Old Owl of the U.S. Senate* (Woodstock, Vt.: The Countryman Press, Inc. 1995), p. 99.

97. Brian L. Porto, *Completing the Revolution: Title IX as Catalyst for an Alternative Model of College Sports*, 8, no. 2 Seton Hall Journal of Sport Law 351, 376 (1998). *See also* Mike Zapler, "Coaches of Major Football Teams Ask Congress to Help Revamp Enforcement of Title IX," *The Chronicle of Higher Education*, January 6, 1995, p. A44.

98. Fulks, *Revenues And Expenses Of Divisions I And II Intercollegiate Athletics Programs*, p. 22.

99. Ibid., p. 40.

100. Ibid., pp. 22, 40.

101. Bill Pruden, "The 'Flutie Factor': Admissions Myth or Miracle?" A paper presented at the Annual Meeting of the Southern Association for College Admission Counseling, Ft. Lauderdale, Fl., April 20–23, 2002.

102. Brian L. Porto, *Completing the Revolution: Title IX as Catalyst for an Alternative Model of College Sports*, 8, no. 2 Seton Hall Journal of Sport Law 351, 417 n. 373 (1998).

103. Pruden, "The 'Flutie Factor': Admissions Myth or Miracle?" p. 3.

104. Zimbalist, *Unpaid Professionals*, p. 171.

105. The results of a poll of college-bound high schools seniors conducted in the spring of 2000 by the Art & Science Group, a research firm located in Baltimore, underscore this point. The poll found that 73 percent of its respondents indicated that their choice of a college had not been influenced by the NCAA division to which their college belonged, and that 37 percent did not even know to which division their college belonged. Even though the poll was conducted within a few weeks of the NCAA men's and women's basketball tournaments, only 16 percent of the respondents knew that Michigan State had won the men's championship and only 10 percent knew that Connecticut had won the women's championship. Similarly, just 16 percent knew that Florida State had been the national champion of college football the previous fall. Welch Suggs, "In Choosing Colleges, Students Give Little Weight to the Quality of Sports Teams, Poll Finds," *The Chronicle of Higher Education*, March 14, 2001.

106. Pruden, "The 'Flutie Factor': Admissions Myth or Miracle?" p. 3.

107. Ibid.

108. Ibid.

109. Sperber, *Beer and Circus*, p. 257.

110. Ibid., p. 259.

111. Josh Saltzman, "College Athletes for Hire? An Interview with Professor William Dowling," *The Rutgers Review* 21, no. 10 (April 11, 2000): 1–7.

112. Ibid.

113. John DiBiaggio, "Cosmetic Change Versus Real Reform," *Academe* 77 (Jan.–Feb. 1991): 21–22.

114. Welch Suggs, "Wins, Losses, and Dollars," *The Chronicle of Higher Education*, October 15, 1999, pp. A61–A62.

115. Ibid.

116. Ibid.

117. Erik Lords, "Trying to Turn 'Hokie Mania' Into Something That Lasts," *The Chronicle of Higher Education*, February 18, 2000, pp. A63–A64.

118. Ibid.

119. Duderstadt, *Intercollegiate Athletics and the American University*, p. 129.

120. Ibid.

121. Paul W. Grimes and George A. Chressanthis, "Alumni Contributions to Academics: The Role of Intercollegiate Sports and NCAA Sanctions," *American Journal of Economics and Sociology* 53, no. 1 (January 1994): 27–40.

122. Ibid.

123. Thomas A. Rhoads and Shelby Gerking, "Educational Contributions, Academic Quality, and Athletic Success," *Contemporary Economic Policy* 18, no. 2 (April 2000): 248–258.

124. Ibid.

125. Robert A. Baade and Jeffrey O. Sundberg, "Fourth Down and Gold to Go? Assessing the Link Between Athletics and Alumni Giving," *Social Science Quarterly* 77, no. 4 (December 1996): 789–803.

126. Ibid.

CHAPTER 4

SEASONS OF SHAME

ACADEMIC CONSEQUENCES OF COLLEGE SPORTS

ACADEMIC FRAUD

A sign that hangs in the men's basketball locker room at Duke reads: "Practice times are as follows. . . . Please schedule class accordingly."[1] This sign conveys in no uncertain terms the message that basketball, not school, is the top priority. The academic schedule must accommodate the athletic schedule, not vice versa.

Duke's basketball coaches are not alone in making this demand. Division I coaches routinely require athletes to subordinate their academic lives to their athletic lives. Damion Davis, a track-and-field athlete at Baylor University, told the *Chronicle of Higher Education*: "They [coaches] always say it's academics [first], then athletics. They're lying. It's athletics, and then academics. You don't perform, you're not here."[2]

Baylor football player Bobby Darnell agreed. Referring to his coaches, he said: "They don't want you thinking about the test you have on Monday, just the 'test' you have Saturday night," namely, the next football game.[3]

In this environment, according to sociologists Patricia and Peter Adler, athletes may become "engulfed" in their athletic role, giving it preeminent status, and may "abandon" their academic role, casting aside the nonathletic goals to which they once aspired.[4] Wherever role engulfment exists, academic fraud is sure to follow.

Academic fraud not only occurs when a student cheats on an exam or submits a plagiarized paper, or when a high school or college coach or administrator falsifies an athlete's transcript, but also occurs whenever a college permits athletes to be something other than full-time college students who are enrolled in degree programs and who pursue their degrees at a reasonable pace. It certainly occurs when coaches arrange course schedules to ensure that athletes will be available for daily practice and that they will earn the grades necessary to remain eligible to compete. Coaches did just that at the Division I college where the Adlers studied the men's basketball team during the late 1980s. One player described his "choice" of a major in the following way: "They never even asked me what major I wanted. They just assumed that I would be a rec [recreation-physical education] major. They're probably right, but you get a certain message when they don't even ask you."[5]

The message, of course, is that one's sport comes first and schoolwork is a minor irritant to which one need only pay enough attention to remain eligible to compete.

At fall registration some years ago, former Drake University provost Jon Ericson witnessed an incident involving a freshman men's basketball player who had received this message. The athlete sat impassively while a representative of the athletic department chose his classes and got him registered. Simultaneously Ericson observed, in stark contrast to the athlete, a young woman student who moved from line to line and negotiated with the registrar as she chose her classes, "engulfed" appropriately in the role of undergraduate.[6]

Athletes also receive the message that their sport comes first when coaches force them to subordinate their academic goals to their athletic responsibilities. One of the Adlers' interviewees recalled the following conversation with a coach, which illustrates this problem vividly. The player said:

> One time I had a paper that was really hard that was due. So I say to Coach Mickey [the "academic" coach], "I'm gonna be a little late to practice because I have to go to the library to do some work on my paper." But he told me, "You'd better be in the gym by three o'clock." I think if they was serious about academics, they would cut you some slack on that.[7]

The athletes whom the Adlers interviewed knew full well why the coaches were more serious about basketball than about academics and why they would not tolerate tardiness in their "classroom." One player, referring to donations from basketball boosters and revenue from the NCAA Tournament, said:

> With that kinda money hanging over the program, how's a coach goin' to tell you, "Don't come to practice if you got a really important paper to do." The University's got too much at stake to let the coaches off the hook, and who has to carry the brunt of the pressure at the bottom? The athaletes [sic]. That's who pays the price.[8]

Another player made the important link between coaches' behavior and athletes' role engulfment. He said:

> In college the coaches be a lot more concerned on winning and the money comin' in. If they don't win, they may get the boot and so they pass that pressure on to us athaletes [sic]. . . . I go to bed every night and I be thinkin' 'bout basketball. That's what college athlaletics [sic] do to you. It take over your mind.[9]

Ironically, academic fraud sometimes occurs even when a college does not stand to earn substantial revenues from sports. A case in point is Marcus LoVett, formerly the star point guard for Oklahoma City University (OCU), a perennial basketball powerhouse in the National Association for Intercollegiate Athletics (NAIA), where visibility is low and profits are rare. LoVett enrolled at OCU in the fall of 1995, after spending his first two years of college at Hutchinson Community College in Kansas and the College of Southern Idaho, respectively.[10] He remained eligible for basketball at OCU in 1995–96 by taking courses in fishing/angling, beginning volleyball, beginning golf, intramural recreation programs, walking/jogging, varsity sports, and the fundamentals of coaching basketball, and postponed until his senior year the more difficult courses that he would need to pass in order to graduate with a degree in physical education. This strategy backfired in December of 1996, when LoVett failed three courses and took an incomplete in two others, causing his GPA to fall below the 2.0 necessary for athletic eligibility under NAIA rules. OCU declared him ineligible to play basketball during the spring semester, whereupon he filed suit in state court in January of 1997, claiming that OCU had (1) broken its promise to have him tested promptly for Attention Deficit Disorder (ADD); (2) failed to provide him with the academic assistance it had promised him, (3) deprived him of a chance to showcase his basketball talents for NBA scouts, and (4) inflicted emotional distress on him.

Whether or not OCU breached a legal duty to Marcus LoVett, it certainly breached a moral duty to him when it permitted him to "major in eligibility" so that he could use his basketball talents to garner notoriety for the university. It is poetic justice that he did garner notoriety for OCU, although not in the way that the university would have preferred. If not for the lawsuit, OCU's complicity in Marcus LoVett's role engulfment might well have remained a closely guarded secret. Instead, the lawsuit shed light on what journalist Alexander Wolff has called "a phenomenon that is widely acknowledged to exist in college sports but rarely seen so starkly: schools hooking an athlete up to an eligibility-support machine until his four years of playing are up."[11]

Linda Bensel-Meyers, formerly professor of English and director of composition at the University of Tennessee at Knoxville, knows how the eligibility support machine works. She charges that at Tennessee, it has enabled athletes to receive excessive assistance from tutors in completing assignments and to enroll in courses and in majors that earn them passing grades, but not a degree or, even more importantly, a meaningful education. According to Bensel-Meyers, the eligibility support machine is at its worst when athletic department personnel oversee the academic tutoring of athletes. She referred to Tennessee specifically, but might as well have referred to Division I colleges generally when she wrote that "[a]cademic improprieties will stop when all academic tutoring . . . is overseen by an academic official . . . , and not someone involved in sports management within the athletics department."[12]

According to Bensel-Meyers, the eligibility support machine not only directs athletes to easy courses and offers excessive assistance in completing assignments but also allows athletes to delay declaring a major so as to avoid degree requirements, and even raises their grades after they complete courses, if that is necessary to ensure continued availability for competition.[13] Her data show that thirty-nine football players who were enrolled in Tennessee's introductory English curriculum in 1995–96 received a total of 105 grade changes during their college years, which far exceeded comparable figures for ordinary students.[14]

If ever the eligibility support machine ran amok, it did so at the University of Minnesota during the 1990s. In March of 1999, *The St. Paul Pioneer Press* reported that Jan Gangelhoff, who was an office manager in the academic services office of Minnesota's athletic department and an undergraduate, had completed more than 100 class assignments for as many as twenty basketball players during a five-year period.[15] That figure was conservative because Gangelhoff estimated that she completed more than four hundred assignments for basketball players at Minnesota between 1993 and 1998.[16] She furnished the *Pioneer Press* with her computer files, which contained more than 225 examples of course work that she had completed for 19 basketball players, dating back to 1994. According to Gangelhoff, the files that she surrendered to the newspaper represented about half of the assignments that she had completed for basketball players, as she had destroyed as many files as she kept.[17]

If Gangelhoff's superiors did not know that she was doing assignments for basketball players, they surely created an environment that encouraged excessive academic assistance to the men's basketball team. Gangelhoff told the *Pioneer Press* that Alonzo Newby, who was the academic advisor to the team, arranged basketball players' course schedules so that they took courses in which she was enrolled or that she had already completed.[18] This was possible because in 1994, at the request of men's basketball coach Clem Haskins, athletic director McKinley Boston transferred Newby from the university's academic counseling department to the men's athletics department. This move made men's basketball the only one of Minnesota's twenty-two sports with an academic advisor who reported to a coach and to the athletic director instead of to the director of academic counseling.[19] Under these circumstances, Jan Gangelhoff was able to complete basketball players' assignments for them for five years without being detected.[20] She did so, she claimed, "because I thought maybe I could teach these kids something."[21] "[The Minnesota basketball coaches] just use these kids up and then they throw them away."[22] She said she hoped that if she worked with the ballplayers, some of her love of learning "might rub off on them."[23]

Gangelhoff was just one cog in the eligibility support machine at Minnesota, though. An NCAA investigation uncovered twenty-five violations of the association's rules by athletic officials at Minnesota, including various forms of academic fraud. Besides facilitating Gangelhoff's activities, Minnesota's Department of Men's Athletics had permitted academically ineligible athletes to compete and had made impermissible special academic arrangements for athletes, namely, admitting them to an interdisciplinary major to which they would not have been admitted had they not been athletes. An academic advisor to the men's athletic department had intimidated a professor into giving an athlete a grade of Incomplete in a course, which allowed the athlete to remain eligible for competition.[24]

The events at Minnesota lend credence to Linda Bensel-Meyers's critique that academic shenanigans are likely to occur whenever athletic officials manage the academic tutoring of athletes. Colleges seem to recognize this now, and many are doing something about it. According to Jack M. Rivas, president of the National Association of Academic Advisors for Athletics and an academic advisor at the University of California at Santa Barbara, "more and more institutions are starting to say that reporting lines should go to some academic office, like the academic vice-chancellor or provost or dean of academic affairs, rather than the athletics department."[25] Minnesota has put its academic counseling department in charge of tutoring for all of its students, including athletes.[26] Tennessee has retained academic support services exclusively for athletes but now requires the tutors and academic advisors who work with athletes to report to the university's provost instead of to the men's and women's athletic directors, respectively.[27] It remains to be seen whether these changes can prevent academic fraud by and for college athletes.

They probably could not have prevented the instances of academic fraud that faculty members committed on behalf of football players at the University of California at Berkeley and at Marshall University several years ago. At Cal-Berkeley in the spring of 1999, Alex Saragoza, an administrator who also taught a course in Chicano Studies, gave two football players, Michael Ainsworth and Ronnie Davenport, bogus credit for his course retroactively in order to preserve their athletic eligibility for the following fall.[28] At Marshall, a professor who served as the strength coach for the football team gave several football players a copy of an exam in advance.[29]

Neither could academic oversight of tutoring have prevented the blatant cheating and plagiarism to which the University of Miami's star wide receiver Andre Johnson has admitted. In February of 2002, Miami's Undergraduate Honor Council—a twenty-two member, student-run disciplinary board—voted to suspend Johnson from school for two semesters, which would have kept him off campus for the 2002–03 academic year and off the national champion Hurricanes' football roster for the 2002 season.[30] The Council imposed the suspension after Johnson admitted to sharing exam answers with two other football players in a sociology course on September 21, 2001, and to later submitting for another sociology course, taught by the same adjunct professor, a term paper that was merely a copy of a promotional description for a book. The professor, a former county prosecutor and judge, chose not to report Johnson to the Honor Council after the first incident, but reported him after the second incident, which occurred less than ninety days later.[31]

Johnson appealed his suspension to the council's three-member Appeals Committee, which consisted of the vice president for student affairs, the vice provost, and the president of the student government. The Appeals Committee reduced Johnson's penalty to a suspension during Miami's two twenty-five-day summer terms, which meant that he could not attend summer school in 2002, and to completion of workshops on values education and proper citation, respectively, upon his return to school in the fall of 2002.[32] The reduced penalty also meant that Johnson would be eligible to play football for Miami during the 2002 season.

To be sure, the Andre Johnson case is nothing new in college sports. Indeed, there is a long, though certainly not proud, tradition of college leaders rescuing a talented athlete from academic oblivion in order to exploit his physical skills for another season. On March 8, 1920, the University of Notre Dame expelled for academic failure its star running back George Gipp, who much preferred playing pool to attending classes. On April 29, 1920, Notre Dame's president allowed Gipp to return to school after eighty prominent local citizens, at the urging of football coach Knute Rockne, presented the president with a petition that urged him to reinstate Gipp.[33]

Still, the Andre Johnson case is instructive for several reasons. First, it shows that undergraduates can react like mature adults and that adult administrators can react like sports-crazed juveniles to egregious academic misconduct by a star athlete. Second, it shows that no amount of bureaucratic restructuring and tinkering with reporting lines can unhook athletes from the eligibility support machine so long as college authorities are determined to pursue fame and fortune through sports. Third, it shows that faculty members have the greatest stake in ending colleges' pursuit of fame and fortune through sports because faculty members bear the greatest responsibility for ensuring academic integrity at their respective institutions.

THE DEVALUATION OF ACADEMICS

Academic fraud grabs headlines and deserves harsh criticism, but it is not the most common, or even the most destructive, academic consequence of big-time college sports. This dubious distinction belongs instead to the many decisions that college athletic departments make daily that sacrifice their athletes' academic well-being on the altar of athletic success. The first such decision is to admit athletes, especially football and basketball players, whose high school grades and standardized test scores are significantly lower than their classmates' grades and test scores.

The average member of a "Top 25" college football or men's basketball team enters college after having graduated in the bottom quarter of his high school class.[34] He is likely to be less prepared for college work than his fellow freshmen, as indicated by the large gaps that often exist between the standardized test scores of all freshmen and those of football or basketball players, especially at academically competitive colleges.[35] For example, at Notre Dame in 1996, the median SAT score of all freshmen was 1310, as opposed to 894 for freshmen football players; at Northwestern, the comparable numbers were 1310 and 1028, respectively, and at Michigan, they were 1240 and 866, respectively.[36] The reason for this disparity, according to Murray Sperber, is that "[o]f the blue-chip football recruits who are out there, only about 300 each year score above 1050 on their SATs."[37] Therefore, academically competitive colleges can be competitive in football, too, only if they are willing to admit athletes whose academic credentials are substantially more modest than those of other freshmen.

James Shulman and William Bowen, who studied the relationship between academics and athletics at thirty colleges, found that at academically competitive private colleges that play big-time sports, the average standardized test scores of football players and of male basketball players were approximately three hundred points lower than those of their classmates.[38] These colleges included Duke, Georgetown, Northwestern, Notre Dame, Rice, Stanford, Tulane, and Vanderbilt. Male high profile athletes at these institutions (football, basketball, and hockey players) also fared worse than most of their classmates with respect to the grades that they earned in college. On average, their class rank was in the eighteenth percentile, which means that 82 percent of their classmates had higher GPAs than they had.[39] More than 80 percent of these athletes ranked in the bottom third of their college class. These figures reflect the efforts of colleges in this group to recruit, simultaneously, some of the most intellectually gifted high school seniors in America and some of their most athletically gifted peers.[40]

Shulman and Bowen's data reflect the ever-increasing intensity of athletic recruiting and the growing pressure that it places on college admissions officers to admit talented athletes, even if their academic skills do not match those of their classmates. Indeed, James Duderstadt has noted that coaches' determination to recruit top athletes has caused them, at least at some colleges, to adopt the practice of negotiating a certain number of "wild card" admissions.[41] This enables coaches to pursue blue-chip athletes and to be confident that the admissions office will admit a predetermined number of them with no questions asked, that is, regardless of their academic credentials.[42]

As if it were not bad enough that colleges recruit and admit athletes with marginal, even meager, academic credentials, college coaches, especially in football and basketball, make matters worse by monopolizing athletes' time and by arranging their academic lives to suit athletic purposes. These circumstances virtually ensure that athletes will not catch up to their classmates academically. Contrary to popular belief, many athletes, even in high-profile sports, enroll in college optimistic about getting an education and graduating. Most of the basketball players whom Patricia and Peter Adler studied were optimistic about their academic prospects in college because they had graduated from high school, they had not thought about what college entailed, and they believed that as college athletes in a high-profile sport, they would receive special treatment in their academic lives.[43]

Unfortunately, they soon discovered that basketball exhausted most of their time and energy, which caused many of them to abandon their schoolwork and to spend their minimal free time sleeping or pursuing a social life.[44] They evidently concluded that the price to be paid for sleeping instead of attending class was substantially lower than the price of being sleepy on the basketball court after a late night of studying. This appears to be a rational, if shortsighted, conclusion in light of a vignette that journalist John Feinstein related in his recent book *The Last Amateurs*.[45] Feinstein has long covered the bloody basketball wars that occur each winter along "Tobacco Road" in the ACC. Recalling a particular ACC contest, Feinstein wrote: "I vividly remember one ACC coach angrily lecture a player during a game because he appeared tired. "You spent too damn much time studying this week!" [the coach] yelled, completely serious."[46]

The basketball players whom the Adlers studied also discovered courses that they needed to complete for their respective majors met in the afternoons during basketball practice, and that the coaches would not allow them to miss or to arrive late for practice in order to attend a class or a laboratory session. This prevented them from majoring in engineering or a natural science, which required attendance at afternoon labs.[47] Stanford basketball player Tony Giovacchini discussed this problem in an interview with a journalist during the 2000–2001 college basketball season. Giovacchini indicated that the demands of basketball forced him to be an "athlete-student," at least during the competitive season. He said:

> Just looking at my class schedule right now, I'm getting far along in my major and there are only a certain amount of classes I can take to finish.

And I have two of them this quarter that I can't take because they meet during practice time. In that regard I have to be an athlete-student.[48]

The need to be an athlete-student persists despite the existence of a rule, which the NCAA adopted in 1991, that limits to four hours per day and twenty hours per week the amount of time that college athletes can devote to practice and competition (combined) during the competitive season.[49] The same rule limits required out-of-season training to eight hours per week. Unfortunately, loopholes reduce the effectiveness of this rule. For example, game days count for a maximum of three hours of athletic participation, even when they require more time than that because of travel and pregame preparations, and the amount of time that an athlete spends warming up individually or being treated by a trainer does not count against the four-hour-per-day limit.[50] Lax enforcement also limits this rule's effectiveness. Most colleges monitor compliance by requiring coaches to keep track of the hours spent in practice and in competition and by requiring players to sign off on the coaches' reports. Athletes do so routinely, if for no other reason than that they fear retribution for questioning a coach's tally even if it understates the time spent on their sport.[51] The penalty for violating the rule does not encourage compliance either. The coach who violates it must merely reduce the amount of practice time in a particular week by twice the amount by which he or she exceeded the limit in an earlier week.[52]

Consequently, according to Ellen Staurowsky, a professor of sports studies at Ithaca College, coaches violate this rule "either in spirit or blatantly on a regular basis."[53] They violate it at least in spirit by scheduling workouts at which attendance is ostensibly voluntary but is, in fact, required for any athlete who wishes to play regularly in competition. One such athlete was the Stanford men's volleyball player who told Murray Sperber in 1998, with respect to "voluntary" workouts, that

> ... [I]t's not like you don't have to show up if you don't want to. We work out as much or even longer now than we did before the rule. ... Also each of us wants playing time and needs to keep ahead of everyone else. We know that the coaches totally monitor who is doing the voluntary work. Guess which players the coaches put in the starting lineup?[54]

Thus, the four-and-twenty-hour rule is a fig leaf that covers the NCAA against charges of exploiting college athletes but offers scant protection to athletes against such exploitation.

It is reasonable to assume, then, that college athletes spend as much time practicing and competing today as they did before the four-and-twenty-hour rule took effect in 1991. Based on this assumption, it is instructive to examine the results of the National Study of Intercollegiate Athletes that the American Institutes of Research (AIR) conducted for the NCAA in 1987–88, which asked college athletes how much time they devoted to practice and competition. Football and basketball players reported that they spent 30 hours per week on their sport in-season and 25.3 hours per week attending or preparing for classes.[55] Athletes who participated in other sports reported that they spent 24.6 hours per week on their sport in-season and 27.2 hours attending or preparing for classes. Students who participated in extracurricular activities other than sports reported that they spent 20.4 hours per week engaged in their main extracurricular activity and 27.6 hours per week attending and preparing for classes. Athletes in all sports reported missing approximately two classes per week during their competitive seasons, approximately one class per week more than their nonathlete classmates missed in order to participate in extracurricular activities.

Football and basketball players reported that during the off-season they spent 17.9 hours per week on their sports and 29 hours per week attending (14.4) and preparing for (14.6) classes.[56] Athletes who participated in other sports reported that during the off-season they spent 15.6 hours per week on their respective sports, 14.2 hours per week attending classes, and 15.3 hours per week preparing for class. "Extracurricular" students, on the other hand, reported spending 11.4 hours per week on their main extracurricular activity during its "off-season," 15.3 hours per week attending classes, and 14.6 hours per week preparing for classes.

These data indicate that prior to the imposition of the four-and-twenty-hour rule, college athletes in general devoted approximately five hours more per week to sports in-season than their nonathlete classmates devoted to extracurricular activities, and that college football and basketball players devoted approximately five hours more per week to sports than other athletes did and nearly ten hours more per week to sports than their nonathlete classmates devoted to their main extracurricular activities. The data also indicate that prior to the four-and-twenty-hour rule, college athletes in general, and football and men's basketball players in particular, spent more hours per week on their respective sports than they spent either attending or preparing for classes, *even during the off-season*. In contrast, students who participated in nonathletic extracurricular activities were able to devote more time to attending, and preparing for classes than they devoted to the band, the orchestra, or the debating team during the off-season.

Consequently, it is easy to see why the NCAA Presidents' Commission asked the AIR to determine how much time college athletes spent on their sports and why the results of the AIR survey prompted enactment of the four-and-twenty-hour rule by the NCAA. Unfortunately, the evidence indicates that the four-and-twenty-hour rule has not reduced the amount of time that athletes are expected to devote to their sports each week. Thus, taking into account the not-so-voluntary workouts that coaches use to evade this rule, it is reasonable to conclude that today's college athletes spend as much time on their sports as did the athletes who participated in the AIR survey, regardless of the rule.

Many of the athletes who participated in the AIR survey suffered adverse academic consequences from devoting long hours each week to their sports. Twenty-seven percent of the football and basketball players and 25.5 percent of athletes who played other sports reported that their participation in sports made it "much harder" for them to earn the grades they were capable of earning had they not participated in sports.[57] The comparable figure for students who participated in nonathletic extracurricular activities was 14 percent. Similarly, 22.2 percent of football and basketball players and 19.3 percent of athletes in other sports said that it was "much harder" for them to "keep up with coursework" than it would have been absent their athletic commitments; only 7.7 percent of the "extracurricular" students said that their nonacademic activities made it much harder for them to keep up with course work than it would otherwise have been.

When asked whether sports made it "much harder" to "make academics your top priority," 21.9 percent of the football and basketball players and 17.1 percent of athletes in other sports agreed; whereas only 11.6 percent of the nonathletes perceived their extracurricular activities in that way. Therefore, it is not surprising that 19.4 percent of the football and basketball players, 16.5 percent of the athletes in other sports, and 9.3 percent of the extracurricular students reported that their respective nonacademic commitments made it "much harder" than it would otherwise have been to "study for exams." Neither is it surprising that 14.2 percent of the football and basketball players, 10.6 percent of the athletes in other sports, and 6.9 percent of the extracurricular students reported that their nonacademic commitments made it "much harder" for them to "prepare for classes." In light of these results, the finding that 11.4 percent of football and basketball players, 5.1 percent of athletes in other sports, and 1 percent of extracurricular students believed that their respective nonacademic activities made it "much harder" for them to "be regarded as a serious student by professors" was not unexpected either.

Such differences also separated football players and men's basketball players at the more athletically successful colleges (defined by win-loss records and strength of opponents over time) from their counterparts at less athletically successful colleges in Division I. Football players and men's basketball players at the more athletically successful colleges were more likely than their counterparts at other colleges to find it "much harder" because they were college athletes to "get the grades [they] were capable of getting" (31.2 percent vs. 23.5 percent); "keep up with course work" (26.4 percent vs. 17.9 percent); "make academics [their] top priority" (25.1 percent vs. 18.7 percent); "study for exams" (23.3 percent vs. 16.1 percent); "prepare for class" (16.5 percent vs. 11.5 percent); and "be regarded as a serious student by professors" (13.4 percent vs. 8.9 percent).[58] The difference continued when the last question was modified to ask whether it was "harder" or "much harder" for football and basketball players to be regarded as serious students by professors. The addition of "harder" as a possible answer caused the percentage of affirmative answers to increase to 62.1 percent for football and basketball players at more athletically successful colleges and to 49.2 percent for their counterparts at other colleges.[59]

The academic difficulties that football and men's basketball players encounter because of the time demands of their sports are compounded by race. That was the conclusion of the AIR study, and more recent social science research has reached the same conclusion. The AIR study observed that African-American football and basketball players "enter predominantly White colleges and universities with somewhat different educational and life experiences than students of other races," and that because of these different experiences, African-American football and basketball players are more likely than their white teammates to suffer from "the effects of the time requirements of football and basketball on course performance."[60] One of these effects was a lower average GPA among African-American football and basketball players (2.16 on a 4.0 scale) than among (1) non-African-American football and basketball players (2.48); (2) African-American students who participated in nonathletic extracurricular activities (2.30); and (3) other African-American students (2.28) at predominantly White colleges.[61] At the same colleges, 16 percent of non-African-American football and basketball players had a GPA below 1.99, the figure that often triggers academic probation, whereas 34 percent of African-American football and basketball players had a GPA below 1.99.[62]

A 1999 study that used the same database as the AIR study reached a similar conclusion. The 1999 study found that football and men's basketball players were more likely than athletes who participated in "non-revenue-producing sports" to repeat a course and to be placed on academic probation.[63] Its authors selected at random a sample of approximately 110 athletes from each of 42 colleges, 21 that belonged to Division I-A, 11 that belonged to Division I-AA, and 10 that belonged to Division I-AAA. The authors found that football players and men's basketball players were considerably more likely than athletes in other sports were to have repeated a course (42 percent vs. 27 percent) and to have been on academic probation (32 percent vs. 16 percent), and that the GPAs of football and men's basketball players were, on average, .30 points lower than those of athletes in other sports (2.31 vs. 2.61).

They found further that these results were the product of two forces; namely, the high concentration of African Americans from educationally disadvantaged backgrounds among football and men's basketball players and time management problems that confront football and men's basketball players of all races. "The achievement gap between revenue and nonrevenue athletes," this study concludes, "is shaped by racial concentration and background attributes, although . . . the gap in performance is also partially a function of institutional pressure having to do with time use in particular, and of levels of competitive intensity."[64] In other words, the competitive intensity of big-time college football and basketball and the time management problems associated with playing these sports hurt both African-American and non-African-American athletes academically. African Americans suffered more, though, because they often entered college at an educational disadvantage compared to their classmates of other races. Thus, many African Americans who play big-time college football and basketball experience an academic double whammy in college; they often enroll less prepared than their white classmates to perform college work, and the demands of their sports not only can prevent them from catching up but can cause them to fall farther behind during their college years.

The culture of the team can also contribute to the academic problems that many African-American football and men's basketball players encounter in college. A recent study of the origins of academic inadequacy focused on eight "academically at-risk" football players at a large public university in the Southeast, all of whom were African Americans.[65] The players observed that throughout their recruitment, their orientation, and their college years, they had received implicit and/or explicit messages from coaches and teammates that academic success was not important, that nobody cared whether football players were good students, and that nobody expected them to be good students. One player recalled that during his recruiting visit, "there was a couple of players, . . . and they said, 'You don't have to go to school, because the teachers are going to take care of you.' "[66] Another player echoed these sentiments, saying:

> I would have done a whole lot better if it weren't for coming in and having a group of people say, "This is the minimum you need to do," and holding your hand here, and holding your hand there. . . . They were already expecting me not to do well, so why should I want to do more?[67]

Prominent among the hand-holding practices, according to several players, was the selection of their courses by an academic advisor to the athletic department.

Still, as one player acknowledged, the athletes participated willingly in these arrangements because the university's low expectations of them as students dovetailed with their own athletic priorities and with their dreams of playing professional football. This player said:

> I think one reason athletes don't do well in school is because they see it as just something you have to do. You get to college because of foot-

ball. Everyone just wants to play pro ball. School is just something you
gotta do to play pro ball. . . . [68]

The jury is still out on whether women's college basketball players are
prone to athletic role engulfment. To be sure, there is evidence to indicate
that they have avoided this trap. For example, the AIR study found that
during the competitive season women basketball players spent more hours
each week than their male counterparts preparing for classes (14 vs.11) and
attending classes (15 vs. 13), although each group spent 26 hours on basketball.[69] In contrast, during the competitive season male basketball players
spent five hours more each week than female basketball players engaged in
social activities (11 vs. 9) and relaxing alone (12 vs. 9). A similar pattern
prevailed during the off-season. Women basketball players spent fewer hours
than their male counterparts training for their sport (14 vs. 16) but more
hours than the men preparing for classes (18 vs. 13) and attending classes
(16 vs. 13).[70] Women basketball players also spent fewer hours than their
male counterparts during the off-season engaged in social activities (13 vs.
16) and relaxing alone (11 vs. 14).

Similarly, a study of ten women basketball players and thirteen women
volleyball players enrolled at a large university in the Midwest found that
even though these women "lived primarily in an athletic peer subculture,"
spending most of their time with teammates, they generally performed well
academically, unlike the male basketball players whom the Adlers studied.[71]
Like the men in the Adlers' study, the women in this study enrolled in
college interested in earning degrees; unlike the men in the Adlers' study,
though, these women retained their academic aspirations and their academic
focus throughout their college years instead of becoming engulfed in the
role of college athlete.

In the words of author Barbara Bedker Meyer, the most immediate reason
for the academic perseverance of the women was that a "pro-intellectual
environment" existed within their respective teams; the women "encouraged
each other academically, took active roles in course selection and program
development, and frowned upon special consideration—from professors and
administrators—as a result of their athletic abilities."[72] There may have been
an underlying reason, though, why these women worked as hard in school
as they did on the court, namely, that in the late 1980s, when they were
playing basketball or volleyball, female college athletes enjoyed neither the
public recognition nor the opportunities for a career in professional sports
that might have caused them to abandon their student role in favor of their
athletic role. Meyer recognized this when she speculated in her conclusion
that the "[a]bsence of pressure and of overemphasis on sport from significant
others may have led the women to evaluate realistically the monetary importance of sport to their future."[73]

In contrast, the evidence that Shulman and Bowen gathered caused them to conclude that "[o]ver time, academic outcomes for women athletes have come to replicate patterns found among the men [who play college sports]."[74] Female "High-Profile Athletes" (i.e., basketball players) at the twelve colleges in Shulman and Bowen's study that play big-time sports had higher high-school grades and standardized test scores than their male counterparts, but they still trailed their classmates on both measures. Female basketball players who entered Duke, Georgetown, Northwestern, Notre Dame, Rice, Stanford, Tulane, and Vanderbilt in the fall of 1989 had SAT scores that were, on average, 240 points lower than those of other freshmen. Female basketball players who entered Miami of Ohio, Michigan, North Carolina, and Penn State in the fall of 1989 had SAT scores that were, on average, 177 points lower than those of other freshmen.[75]

Shulman and Bowen also discovered that a gap existed between women athletes generally and their female classmates with respect to class rank. The women athletes who entered the colleges in this sample in the fall of 1989 ranked in the forty-sixth percentile of their college graduating class, whereas the average GPA of all women students who entered the same colleges at the same time put them in the fifty-third percentile.[76] Moreover, the academic performance of women athletes who entered these colleges in 1989 was inferior to that of their predecessors who entered the same colleges in 1976. The 1976 entrants, who were less likely than the 1989 entrants to have been recruited by a coach, were also less likely than their female classmates who were not athletes to rank in the bottom third of their college class on graduation day. Among the 1976 entrants, 30 percent of the women athletes and 33 percent of the women who were not athletes ranked in the bottom third of their class at graduation.[77] Among the 1989 entrants, though, 39 percent of the women athletes and 29 percent of the women who were not athletes ranked in the bottom third of their class at graduation.

Moreover, the women athletes among the 1989 entrants not only earned lower grades than both their female classmates and the women athletes who entered the same colleges in 1976, they even earned lower grades than one would have predicted based on their high school grades and SAT scores.[78] In this respect, the women athletes who entered college in 1989 mirrored the male athletes who entered college with them. Thus, even at academically prestigious colleges, by the early 1990s the increased visibility and competitive intensity of women's sports had apparently contributed to a decline in the academic performance of women athletes. They were better athletes than their predecessors who entered college in 1976 had been, but they were less able than the women athletes of 1976 to compete with their peers in the classroom and the laboratory.

Shulman and Bowen suggest that the major reason for these findings is that an "athletic culture," which "[t]ends to separate athletes from other students and exacerbates the problems of academic performance," exists today among both male and female athletes in all sports, and even at academically competitive colleges.[79] The anti-intellectualism of this culture may be more responsible for the disappointing academic performance of many college athletes than the time commitment necessary to play a big-time college sport. The best evidence for this statement is the finding by Shulman and Bowen that "[students] who stayed up late editing the [college] newspaper, played in the orchestra, or participated in student government did not suffer the same academic penalty for their activities as those who played sports; in fact, the 'extracurriculars' finished much higher in the class, on average, than students in general."[80]

Unfortunately, the increased visibility of women's college sports generally, the growing commercial viability of women's college basketball particularly, and the presence of women's professional leagues in basketball and soccer threaten to strengthen the athletic culture among female college athletes, which bodes ill for their academic performance. Basketball players face the greatest risk of role engulfment. According to James Duderstadt:

> There are signs that women's basketball is moving down the same road to excessive commercialism that characterizes the men's program, complete with the March Madness of the NCAA Championship. There is increased pressure on admissions offices to admit at-risk female athletes, just as there has been for men.[81]

Several signs of excessive commercialism were evident at the 2002 women's Final Four in San Antonio. The site of the two semifinal games was the 30,000-seat Alamodome, where even a ticket for the top row cost $90, and seats closer to the floor cost $120 apiece. In 2003 the women's Final Four took place in Atlanta's Georgia Dome, where 53,000 fans watched the men's Final Four in 2002. ESPN broadcast all sixty-three games of the women's tournament in 2003. In this environment, it is not surprising that Pat Summit, the head coach of the women's basketball team at Tennessee, one of the participants in the 2002 women's Final Four, earns approximately $550,000 a year. Says Duke coach Gail Goestenkors, "We've come a long, long way, and we're still growing."[82]

Bigger is not necessarily better, though. Growth has costs, and in college sports the highest cost of growth is the tendency of the athletic culture to shove academic values aside. It is not surprising that a modern college coach, such as Gail Goestenkors, would sing the "bigger is better" anthem of the athletic culture because the modern method of hiring coaches, especially in Division I, helped to create this culture. Thirty years ago, head coaches of college teams hired as assistants former high school coaches, who often had master's degrees and several years of classroom teaching experience. Today, head coaches hire assistants who have recently finished their playing days, are clever and tenacious at recruiting athletes, but have neither a graduate degree nor teaching experience.[83] This is possible because there are virtually no educational criteria for becoming a college coach. A study that the National Association of Athletics Compliance Coordinators' Committee on Athletics and Higher Education published in 1993 found that only 49 percent of coaches at Division I colleges possessed a master's degree.[84]

Thus, many college coaches see themselves not as educators, but instead, as managers of athletic-entertainment enterprises, which can make them insensitive, even hostile, to their players' academic needs and responsibilities. Under these conditions, both male and female college athletes can become engulfed in their athletic role, to the detriment of their academic role. The long-term consequences of this choice can be tragic.

THE PRICE OF IGNORANCE

College athletes pay a high price for ignoring their academic needs during their athletic careers. One reflection of this is low graduation rates among football players and men's basketball players at colleges that belong to Division I of the NCAA. The association reports annually to the federal Department of Education the percentages of students in general, and of athletic scholarship recipients in particular, who have earned degrees at its member institutions within six years of their enrollment.[85] In 2001 the NCAA reported that 51 percent of the football players and 40 percent of the male basketball players who entered Division I colleges in 1994–95 had graduated within six years.[86] In comparison, 58 percent of all athletic-scholarship recipients, 54 percent of all male students, 59 percent of all female students, and 65 percent of all women basketball players who entered these colleges in 1994–95 had graduated by 2001.[87] In 2000 the NCAA reported that 48 percent of the football players and 42 percent of the male basketball players who entered Division I colleges in 1993–94 had graduated within six years.[88] During the same time period, 60 percent of all athletic-scholarship recipients, 54 percent of all male students, 59 percent of all female students, and 63 percent of all women basketball players earned bachelor's degrees.[89]

The graduation rates of football players and men's basketball players are disheartening because as recipients of athletic scholarships, they do not have to pay to attend classes, and they have easy access to tutoring and other academic support services. Therefore, these athletes are less likely than other students to leave college for financial reasons, and they are more likely to find help with which to overcome academic shortcomings. Thus, it is reasonable to expect that football players and male basketball players, like female basketball players, would be more likely, not less likely, than their nonathlete classmates to graduate from college within six years. Unfortunately, quite the opposite is true.

To be sure, some colleges in Division I have compiled admirable records with respect to the graduation of their athletes. For example, *The Chronicle of Higher Education* reported that all of the African-American football players who enrolled at the University of New Hampshire between 1991–92 and 1994–95 had graduated by 2001, as had all of the male basketball players at Stanford and all of the female basketball players at Lehigh, Loyola of Maryland, Miami of Ohio, Santa Clara, Siena College, Wisconsin, Wagner College, and Wofford College during the same time period.[90] Each of these categories included at least six athletes. Other colleges, though, have compiled deplorable records in this regard. For example, *The Chronicle of Higher Education* also reported that *none* of the male basketball players who enrolled at Cal. State–Sacramento, Jackson State, Arkansas, the University of Louisiana at Lafayette, Memphis, Nevada-Las Vegas, Oklahoma, or Virginia Commonwealth between 1991–92 and 1994–95 had graduated by 2001. *None* of the African-American male basketball players who enrolled at Florida State, Georgia Tech, Jacksonville State, Louisiana Tech, Oregon State, Southwest Missouri State, Tennessee Tech, Texas Tech, Cincinnati, Colorado, Louisville, Minnesota, Oregon, Wyoming, or Western Illinois during this period had graduated by 2001, either. Each category contained at least six athletes. Indeed, at forty-two colleges, including eight that earned bids to the 2001 NCAA Men's Basketball Tournament, no black male basketball player who enrolled between 1991–92 and 1994–95 had graduated by 2001, and at fifteen colleges, no player who enrolled during these years had earned a degree by 2001.

Still, low graduation rates are not the only indicator that playing big-time college sports can be detrimental to academic success. The AIR study, for example, found that for males, playing college football or basketball on a team that had enjoyed a favorable won-lost record against comparable teams over time was associated with an increased likelihood of a "low academic performance."[91] A low academic performance included a GPA of less than 2.0 and either having been on academic probation or having missed an average of at least two classes per week in-season and out-of-season.[92] A male who had a 50 percent likelihood of a low academic performance (based on his high school grades, SAT score, and six other factors that the authors examined) without playing big-time college football or basketball increased that likelihood to 57.5 percent by playing big-time college football or basketball.[93]

Not surprisingly, the AIR study also found that playing college football or basketball on a traditionally successful team was associated with a decreased likelihood of a "high academic performance."[94] A high academic performance included having a GPA of at least 2.5, having never been on academic probation, and having missed an average of no more than one class per week, both in-season and out-of-season.[95] A male who had a 50 percent likelihood of a high academic performance without playing big-time college football or basketball decreased that likelihood to 31.8 percent by playing big-time college football or basketball.[96]

Women basketball players did not suffer as much academically from playing a big-time college sport as football and men's basketball players did. Women who played big-time college basketball were, like their male counterparts, less likely to achieve a "high academic performance," but unlike their male counterparts, their participation in sport at a high level did not increase the likelihood that they would turn in a "low academic performance."[97]

Similar results emerged from a subsequent study that sought to estimate the effects of athletic participation on the reading comprehension, mathematics, and critical thinking skills of freshmen at eighteen four-year colleges, some of which play sports in Division I. The study compared the scores that 2,416 students achieved on the Collegiate Assessment of Academic Proficiency (CAAP) on two occasions; namely, in the fall of 1992, shortly before their freshmen year began, and in the spring of 1993, as their freshman year ended.[98] It found that among males, both nonathletes and athletes who participated in sports other than football and basketball showed modest gains in reading comprehension and in mathematics between the beginning and the end of their freshman year in college. Among females, both athletes and nonathletes gained in reading comprehension, but the athletes' gain was less than half the size of the nonathletes' gain.

Conversely, males who played football and basketball showed modest declines in both reading comprehension and mathematics during their freshman year. Most males in this study progressed in reading comprehension and mathematics during their freshman year in college, but males who played football and basketball regressed during the same time period. This disparity between football and basketball players, on the one hand, and their male classmates, on the other, remained even when the authors "controlled for"— that is, compared—only freshman males who were similar with respect to their "precollege academic motivation," age, ethnicity, "family social origins," "credit hours taken as freshmen," and residence (i.e., on-campus or off-campus). Therefore, playing football or basketball, not socioeconomic status, accounts for the decline in cognitive skills among certain males during their freshman year in college. These results are troubling because, as the authors note, "initial academic disadvantages become cumulative over time, [therefore] one might anticipate that such modest freshman-year disadvantages would become more pronounced during the course of one's college career."[99] Put simply, football players and men's basketball players are likely to finish college farther behind their classmates in reading comprehension and mathematics than they were when they enrolled.

To make matters worse, this "negative learning impact" on males of playing football and basketball seems not to be limited to big-time sports colleges. The authors found that playing football or basketball had the same effect on the reading comprehension and mathematical skills of male freshman at Division II and III colleges as it had on the reading comprehension and mathematical skills of their counterparts at Division I colleges. Moreover, the effect of playing football or men's basketball was the same at colleges where freshmen had high reading comprehension and mathematics scores on the CAAP as it was at colleges where freshmen registered modest scores in both of these categories. This finding led the authors to suggest that the negative learning impact on males of playing college football or basketball was a product of the culture of those sports, not of the competitive level at which one played them. "It may be," the authors concluded, "that football and basketball teams constitute campus subcultures that attach less value to academic achievement than do other sports."[100]

Education is not only about academic achievement, though. It is also about personal growth; namely, becoming familiar with people, ideas, events, and cultures that one previously was unaware of, ignored, or misunderstood. College athletes do not perform well on this measure of education, either, according to psychologists Nancy Cantor and Deborah Prentice, whose survey of sophomores at three eastern colleges led them to conclude that athletes experience less personal growth in college than their classmates. According to Cantor and Prentice:

> Compared with other students, athletes report having grown less as people at college and having spent limited time at cultural events, pursuing new interests, or meeting new people from different backgrounds. . . . Time pressure is not wholly responsible for these deficits, as other students who are equally active in extracurricular pursuits make time for more of the . . . broadening activities.[101]

It is unclear whether athletes tend not to pursue a well-rounded college education only because their sports make excessive demands on their time or also because the athletic culture rejects symphony concerts and poetry readings.[102] It is clear, though, that when playing a sport either consumes so much of a student's time or becomes a student's entire identity, college sports are not the healthy, constructive adjunct to the educational process that they can and should be. Four years of playing basketball or football, and poker or gin rummy, with one's teammates hardly amount to a well-rounded college education.

Playing basketball or football, though, can make one a celebrity, and the glare of celebrity may outshine academic achievement and personal growth for college athletes, causing them to focus all their attention on the present, to the probable detriment of their futures. Several of the basketball players whom the Adlers studied fell victim to the glare of celebrity, in part because journalists made the players believe that alumni, boosters, and area residents were watching them closely and counting on them to have a successful season. These players inferred from the journalists' attention that "their actions were more important than those of the ordinary person, and that being in the limelight of public attention was where they belonged."[103] For example, one player said: "I've got two finals tomorrow and one the next day. I should be up in the room studying right now. But how can I get my mind on that when I know I've got to guard Michael Jordan tomorrow night?"[104]

The glare of celebrity is brief for most college athletes, though. Athletic eligibility ends quickly, and unless a professional contract awaits, the athlete who has neglected academics and personal growth in favor of the athletic role will face a rapid and dramatic loss of personal identity. This is common because only about 310 of the 50,000 football players (3.3 percent) at NCAA-member colleges earn a position on an NFL team and only about 50 of the 13,000 basketball players (1.9 percent) at NCAA-member colleges earn a position on an NBA team each year.[105] One player in the Adlers' study who lost his athletic identity after college began to re-think his lifelong focus on sports. He said:

> If I had a child, I would try to steer him towards something else other than athaletics, [sic] because it's a dream that we live as athaletes [sic], it's a fantasy, and after your senior year I really recognized that the fantasy was coming to an end, and all the crowd cheering and the boosters there, it was all going to come to an end. And I'm glad I realized that early my senior year because [the boosters] were looking toward the freshmen and the sophomores and the younger kids, and I thought that I was one of their favorites somewhat out here, and it's really, you really crash, you really come down to earth quick.[106]

To add insult to injury, the college athlete who becomes engulfed in the athletic role and neglects academic matters may discover that when athletic eligibility ends, so does the best chance to pursue a college degree affordably and to prepare for a profession that will bring personal satisfaction and financial self-sufficiency. College fails to expand either the personal horizons or the professional prospects of such athletes, even though it has the opposite effect on most students.

Colleges also pay a high price for subordinating athletes' academic needs to the pursuit of national championships and bids to bowl games and the NCAA Basketball Tournament. A tarnished image is likely to be part of that price. James Duderstadt observed that:

> Nebraska can win all the national championships it wishes, and it will never catch fair Harvard's eye. Indeed, fame in athletics is often paradoxical, since it can attract public scrutiny, which can then uncover violations and scandal.[107]

A college need not experience violations and scandals, though, in order to see its image tarnished by sports; the perception by alumni and friends that a college overemphasizes sports to the detriment of academic life can produce the same result. When this happens, the college will suffer damage, not only to its academic reputation but also to its relationship with those alumni and friends, which, ironically, the pursuit of athletic success was designed to enhance.

Shulman and Bowen asked a representative sample of graduates from twelve colleges that play big-time sports what emphasis their colleges currently placed on intercollegiate athletics and what emphasis these colleges should place on intercollegiate athletics. The graduates, men and women who enrolled in college in 1976, expressed a desire to see their colleges put less emphasis on intercollegiate athletics. The graduates of the public institutions in the sample (Miami of Ohio, Michigan, North Carolina, and Penn State) felt strongly that their colleges overemphasize sports, as their high negative scores on these questions (desired emphasis minus perceived current emphasis = −0.98) indicate.[108] The graduates of the private big-time sports colleges in the sample (Duke, Georgetown, Northwestern, Notre Dame, Rice, Stanford, Tulane, and Vanderbilt) also thought that their colleges overemphasized sports, although they were not as negative as their counterparts at the public colleges were (desired emphasis minus perceived current emphasis = −0.46).

These attitudes have important financial implications for colleges. Shulman and Bowen found that among the graduates who had entered the aforementioned colleges in 1951 and 1976, respectively, the big donors (i.e., top 5 percent of their class in donations), male and female, wished to see a reduced emphasis on sports. This was especially true of graduates of the private colleges in the sample that play big-time sports. The differences between the desired emphasis and the perceived degree of emphasis on sports at these colleges were −.15 for the 1951 men, −.29 for the 1976 men, and −.41 for the 1976 women.[109] Therefore, Shulman and Bowen concluded not only that "there is no evidence to suggest that 'paybacks' [to colleges for success in sports] will come in the form of enhanced generosity by alumni/ae," but, indeed, that "at the most intensive level of play [NCAA Division I-A], winning appears to have had, if anything, a modest *negative* effect on the overall amount of alumni giving."[110]

Shulman and Bowen also asked graduates who had entered college in 1951, 1976, and 1989, respectively, how much emphasis their colleges placed and should place on intercollegiate athletics, faculty research, alumni concerns, a diverse student body, a broad liberal arts education, other extracurricular activities, intellectual freedom, residential life, and teaching undergraduates. The item that received the highest positive score, indicating the graduates' desire that it receive more emphasis, was teaching undergraduates (0.70), and the only items that received negative scores, indicating a desire for less emphasis, were intercollegiate athletics (−0.32) and faculty research (−0.26).[111] Evidently alumni wish to see their colleges reduce their emphases on sports and research because both activities divert human and financial resources from undergraduate teaching and learning. Perhaps the alumni also want their colleges to pay less attention to sports and research because both endeavors cause colleges to create and to market myths; namely, that student-athletes are interested primarily in their studies, and that teacher-scholars are interested primarily in undergraduate teaching, despite compelling evidence to the contrary. The analysis of myths is an appropriate focus for higher education, but the creation and the promotion of them is the opposite of higher education.[112]

The myths about student-athletes don't fool the American public, though, as recent poll results indicate. A poll of 850 adults that the American Council on Education made public in January 2001 indicated that 56 percent of the respondents believed that colleges place "too much emphasis" on intercollegiate athletic programs, and that only five percent believed that colleges place "too little emphasis" on such programs.[113] A poll of 1,000 adults between the ages of twenty-five and sixty-five that the *Chronicle of Higher Education* published in 2003 revealed that 67 percent of the respondents agreed: "Four-year colleges and universities put too much emphasis on sports," while only 35 percent agreed: "Sports should be a priority for universities."[114] These results show that when colleges shortchange undergraduate education in pursuit of athletic fame and fortune, they sacrifice their integrity, which is their most valuable asset.

Public cynicism about college sports will persist and colleges will continue to sacrifice their integrity by pursuing athletic success at the expense of undergraduate education as long as coaches and athletic directors feel pressure to earn money from sports. Such pressure lies at the heart of the commercial model of college sports. While the commercial model reigns supreme, athletic fame and fortune will trump the academic needs of college athletes, notwithstanding a decision by the NCAA in October of 2002 to increase the number of hours that athletes must complete in order to remain eligible for sports.[115] Indeed, this decision by the association's board of directors, which consists of college presidents, is likely to increase public cynicism about college sports.

On the one hand, it requires athletes who enter college beginning in August of 2003 to complete 40 percent of the courses they need for a degree by the start of their third year in college, 60 percent by the start of their fourth year, and 80 percent by the beginning of their fifth year, up from the 25–50–75 percent standard that existed previously.[116] On the other hand, in an effort to reduce the influence of standardized test scores on athletic eligibility, this decision modifies the sliding scale of test scores and high school grades that determines eligibility and permits athletes who score as low as 400 on the SAT (no correct answers) to be eligible to play as freshmen if their high school GPAs in fourteen core courses (up from thirteen previously) are 3.55 or higher.[117]

The second provision invites high school teachers and administrators to inflate athletes' grades in order to compensate for low scores on standardized tests. The two provisions, taken together, invite academic fraud by college athletes and officials because they permit the admission of athletes who are even less prepared for college academically than their predecessors; yet they expect these athletes to make more rapid progress toward a degree than previous rules required.[118] College coaches and athletic administrators will figure out how to evade these new academic progress requirements, just as they have figured out how to major in eligibility and how to work around the four-and-twenty-hour rule. Thus, it is necessary to release the financial pressure on coaches and athletic directors in order for athletes to be students, coaches to be educators, and college sports to be compatible with the goals of higher education.

The participation model is the valve that can release the pressure because it recognizes that sports have no educational merit, and hence, do not belong in academic institutions unless they are compatible with intellectual inquiry, career preparation, and personal growth. John Gerdy has written that: "[S]port is not educational simply because it is sport. Rather, it is the environment within which sports participation occurs that influences the educational, moral, and ethical development of participants."[119]

If the participation model is the valve that can release the pressure to profit from sports, Title IX is the wrench that will open the valve. Later chapters will discuss Title IX and the participation model as key components of a solution to the problems in college sports. First, though, it is necessary to discuss the social consequences of big-time college sports, which is the task of chapter five.

NOTES

1. Sarah E. Gohl, *A Lesson in English and Gender: Title IX and the Male Student-Athlete*, 50 Duke Law Journal 1123, 1139 (2001).

2. Alex P. Kellogg, "For Athletes, How Much Practice Time Is Too Much?" *The Chronicle of Higher Education*, June 1, 2001, pp. A33–A34.

3. Ibid.

4. Patricia A. Adler and Peter Adler, *Backboards and Blackboards: College Athletes and Role Engulfment* (New York: Columbia University Press, 1991), pp. 27–28.

5. Ibid., p. 67.

6. Katie Funk, "Academic Reform Group Seeks Sweeping Changes in Education of College Athletes," *The Kansas City Star*, June 24, 2000 [available at http://www.kcstar.com/item/pages/sports.pat,sports/37748f 9e.624,.html].

7. Adler and Adler, *Backboards and Blackboards*, p. 150.

8. Ibid., p. 84.

9. Ibid., p. 85.

10. Alexander Wolff, "School's Out," *Sports Illustrated*, February 24, 1997, pp. 60–66.

11. Ibid.

12. Welch Suggs, "A Professor's Challenge to Sports at Tennessee," *The Chronicle of Higher Education*, July 21, 2000, pp. A37–A38.

13. Associated Press, "Professor Feels Like A 'Pariah' on Tennessee Campus," *The Valley News* (West Lebanon, N.H.), September 19, 2000, p. B7.

14. Welch Suggs, "A Professor's Challenge to Sports at Tennessee," *The Chronicle of Higher Education*, July 21, 2000, pp. A37–A38.

15. Welch Suggs, "Once Again, U. of Minnesota Asks Why Its Athletes Are Scandal-Prone," *The Chronicle of Higher Education*, July 16, 1999, pp. A41–A42.

16. George Dohrmann, "U Basketball Program Accused of Academic Fraud," *St. Paul Pioneer Press*, March 10, 1999 [available at http://www.pioneerplanet.com/uofm/docs/0310gophers.htm].

17. Ibid.

18. Ibid.

19. George Dohrmann, " 'Experiment': Haskins Sought Counselor's Move to Athletic Staff," *St. Paul Pioneer Press*, March 10, 1999 [available at http://www.pioneerplanet.com/uofm/docs/0310goside.htm].

20. Welch Suggs, "Scandals Force Colleges to Reassess Roles of Academic Advisors for Athletes," *The Chronicle of Higher Education*, December 3, 1999, pp. A51–A53.

21. Judith Yates Borger and Laura Billings, "Gangelhoff: 'I Thought Maybe I Could Teach These Kids,' " *St. Paul Pioneer Press*, March 12, 1999 [available at http://www.pioneerplanet.com/uofm/docs/0312jan.htm].

22. Ibid.

23. Ibid.

24. Welch Suggs, "NCAA Gives Minnesota 4-Year Probation for Academic Fraud," *The Chronicle of Higher Education*, November 3, 2000, p. A49. In April of 2002, Minnesota announced that as part of its efforts to save $9.5 million over five years, it would merge its men's and women's athletic departments into one department. Welch Suggs, "U. of Minnesota Reorganizes Athletics Program and Cuts 3 Teams," *The Chronicle of Higher Education*, April 26, 2002, p. A44.

25. Welch Suggs, "Scandals Force Colleges to Reassess Roles of Academic Advisors for Athletes," *The Chronicle of Higher Education*, December 3, 1999, pp. A51–A53.

26. Ibid.

27. Welch Suggs, "Tennessee Restructures Tutoring Program," *The Chronicle of Higher Education*, June 23, 2000, p. A53.

28. Welch Suggs, "UC-Berkeley Is Among 2 Colleges Accused of Academic Problems Involving Athletes," *The Chronicle of Higher Education*, February 28, 2001 [available at http://chronicle.com/daily/2001/02/2001022804n.htm].

29. Welch Suggs, "NCAA Punishes 3 Colleges for Rules Violations," *The Chronicle of Higher Education*, January 11, 2002, p. A49.

30. Kirk Nielsen, "End Run," *Miami New Times*, March 7, 2002 [available at http://miaminewtimes.com/issues/2002-03-07/metro.html/1/index.html].

31. Ibid.

32. Ibid.

33. Murray Sperber, *Shake Down The Thunder: The Creation of Notre Dame Football* (New York: Henry Holt and Company, 1993), p. 107. Ronald Reagan immortalized George Gipp with his portrayal of the great Notre Dame athlete in the 1940 film *Knute Rockne—All-American*. Murray Sperber, *Onward to Victory: The Crises That Shaped College Sports* (New York: Henry Holt, 1998), pp. 17–18.

34. Jim Naughton, "Athletes on Top-Ranked Teams Lack Grades and Test Scores of Other Students," *The Chronicle of Higher Education*, July 25, 1997, pp. A43–A44.

35. Ibid.

36. Mike Rubin, "Personal Fouls," *The Village Voice*, January 1, 1997, p. 22.

37. Jim Naughton, "Athletes on Top-Ranked Teams Lack Grades and Test Scores of Other Students," *The Chronicle of Higher Education*, July 25, 1997, pp. A43–A44.

38. James L. Shulman and William G. Bowen, *The Game of Life: College Sports and Educational Values* (Princeton, N.J.: Princeton University Press, 2001), p. 47.

39. Ibid., p. 64.

40. Ibid.

41. James J. Duderstadt, *Intercollegiate Athletics and the American University: A University President's Perspective* (Ann Arbor, Mich.: The University of Michigan Press, 2000), pp. 193–194.

42. Ibid.

43. Adler and Adler, *Backboards and Blackboards*, p. 62.

44. Ibid., p. 73.

45. John Feinstein, *The Last Amateurs: Playing for Glory and Honor in Division I Basketball* (Boston: Little, Brown and Company, 2000).

46. Ibid., p. xix.

47. Adler and Adler, *Backboards and Blackboards*, p. 148.

48. Carter Strickland, "Integrity on Trial," *Spokesman Review* (Spokane, WA), May 6, 2001, p. C9 [available at www.spokesmanreview.com/archives].

49. NCAA Operating Bylaws, Article 17.1.5, Time Limits for Athletically Related Activities, reprinted in NCAA, *2002–03 NCAA Division I Manual* (Michael V. Earle, ed., 2002), p. 221. *See also* Alex P. Kellogg, "For Athletes, How Much Practice Time Is Too Much?" *The Chronicle of Higher Education*, June 1, 2001, pp. A33–A34.

50. Alex P. Kellogg, "For Athletes, How Much Time Is Too Much?" *The Chronicle of Higher Education*, June 1, 2001, pp. A33–A34.

51. Ibid.

52. Ibid.

53. Ibid.

54. Murray Sperber, *Beer and Circus: How Big-Time College Sports Is Crippling Undergraduate Education* (New York: Henry Holt and Company, 2000), p. 31.

55. Robert J. Rossi and Terry Armstrong, Studies of Intercollegiate Athletics: Report No. 1: *Summary Results from the 1987–88 National Study of Intercollegiate Athletes* (Palo Alto, Cal.: Center for the Study of Athletics, American Institutes for Research, 1988), p. 26.

56. Ibid., p. 27.

57. Ibid., p. 46.

58. Ibid., p. 47.

59. Ibid., p. 48.

60. Robert J. Rossi and Terry Armstrong, Studies of Intercollegiate Athletics: Report No. 3: *The Experiences of Black Intercollegiate Athletes at NCAA Division I Institutions* (Palo Alto, Cal.: Center for the Study of Athletics, American Institutes for Research, 1989), p. 41.

61. Ibid., p. 43.

62. Ibid., p. 44.

63. Tanya R. Upthegrove, Vincent J. Roscigno, and Camille Zubrinsky Charles, "Big Money Collegiate Sports: Racial Concentration, Contradictory Pressures, and Academic Performance," *Social Science Quarterly* 80, no. 4 (December, 1999): 718–737.

64. Ibid.

65. Kirsten F. Benson, "Constructing Academic Inadequacy: African American Athletes' Stories of Schooling," *The Journal of Higher Education*, 71, no. 2 (March/April, 2000): 223–246.

66. Ibid.

67. Ibid.

68. Ibid.

69. Robert J. Rossi and Terry Armstrong, *Studies of Intercollegiate Athletics: Report No. 4: Women in Intercollegiate Athletics at NCAA Division I Institutions* (Palo Alto, Cal.: Center for the Study of Athletes, American Institutes for Research, 1989), p. 33.

70. Ibid., p. 34.

71. Barbara Bedker Meyer, "From Idealism to Actualization: the Academic Performance of Female Collegiate Athletes," *Sociology of Sport Journal* 7 (1990): 44–57.

72. Ibid.

73. Ibid.

74. Shulman and Bowen, *The Game Of Life*, p. 155.

75. Ibid., pp. 133–134.

76. Ibid., pp. 142–143.

77. Ibid., pp. 144–145.

78. Ibid., p. 155.

79. Ibid., p. 82.

80. Ibid., p. 70.

81. Duderstadt, *Intercollegiate Athletics and the American University*, p. 211.

82. "Women's Final Four Is Now a Big Sell," *The New York Times*, April 1, 2002, p. D5.

83. John Gerdy, *The Successful College Athletic Program: The New Standard* (Phoenix: Oryx Press, 1997), p. 93.

84. Ibid., p. 100.

85. Welch Suggs, "Graduation Rate for Male Basketball Players Falls to Lowest Level in a Decade," *The Chronicle of Higher Education*, September 21, 2001, pp. A34–A36. This measure is controversial because it counts against a college's graduation rate athletes who transfer to other colleges or who leave college early to become professional athletes while in good academic standing at the college from which they departed. Some coaches at Division I colleges would like the NCAA to replace this "unadjusted" measure of graduation rates with an "adjusted" measure, which would exclude from the measurement of a college's graduation rate those athletes who left the college in good academic standing. The adoption of the adjusted measure would improve the graduation rates of some colleges, but it is a less accurate indicator than the present method is of whether a college recruits athletes who are also serious students and helps them to meet their academic goals within a reasonable

period of time. The adjusted method would also reward colleges where the football and basketball teams are merely brief stops for future professional athletes, and where coaches revoke the scholarships of athletes whose athletic performances do not meet expectations, because it would exclude both types of athlete from the calculation of graduation rates. Thus, the present method of measuring graduation rates, despite its imperfections, is preferable to the alternative because it is more compatible with the stated aims of higher education. *See:* Bruce I. Mallette, "Evaluating Academics in Intercollegiate Athletics: Methodological Issues," in Bruce I. Mallette and Richard D. Howard, eds., *Monitoring and Assessing Intercollegiate Athletics* (San Francisco: Jossey-Bass Publishers, 1992), p. 66.

86. Welch Suggs, "Graduation Rate for Male Basketball Players Falls to Lowest Level in a Decade," *The Chronicle of Higher Education*, September 21, 2001, pp. A34–A37.

87. Ibid.

88. Welch Suggs, "Graduation Rates for Athletes Hold Steady," *The Chronicle of Higher Education*, December 1, 2000, pp. A47–A49.

89. Ibid.

90. Welch Suggs, "Graduation Rate for Male Basketball Players Falls to Lowest Level in a Decade," *The Chronicle of Higher Education*, September 21, 2001, pp. A34–A37.

91. American Institutes for Research, *Studies of Intercollegiate Athletics: Report No. 7: Academic Performance and College Sports* (Palo Alto, Cal.: American Institutes for Research, 1992), p. 6.

92. Ibid., p. 18.

93. Ibid., p. 30.

94. Ibid., p. 6.

95. Ibid., p. 18.

96. Ibid., p. 30.

97. Ibid.

98. Ernest T. Pascarella, Louise Bohr, Amaury Nora, and Patrick T. Terenzini, "Intercollegiate Athletic Participation and Freshman-Year Cognitive Outcomes," *Journal of Higher Education* 66, no. 4 (July/Aug. 1995): 369–387.

99. Ibid.

100. Ibid.

101. Nancy E. Cantor and Deborah A. Prentice, "The Life of the Modern Day Student-Athlete: Opportunities Won and Lost," a paper presented at the Princeton Conference on Higher Education, March 21–23, 1996, p. 23 (quoted in Shulman and Bowen, *The Game Of Life*, p. 74).

102. The time demands of college sports, especially in Division I, certainly contribute to the narrowly focused lives that many college athletes lead, though. *See* Darren Bilberry, "The Myth of Athletics and Educational Opportunity," in John R. Gerdy, ed., *Sports in School: The Future of an Institution* (New York: Teachers College Press, 2000), pp. 91–101.

103. Adler and Adler, *Backboards and Blackboards*, p. 92.

104. Ibid., p. 167.

105. Sarah E. Gohl, *A Lesson in English and Gender: Title IX and the Male Student-Athlete*, 50 Duke Law Journal 1123, 1134 (2001). Another estimate is even less optimistic. It states that only 2 percent of college football players earn positions

on NFL teams and that only 1.3 percent of college basketball players earn positions on NBA teams. *See* Carter Strickland, "Integrity on Trial," *The Spokesman Review* (Spokane, WA.), May 6, 2001, p. C9 [available at http://www.spokesmanreview. com/archives]. Regardless of which estimate is the more precise one, the prospects for a career in the NFL or the NBA are bleak; therefore, all but a few college football and basketball players will lose their athletic identity, and the celebrity that accompanies it, when their college eligibility ends.

106. Adler and Adler, *Backboards and Blackboards*, p. 181.

107. Duderstadt, *Intercollegiate Athletics and the American University*, p. 146.

108. Shulman and Bowen, *The Game Of Life*, p. 202.

109. Ibid., pp. 217–218.

110. Ibid., p. 223.

111. Ibid., pp. 200–201.

112. Allen Sack and Ellen Staurowsky expressed a similar idea when they wrote that "[t]he major task of a university is to challenge falsehood and ideology, not to perpetuate them." Allen L. Sack and Ellen J. Staurowsky, *College Athletes For Hire: The Evolution and Legacy of the NCAA's Amateur Myth* (Westport, Conn.: Praeger, 1998), p. 92.

113. Mary Beth Marklein, "Colleges' Sports Success Is Not a Major Draw," *USA Today*, March 20, 2001 [available at http://www.usatoday.com/life/2001-03-20-college-sports.htm].

114. Welch Suggs, "Sports as the University's 'Front Porch'? The Public Is Skeptical," *The Chronicle of Higher Education*, May 2, 2003, p. A17.

115. Welch Suggs, "NCAA Approves New Academic Standards for Athletes," *The Chronicle of Higher Education*, November 1, 2002 [available at http://chronicle. com/daily/2002/11/2002110103n.htm].

116. Ibid.

117. Ibid. In April of 2003, the NCAA's Division I Management Council approved an increase in the number of core high school courses that one must complete satisfactorily in order to compete in sports as a college freshman. If the NCAA's Board of Directors approves this proposal, the minimum number will increase to sixteen in 2008–2009. *See* Welch Suggs, "NCAA Announces Tougher High-School Standards for Athletes Seeking College Eligibility," *The Chronicle of Higher Education*, April 16, 2003 [available at http://chronicle.com/daily/2003/04/2003041601n.htm].

118. Tom Farrey, "It's All Academic Now," *ESPN.com*, October 31, 2002 [available at http://espn.go.com/columns/farrey_tom/1453693.html].

119. John R. Gerdy, "Want Value for Education Dollars? Try Music!" in John R. Gerdy, ed., *Sports in School: The Future of an Institution* (New York: Teachers College Press, 2000), p. 135.

CHAPTER 5

SEASONS OF PAIN

SOCIAL CONSEQUENCES OF COLLEGE SPORTS

LOST SOULS

When President Hutchins of the University of Chicago observed that a college that acts in pursuit of money "must lose its soul and frequently does not get the money" (see Chapter 3), he was correct on both counts.[1] Chapter 3 showed that most Division I colleges do not earn a profit from sports. This chapter will show that Division I colleges have lost their souls in the pursuit of athletic fame and fortune by exploiting athletes and by tolerating coaches' and athletes' deplorable behavior in return for bowl bids and tournament invitations. As a result, the American public is dubious about the role of sports in higher education.

One way in which big-time college sports exploit athletes is by requiring them to train intensely year-round. Michael Goforth, head athletic trainer at Virginia Tech, has described the year-round schedule of the Hokies' football team as follows:

> We've got the bowl game in January, then spring practice starts, what, six weeks later? And in between that, a lot of kids have surgery. Then after spring ball, it's [weight]lifting, then summer workouts, then we're back here in the fall.[2]

This schedule instills a single-mindedness that makes athletic life more important than academic life. Consequently, even athletes who are good students sacrifice educational opportunities, such as internships, in order to train for next season. Coaches are unapologetic about such sacrifices because they want their athletes to "stay focused" on sport. Boyd Epley, the director of athletic performance (i.e., strength and conditioning coach) at Nebraska, says: "I'm not sure how you compete when you lose focus, go off, and do internships."[3]

Mr. Epley need not worry whether his players can compete successfully for jobs or for admission to graduate or professional schools; his job requires him to care only about how well they compete in football. No such tie binds R. Scott Kretchmar, a sports ethicist at Penn State, who is critical of the educational and psychological consequences of the year-round training schedules to which big-time college athletes now adhere. Says Kretchmar:

> What bothers me" [about the year-round schedule], is the narrowness, the illiberal nature of the education. It forces parents and children to make an unfortunate choice—either to forfeit opportunities to be a varsity athlete, or on the other hand becoming unduly narrow, specialized, and risking burnout to get a college scholarship and perhaps a professional experience.[4]

It can also force a college athlete to become single-minded about sport or risk incurring the wrath of his coach.

In this atmosphere coaches can become so determined to win that they will abuse their athletes emotionally and physically if they think that such behavior will ensure competitive success. The clearest example of this is Texas Tech basketball coach Bob Knight. Knight is the former coach at Indiana University whose 2.3-second handhold on the neck of Hoosier guard Neil Reed may be the best known example of physical abuse of a player by a college coach. The public disclosure during the spring of 2000 of a videotape that revealed this incident led to an investigation by Indiana's board of trustees that found that in his twenty-nine years in Bloomington, Knight had engaged in a "pattern of inappropriate behavior," including physical abuse of his athletes and colleagues, that was "persistent and systematic."[5] These revelations were not sufficient in the trustees' eyes to cost the coach his job, but they spawned a long overdue "zero tolerance" policy that Knight soon violated when he grabbed the arm of a student who greeted him by saying, "Hey, what's up, Knight?" and admonished the student to address him as "Coach Knight" or "Mr. Knight."[6]

Unfortunately, Knight's methods are not unique to him. Neither are they exclusive to male coaches, as Nicole Vallieres discovered when she began playing varsity women's basketball at the University of Massachusetts in the fall of 1997. According to court papers, Coach Joanie O'Brien's verbal and physical intimidation of her players began on the first day of formal practices. They charge that O'Brien yelled at players, "Are you stupid or something? What the f—— is wrong with you that you cannot understand this f——ing concept?" and that she grabbed players "so tightly that red marks would appear on their arms," and "pull[ed] or push[ed] them to the position in which she wanted them on the court." Nicole claims that she had a welt on her body where Coach O'Brien slapped her. Depressed and unable to concentrate on her schoolwork, Nicole left UMass after her freshman year and transferred to another college.[7]

College athletes are not always victims, though; they can be villains, too. Police arrested at least 175 athletes from Division I-A colleges between August 1, 1997, and August 1, 1998, most often for violence against others, including forty instances of assault and battery, eleven instances of rape or sexual assault, and eleven instances of domestic abuse (i.e., an assault of a wife or girlfriend).[8] Colleges have long been remarkably tolerant of criminal behavior by their athletes. A case in point is Marcus Webb, who, in 1992, while he was a member of the Boston Celtics, pled guilty to third-degree sexual assault after having been charged with the rape of a female college student whom he had dated. Webb played college basketball at the University of Alabama, where he rarely attended classes, was arrested twice, was named as the defendant in a paternity suit, and collected enough speeding tickets to cause the state of Alabama to suspend his driver's license, which it later revoked when he drove with a suspended license. The university did not punish Webb for these transgressions until his exasperated coach finally suspended him just before the start of his senior season, whereupon Webb left college to play professional basketball.[9]

Colleges are still reluctant to punish criminal behavior by athletes. For example, in early December 2001, a female student at the University of Colorado reported to police that she was the victim of a gang rape at a party in her apartment that six football players and 15 recruits attended. An investigation ensued, but the football players all played in the Fiesta Bowl on New Year's Day, 2002.[10] This reluctance to punish athletes for criminal behavior is not surprising, because the same pressures for athletic success that cause colleges to admit and retain athletes who are academically deficient cause them to admit and retain athletes who are not solid citizens. Former Brigham Young University football coach LaVell Edwards acknowledged this when he observed:

> We're all trying to be as honorable as we can. Still, it's tough to turn a real good ballplayer loose. If you've got a guy who's going to make a difference on your ball club, you're not going to be as objective about him, because you want him around. The bottom line is [that] your job's at stake.[11]

Perhaps the strongest evidence, though, that colleges have lost their souls in the pursuit of athletic fame and fortune is that at any given time in recent decades, numerous colleges have been "on probation"; that is, under penalty by the NCAA for having violated its rules. Between 1952 and 1985, the NCAA penalized 150 colleges either for recruiting violations or for having provided improper benefits to their athletes.[12] Between 1974 and 1994, the NCAA penalized 50 percent of the colleges that play football in either Division I-A or Division I-AA and that play basketball in Division I.[13] During the 1980s an average of 16 of the 106 colleges that played football in Division I-A were on probation each year, an increase of seven colleges over the average annual total during the 1970s.[14] According to former NCAA executive director Walter Byers:

> Violations [of NCAA rules] are so prevalent that they have become classified as secondary and major by the NCAA. The secondary cases have become an industry within themselves. There were 150 such cases in 1987. In 1993, there were 900, a fivefold growth. Approximately 75 to 80 percent involve NCAA Division I members. Major cases have remained static, averaging about 22 per year during the same period.[15]

During the 1990s the NCAA penalized more than half of the members of Division I-A for either secondary or major violations of association rules.[16] The beat goes on in the new millennium; consider, for example, the Southeastern Conference (SEC) during 2002. The NCAA put Alabama and Kentucky on probation for major recruiting violations. Louisiana State University (LSU) self-reported to the NCAA minor violations in athletic recruiting and in its tutoring program for athletes.[17] Arkansas self-reported the payment of excessive wages to athletes by a sports booster. The NCAA and the conference office investigated allegations that a Tennessee booster from Mobile, Alabama, used a sportswriter to funnel illegal payments to Mobile resident and former Tennessee quarterback Tee Martin.[18] The investigation ended early in January of 2003 when the NCAA cleared the university of wrongdoing because the evidence was insufficient to indicate that the alleged benefactor was a booster or that any booster had provided money to Martin. On the other hand, the NCAA noted that it was likely that Martin, who now plays professionally and is beyond the NCAA's reach, had violated the association's amateurism bylaw by receiving improper financial assistance while he played for the Volunteers.[19] The University of Georgia may not be as fortunate as Tennessee. It faces allegations that a former assistant coach gave A grades in a course he taught to several players who never attended a class and that coaches gave money to players in violation of NCAA rules.[20] The association and the university were investigating these allegations in the spring of 2003.

Under these circumstances it is no surprise that polls taken during the past decade or so (see Chapters 1 and 4, respectively) show that many Americans agree with President Hutchins that colleges lose their souls when they seek fame and fortune through sports. In the most recent poll, the results of which were published in *The Chronicle of Higher Education*, 67 percent of the respondents said that colleges place "too much emphasis" on intercollegiate athletic programs, and only 33 percent said that sports should be "a priority" for colleges.[21]

ATHLETES AS VICTIMS

One reason for the public's misgivings about college sports is the colleges' long-standing practice of using athletes' services for four years, then casting them off without a degree or any marketable skills other than athletic talent, which will take only a small percentage of them to careers in professional sports. The principal victims of this practice have been African-American males, who are often the stars of college football and basketball teams, but who are just as often casualties of commercialized college sports. The best evidence that commercialized college sports have treated African-American males badly is their low rate of graduation. Only 42 percent of African-American male athletes who enrolled in a Division I college as freshmen in 1994–95 had graduated by 2001.[22]

Most African Americans exhaust their collegiate athletic eligibility without having obtained either a college degree or a professional sports contract, which can complicate the transition to postcollege life. Dr. Billy Hawkins, who has counseled African-American college athletes, writes:

> Black communities have witnessed too many young Black males that did not make it professionally or educationally return home with little employable skills because they spent the past 3–5 years honing skills at a university that are not employable outside of professional sports.[23]

African-American athletes who fail to win professional sports contracts not only may have to shed their childhood dreams and their athletic identities after college but also may have to let go of the perception that sports are a viable avenue to financial success and social prominence in America. A survey that the Center for the Study of Sport in Society at Northeastern University in Boston conducted several years ago found that 66 percent of African-American males aged thirteen to eighteen believed that they could earn a living as an athlete; the comparable figure for white males in that age group was 33 percent.[24] This survey also found that African-American parents were four times more likely than white parents to believe that their children could be professional athletes.[25]

At first blush, the optimism with which African Americans view their prospects, and the prospects of their children, for careers in professional sports may seem reasonable because 80 percent of NBA players and 67 percent of NFL players are African Americans.[26] Furthermore, African Americans, unlike whites who belong to the middle and upper classes, have not enjoyed the luxury of participating in sports for their inherent physical and psychological benefits. On the contrary, their traditional exclusion from the professions in America long ago caused them to view participation in sports as a viable means of social and economic advancement, indeed, perhaps the most viable means of achieving those ends. Consequently, African-American athletes often view college sports as a type of employment wherein one offers his physical skills to a college in return for room, board, tuition, and other tangible benefits.[27] According to this view, sports are neither recreation nor a vehicle for broadening one's education, but rather, in the words of Professor John Hoberman of the University of Texas, "a ritual of survival that reenacts a visceral African-American determination to persevere."[28]

Unfortunately, this view of sports ignores the enormous odds that exist against earning a living by playing games, even for a talented African-American athlete. There are fewer than 3,400 male professional athletes in team sports, and there are approximately 50.2 million American males who are between the ages of fifteen and thirty-nine, of whom approximately 6.2 million are black. This means that the odds of an African-American male becoming a professional athlete are one in five thousand, which is why there are twelve times as many black lawyers and fifteen times as many black doctors in America as there are black professional athletes.[29] Even in basketball, where African Americans dominate top college teams and professional teams, only 1 in 250 Division I college players will win a job in the NBA.[30]

These odds have prompted some African-American professionals to criticize the emphasis that African-American males attach to athletic prowess, both as a symbol of masculinity and as an engine of economic opportunity. For example, Professor Henry Louis Gates, Jr., who chairs the Afro-American Studies program at Harvard, observed:

> An African American youngster has about as much chance of becoming a professional athlete as he or she does of winning the lottery. The tragedy of our people, however, is that few of us accept the truth. . . . The blind pursuit of attainment in sports is having a devastating effect on our people.[31]

Similarly, Professor Harry Edwards, a sports sociologist at the University of California-Berkeley, has said: "You have a better chance of getting hit by a meteorite in the next ten years than [of] getting work as an athlete."[32] Despite such long odds, notes Dr. Alvin Poussaint, a psychiatrist who teaches at the Harvard Medical School, "[t]here is an overemphasis on sports in the black community, and too many black students are putting all their eggs in one basket."[33]

Ironically, in putting all their eggs in one basket, young African Americans disregard not only the long odds against a professional sports career but also the reality that the academic basket holds many more eggs than the athletic basket holds. NCAA-member colleges award approximately $600 million in athletic scholarships each year, as opposed to $49.7 billion in academic scholarships, including minority scholarships and merit-based assistance.[34] Thus, athletic scholarships are neither the only means nor even the best means by which young African Americans can attend college.

Indeed, athletic scholarships preserve unfortunate stereotypes about black male athletes; namely, that they enjoy a physical superiority over men of other races, but suffer, simultaneously, from an intellectual inferiority to men of other races. According to sports sociologist D. Stanley Eitzen:

> A major unintended consequence of the situation in which African American athletes find themselves is that their individual adaptations—denigrating education, opting for easy courses and majors, not making progress toward a degree, emphasizing the athletic role, and eventually dropping out of education without a degree—reinforce the very racial stereotypes that an integrated education is meant to negate.[35]

John Hoberman refers to these stereotypes as the "Law of Compensation," which maintains that there is an inverse relationship between cognitive skills and muscular coordination; that is, between intellectual ability and athletic prowess.[36] He argues that "African-American athleticism" has helped to perpetuate it by "making athletes the most prominent symbols of African-American achievement," thereby ensuring "the invisibility of the black middle class," and preventing young black men from identifying role models other than athletes and entertainers.[37]

Data indicate that the Law of Compensation is alive and well in America. A questionnaire survey of 869 undergraduates and graduate students conducted at Indiana University by sports sociologist Gary Sailes found that (1) almost 12 percent of the respondents believed that black athletes were not as intelligent as white athletes; (2) slightly more than 20 percent of the respondents believed that black athletes were physically superior to white athletes; and (3) slightly more than 33 percent of the respondents believed that blacks were better athletes than whites.[38] Under these circumstances, according to Professor Hoberman, the "intense peer pressure" among young black males that "equates academic excellence with effeminacy and racial disloyalty and identifies 'blackness' with physical prowess" is catastrophically self-defeating for the socioeconomic prospects of African Americans.[39] Those prospects prompted filmmaker John Singleton to state, bluntly, in 1994: "Enough of basketball. Our children need assets like technology that will lead us into the next century. And they need to learn that it's cool to learn this technology."[40]

Colleges are not to blame for young African-American males' preoccupation with sports, but they certainly deserve criticism for seeking to exploit it by convincing black high school athletes that an athletic scholarship is the only means by which they can obtain a college education. This message is financially inaccurate in light of the many other sources of financial assistance that are available for economically disadvantaged students. It is also educationally inaccurate, if not unethical, in light of the enormous demands that playing a big-time college sport makes on an athlete's time.[41] Thus, some African-American male athletes are complicit in their own victimization because they have based their postcollege plans on their athletic prowess, but many coaches are co-conspirators for having validated the misconception that the only road from the outhouse to the penthouse runs through the field house. These coaches mortgage the futures of vulnerable young people to the short-term pursuit of the colleges' and the coaches' own athletic fame and fortune.[42]

To make matters worse, African-American athletes are often victims of social isolation on overwhelmingly white campuses. This is not surprising, considering the small number of African-American students who are enrolled at many Division I colleges and the high percentage of that number who are athletic scholarship recipients. Nationwide, approximately one of every nine African-American male students enrolled at a Division I college holds an athletic scholarship. The comparable figure for whites is one in fifty.[43] African Americans are only 6.6 percent of the undergraduate population at Division I colleges, but they are 46 percent of the football players and 60 percent of the basketball players at these colleges.[44] At Notre Dame, blacks were 55 percent of the football team, but just 3 percent of the student body in 1998.[45]

Still, not only their small numbers isolate African-American athletes from the rest of the student body on Division I campuses; the difference between their socioeconomic circumstances and those of most of their white classmates has the same effect. Billy Hawkins has analogized the lives of African-American athletes, who "must travel to distant colleges to use their athletic abilities in return for a scholarship," to "the rotation by migrant laborers between home and work locations."[46] According to Hawkins, this rotation between largely black, low-income communities at home and largely white, middle- and upper-income campus communities contributes to the isolation and the low graduation rates of African-American athletes.[47]

Ample evidence supports Hawkins's assertion that the socioeconomic circumstances of black athletes differ from those of their white classmates and contribute to the social and academic difficulties that black athletes often encounter in college. The American Institutes for Research study of Division I athletes, which chapter 4 introduced, said: "Because of their backgrounds, their participation in athletics, and the small numbers of other Black students on predominately White campuses, Black student-athletes are likely to face personal challenges in college that are beyond those faced by other student-athletes."[48]

The AIR study measured the socioeconomic status of black and white athletes and nonathletes by averaging the values of four variables, including annual family income, father's education, mother's education, and father's occupation (or mother's occupation if the student did not indicate father's occupation on the completed questionnaire). The data showed that 49 percent of black football and basketball players, but just 13 percent of their teammates of other races, ranked in the lowest 25 percent of the sample with respect to socioeconomic status. The data also showed that 35 percent of the African Americans who played sports other than football and basketball, and 44 percent of the African Americans who participated in extracurricular activities other than varsity sports, ranked in the lowest 25 percent of the sample on socioeconomic status.[49]

Almost two-thirds of the African-American football and basketball players surveyed reported that they had twenty-five dollars or less each month with which to meet personal expenses.[50] The authors concluded that black athletes at Division I colleges suffered from the combined effects of social isolation and economic disadvantage. They observed: "Black student-athletes may need the most to get off campus once in a while to visit with family and friends, but may find few opportunities to do so."[51]

This need is reflected in the responses by black athletes to questions concerning their feelings of isolation on campus. At colleges where African Americans made up less than 4 percent of the student body, 69 percent of African-American football and basketball players sensed that they were different from other students; 51 percent felt racially isolated; 50 percent felt that they lacked control over their lives; 33 percent experienced racial discrimination; and 27 percent believed that they were isolated from other students.[52] At colleges where African Americans comprised more than 4 percent of the student body, these numbers declined somewhat, as 63 percent of African-American football and basketball players sensed that they were different from other students; 39 percent felt racially isolated; 49 percent felt that they lacked control over their lives; 27 percent experienced racial discrimination; and 30 percent said that they felt isolated from other students.[53]

Moreover, African-American football and basketball players not only *felt* isolated from other students but also *were* isolated from other students by their socioeconomic backgrounds, the demands of their participation in big-time sports, and their choices of how to spend leisure time. They reported spending most of their leisure time with teammates.[54] They belonged to fewer social and activity groups than other African-American students. They were most likely to belong to religious clubs or fellowships (24 percent), but they also belonged to service organizations (8 percent), interest or hobby clubs (7 percent), social fraternities or sororities (7 percent), and political organizations (4 percent).

This social isolation deprives African-American athletes of the opportunities for personal growth and career enhancement that can result from collegiate friendships that cross class and cultural lines. Its most tragic consequence, though, may be unrealistic views about one's academic progress in college and career prospects after college. The AIR study found that 39 percent of African-American football and basketball players at mostly white colleges who regarded earning a degree as being of the greatest importance had GPAs of 1.99 or below. In contrast, only 15 percent of their teammates of other races who said that earning a degree was of the greatest importance had GPAs of 1.99 or below. The study also found that approximately 35 percent of African-American football and basketball players at mostly white colleges who said that they would almost certainly attend graduate or professional school had GPAs of 1.99 or below, which would make it difficult for them to graduate from college and almost impossible for them to attend graduate or professional school. Only 11 percent of their teammates of other races who said that they would almost certainly attend graduate or professional school had GPAs of 1.99 or below.[55]

Finally, 37 percent of African-American football and basketball players at mostly white colleges who expected at age forty to be employed in the most prestigious and lucrative career fields (e.g., medicine, law, engineering) had GPAs of 1.99 or below. In contrast, only 14 percent of their teammates of other races who had such lofty career expectations had such low grades.[56] A GPA of 1.99 or below makes entry into prestigious and lucrative career fields unlikely because such entry almost always requires high undergraduate grades, and it often requires graduate or professional training, too, for which one who struggled through college probably will not qualify.

Thus, the isolation that many African-American athletes experience at predominately white Division I colleges apparently contributes to misconceptions among a sizable segment of these athletes about their career prospects after college. By promoting delusions of future success, social isolation sets black athletes up for failure and disappointment when their athletic eligibility ends. It also reinforces the adverse effects of inadequate academic preparation, low socioeconomic status, unfamiliarity with campus culture, and the time demands of playing big-time sports, thereby depriving African-American athletes of the opportunities for personal growth, intellectual development, and career preparation that college promises to all students.

Nevertheless, African-American males are not the only victims of commercialized college sports, and the denial of educational opportunities is not the only form of victimization that college athletes experience. White middle-class women can be victims, too, and their victimization can take the forms of physical and psychological abuse and substandard medical care. Kara Trent discovered that when she played women's basketball for the University of Massachusetts in 1997–98.

Coach Joanie O'Brien should have been thrilled to have Kara and teammate Nicole Vallieres on her team. Kara, a four-year starter at Sandwich High School on Cape Cod, was an Atlantic Coast League All-Star from 1994–1997, a Cape Cod All–Star during the same period, and a *Boston Globe* All-Scholastic selection in 1997. She also had a 4.0 GPA, was a member of the National Honor Society, and was the president of a service organization.[57] Harvard, Dartmouth, and Cornell all accepted her, but she spurned the Ivy League in favor of the big-time basketball atmosphere at UMass.

Nicole was multitalented, too. Indeed, she played high school basketball for *five years*, as she became a starter at Hoosac Valley High School as an eighth-grader. Amazingly, she was also her team's top scorer and rebounder and assists leader that year, and the first eighth-grader in the history of girls' basketball in Massachusetts to be named to the All-Western Massachusetts team. Three years later, in the summer of 1996 she was named the outstanding female athlete of the Bay State Games. Nicole was nearly a straight-A student in high school, and she belonged to the National Honor Society. In 1997 she spurned non-scholarship offers from Colgate and Dartmouth, an offer of an appointment to West Point, and athletic scholarship offers from Vanderbilt and Boston University in order to accept a basketball scholarship to UMass.[58]

If Coach O'Brien appreciated having Kara and Nicole on her team, she had an odd way of showing that appreciation. Both women later charged in a lawsuit that O'Brien frequently became angry at them and their teammates during practice sessions, and that she grabbed them violently by the necks of their jerseys and screamed in their faces while she pulled them to the places on the court where she thought they should be.[59] Nicole became depressed, saw her grades fall, and ended a relationship with a young man to whom she had been close for six years. Kara later told *The Boston Globe* that she experienced "constant emotional distress and turmoil due to [Coach O'Brien's] verbal abuse."[60]

Kara also charged that she received poor medical care at UMass. During her freshman season she sustained a knee injury. The team trainer and the team doctor both assured her it was merely "jumper's knee," a form of tendonitis, which they treated with ice and ibuprofen. She needed to use a special heating pad at halftime in order to prevent the knee from becoming stiff. According to court papers, Coach O'Brien told her to "stop being a f——ing baby and suck it up!" Despite the injury, she started at point guard and appeared in all 30 games during a season in which the Minutewomen won the eastern division of the Atlantic 10 Conference and earned a bid to the NCAA Tournament. Those achievements did not ease the pain in her knee, though; so during the summer of 1998 she consulted her family doctor, who ordered an MRI, which revealed a torn patella tendon that required surgery. She was still undergoing postoperative rehabilitation when she returned to UMass for her sophomore year.

Kara contends that her return to college brought a resumption of abuse from Coach O'Brien. She says that instead of apologizing for having underestimated the seriousness of her injury, O'Brien was "furious" at her for having consulted her family doctor, and criticized her repeatedly for having had surgery too late in the summer to be ready to play when the basketball season began.[61] To make matters worse, before the new season began, Coach O'Brien dismissed Kara's friend Tory Grant from the team, which Kara thought was unfair and unwarranted. She left the team shortly thereafter.

Disappointment and disillusionment can be the beginning of wisdom, and Kara Trent was a voice of wisdom about big-time college sports when she spoke to a *Boston Globe* reporter early in 2001. She said:

> The top priority should be to have fun. And that's all. Because when you stop having fun, you shouldn't be playing. It's not a job. People say: "You're on scholarship. You listen to your bosses." Well, no. I would hope I would never have to go into a workforce and have bosses put their hands on me. Or speak to me like [Coach O'Brien did]. Kids need to remember it's a sport. It's not life. It can do a lot of things to enhance your life, but there is life after basketball.[62]

The wisdom in this statement lies in its recognition that the principal beneficiaries of college sports ought to be the participants, and that the games ought to be organized in such a way as to enhance the educational experiences of college athletes. Kara's statement is not only wise, but also optimistic because it offers hope that from victimization a collegiate sports system that is rooted in education instead of in commerce can emerge.

Coaches' ambitions cannot account for all of the victimization of college athletes. Other factors, including NCAA rules, increase the likelihood that athletes will forfeit educational opportunities in order to compete in sports and that coaches and athletic administrators will mistreat athletes. Two NCAA rules in particular facilitate the victimization of college athletes. One rule makes freshmen eligible to compete in varsity sports, and another rule permits a college to award (and to revoke) athletic scholarships on an annual basis even though most students will need four or five years to earn a degree.[63]

It was not always this way. Until 1968 freshmen were ineligible for varsity competition in all sports. Typically, freshman teams played abbreviated competitive schedules. At the 1968 NCAA Convention, delegates voted by a narrow margin (163–160) to make freshmen eligible for varsity competition in all sports except football and basketball. Delegates to the 1972 NCAA Convention voted to extend freshman eligibility to football and basketball.[64]

In so doing, the delegates saved their institutions the cost of maintaining separate freshman teams, but they forced freshman athletes, including those who were marginal students, to meet the new and substantial demands of college class work and big-time sports simultaneously. Moreover, varsity eligibility sometimes resulted in freshmen playing in one or more college football games before they had ever attended a college class, which suggested to them that their principal reason for being on campus was to participate in sports. It is no wonder, then, that some athletes become engulfed in the athletic role soon after they arrive on campus. It is also no wonder that when their collegiate eligibility ends, they may become victims of their role engulfment, especially if they have suffered career-ending injuries or have failed to obtain professional sports contracts. The NCAA bears some responsibility for the human tragedy that can occur when athletes exhaust their athletic eligibility without having earned a college degree or acquired marketable skills. This is because its freshman-eligibility rule fosters the athletic role engulfment that produces this tragedy. NCAA rules should seek to prevent, not to promote, athletic role engulfment.

Annually renewable athletic scholarships also can victimize college athletes. Prior to 1973, athletic scholarships were valid for four years, which meant that coaches could not take them away from athletes who suffered career-ending injuries or who failed to develop satisfactorily as power forwards or offensive tackles. At the 1973 NCAA Convention, however, more than two-thirds of the delegates voted to make athletic scholarships annually renewable, which, according to former executive director Walter Byers, legitimized "the one-year freshman tryout."[65]

This rule epitomizes the triumph of commercial values over educational values in college sports. It permits coaches, in effect, to "fire" athletes who, as a result of injuries or limited physical talent, cannot perform up to the coaches' standards. Annually renewable athletic scholarships operate like employment contracts that permit employers to fire employees for doing unsatisfactory work. At first blush, this arrangement may seem reasonable because college sports are a large commercial enterprise today. A closer look though, reveals that annually renewable scholarships are indefensible, in part because they are incompatible with the Principle of Amateurism that is a core component of the NCAA Constitution. This principle states as follows:

> Student-athletes shall be amateurs in an intercollegiate sport, and their participation should be motivated primarily by education and by the physical, mental and social benefits to be derived. Student participation in intercollegiate athletics is an avocation, and student-athletes should be protected from exploitation by professional and commercial enterprises.[66]

The principle is right; student participation in college sports *should* be an avocation. That is precisely why the practice of renewing scholarships annually is wrong; it treats what is properly an avocation as a vocation by letting coaches deny financial aid to players who do not perform adequately on the field or the court, regardless of their character or academic standing.

Moreover, annually renewable scholarships are incompatible with higher education's core purpose—namely, long-term human development—because their only plausible justifications are short-term athletic and commercial success.[67] There is surely no sound educational reason for annual renewal. Annually renewable scholarships also give coaches dictatorial power over the lives of college students, enabling coaches to dismiss athletes who question their authority, even when there is ample justification for doing so. Finally, they save coaches from the adverse consequences of their sloppy recruiting or ineffective teaching, while forcing young athletes to pay a high price for coaches' limitations as recruiters or teachers. Other college teachers must teach the students who enroll in their classes as best they can, so it is reasonable to expect coaches to do the same, especially since coaches, unlike professors of chemistry, art, or electrical engineering, have recruited their students personally.

Annually renewable athletic scholarships are also legally indefensible. Athletic scholarships are not employment contracts, so they ought not to mirror employment contracts by permitting coaches to dismiss athletes for performing unsatisfactorily. The NCAA insists that athletic scholarships are not employment contracts when the issue is whether college athletes should receive wages, be able to unionize, or qualify for workers' compensation. In other words, the NCAA does not want college athletes to be "employees" when that status would cost it and its member institutions money; however, it is willing to treat them as employees when doing so benefits coaches and athletic directors but victimizes the athletes themselves. This double standard is unacceptable. If athletic scholarships are not employment contracts for purposes of wages, unionization, and workers' compensation, they should not operate like employment contracts for purposes of "firing" injured or insufficiently talented athletes.

All the forms of victimization of college athletes discussed above are the offspring of the marriage between athletic commerce and higher education. They will continue as long as colleges seek to achieve public visibility and financial health through athletic success. Therefore, the only way to end these forms of victimization is to arrange a divorce between athletic commerce and higher education. This divorce may also be the best means of ending the victimization of other students, especially women, by college athletes, which is one of the subjects of the following section.

ATHLETES AS VILLAINS

Criminal behavior by athletes has been a major social cost of big-time college sports in recent years. In 1995, for example, 220 college athletes were the subjects of criminal proceedings for alleged crimes that ranged from illegal gambling to manslaughter. In 1995 and 1996 a total of 112 college athletes faced charges of sexual assault or domestic violence; most of the victims were female college students.[68] At the University of Nebraska in 1994–95, 7 starters and one reserve on the football team were charged with or convicted of violent crimes, including sexual assault, domestic assault (on a former girlfriend), firing a gun into an occupied car, theft, and even attempted murder.[69] At Arizona State University in February of 1996, police arrested 3 basketball players for sexual assault. The victim consented to have sex with one of the athletes, whereupon 2 teammates forced themselves on her unexpectedly. One of them brandished a gun when the victim spurned his advances.[70]

As these examples indicate, women are often the victims of criminal behavior by college athletes. Hard data support this assertion. Research conducted by Todd Crosset of the University of Massachusetts and several colleagues found that athletes were over-represented among the male students who were reported to campus judicial affairs offices for having committed acts of violence against female students. Crosset and his colleagues examined the records of judicial affairs offices at ten Division I colleges from 1991 through 1993. The records revealed that during the three-year period athletes were 3 percent of the male student population at the colleges surveyed, but were 35 percent (seven of twenty) of the men about whom judicial affairs offices received reports of "battering" (i.e., domestic assault).[71] These results are consistent with the results of an earlier study by Crosset and his colleagues that indicated that from 1991 through 1993, athletes were 3.3 percent of the male students at thirty Division I colleges surveyed but were 19 percent of the alleged perpetrators (a total of 69) about whom campus police departments and judicial affairs offices received reports of sexual assaults.[72]

The two sets of results taken together led the researchers to conclude that "[t]he press has overstated the problem of athletes and violence against women, but the evidence, nonetheless, suggests an association between athletic involvement and violence against women."[73] Consequently, they added that "[t]he contention that athletes' violence against women only appears to be a problem because athletes are being targeted by the media is not supported by the findings."[74]

Colleges increase the likelihood of violence against women by recruiting athletes who have behaved violently in the past and by failing to punish them swiftly and severely when they behave violently on campus. A case in point is the recruitment by former University of Georgia basketball coach Jim Harrick of point guard Tony Cole, whom the university suspended from the basketball team in April of 2002 after his indictment on charges of aggravated assault with intent to rape.[75] Before he enrolled at Georgia, Cole attended the Community College of Rhode Island (CCRI), where two women filed a complaint with the college stating that between December of 1999 and February of 2000, when they worked part-time in the athletic department, Cole sexually harassed them by groping them and by making threatening comments to them when they spurned his advances. In March of 2000, CCRI expelled Cole after his arrest for trespassing at a basketball game at the University of Rhode Island, where officials had previously barred him from the campus.[76] Coach Harrick claimed that he was unaware of Cole's previous disciplinary problems, including his expulsion from CCRI and an outstanding warrant for his arrest for failing to appear in court on the trespassing charge.[77]

The NCAA does not sideline athletes for off-the-field violence. NCAA rules can declare an athlete ineligible to compete for engaging in substance abuse or gambling, but there is no rule that can render an athlete ineligible for conduct such as rape or domestic assault.[78] As a result, the decision to punish or not to punish usually is the responsibility of the college, which may mean that it is left up to the athletic director or the coach, both of whom are typically reluctant to declare an athlete ineligible for competition.

Nobody knows that better than Christy Brzonkala, who was the victim of repeated sexual assaults on the night of September 21 and in the early morning hours of September 22 in her dormitory room at Virginia Tech, where she had begun her freshman year just a few weeks earlier. She had met the two men who assaulted her only a half hour before the assault, and knew only their first names until five months later, when she discovered that they were football players Antonio Morrison and James Crawford.[79] Late in April 1995, Brzonkala filed a complaint against Morrison and Crawford pursuant to Virginia Tech's sexual assault policy, which the university had made available to students less than two months earlier. She relied on the university to investigate and punish the two athletes, because she believed that her failure to preserve physical evidence of the assaults prevented her from filing criminal charges against them.[80]

In May 1995 a hearing took place to consider Brzonkala's charges. During the hearing, Antonio Morrison admitted that he had had sexual contact with Brzonkala even though when he had asked her to have sex with him, she had twice told him no! The university's judicial committee found Morrison guilty of sexual assault, and it suspended him from school for two semesters. An appeal officer upheld this punishment.[81]

Morrison's unsuccessful appeal should have ended the university's proceedings in this case because the guidelines for its judicial system stated expressly that the "Appeal Officer's decision is final."[82] Unfortunately for Christy Brzonkala, though, the process was not over yet. Two university officials contacted her during the summer of 1995 and requested that she participate in another hearing because (1) Morrison's attorney had threatened to sue the university for depriving him of his constitutional right to due process by using unfair procedures in prosecuting him; (2) Morrison claimed that the sexual assault policy under which he had been charged was invalid because it was not printed in the Student Handbook; (3) the university would not defend against the threatened lawsuit; and (4) it was necessary to hold a new hearing in order to charge Morrison under the old abusive conduct policy instead of the new sexual assault policy.[83] The university's refusal to defend its disciplinary proceedings against a possible lawsuit forced

Brzonkala to agree to an additional hearing if she hoped to see Morrison punished, even though, as a federal judge later observed, attorneys for the university knew that Morrison's due process arguments were "groundless under Virginia law."[84]

If ever a disciplinary hearing was stacked against a victim, it was the second hearing of Christy Brzonkala's complaint against Antonio Morrison. The university refused a request by Brzonkala's attorney for a tape recording of the first hearing on the ground that it was part of Morrison's "educational records," so federal privacy law precluded its disclosure. University officials warned Brzonkala not to mention James Crawford during the hearing because they had dismissed him from the disciplinary process for lack of evidence after he denied having assaulted her. She could not even obtain sworn affidavits from witnesses in her favor because the hearing occurred during summer vacation, when the witnesses were off campus.[85] Despite these procedural obstacles, the judicial committee again found Morrison guilty, and it reimposed the two-semester suspension. Morrison appealed, though, and the university's provost reversed the decision of the judicial committee, finding that he was guilty only of "using abusive language," for which his punishment would be required attendance at a one-hour seminar on how to behave in an educational setting.[86] He would return to campus for the fall term with his athletic eligibility intact.

The final insult to Christy Brzonkala was that no employee of the university notified her that Morrison's second appeal was successful and that he would return to school for the fall 1995 term. She learned this by reading a newspaper article, after which she cancelled her plans to return to Virginia Tech.[87]

To its credit, Virginia Tech adopted a recruiting policy in 1997 that requires recruiters to "interview the person within each high school, apart from the coaches, who is in the best position to know the recruit's personal background," and to ask that person about the recruit's conduct, including "fighting, alcohol or drug abuse, class attendance, violations of the law, respect for authority, respect for others, and social skills."[88] Other colleges have taken steps to prevent the recruitment of athletes who have criminal records. Fresno State now forbids its coaches to recruit an athlete who has been convicted of a felony, and coaches who seek to recruit athletes who have misdemeanor convictions must obtain approval from the athletic director before proceeding. State colleges in Idaho must abide by a state board of education rule that prohibits them from recruiting an athlete who has been convicted of a felony or of a juvenile offense that corresponds to a felony in adult court. Exceptions are allowed, but the college's president must approve them and report them to the board of education.[89]

Colleges should investigate their recruits' gambling habits, too. Gambling by college athletes is a persistent problem, as is reflected in their arrests in recent years for betting on college football (Boston College) and for point shaving (Arizona State and Northwestern). In December of 1997 two former Arizona State basketball players pled guilty to conspiracy to commit sports bribery during the 1993–94 season.[90] In March of 1998 a federal grand jury in Chicago indicted two former Northwestern basketball players on charges of shaving points in three games during the 1994–95 season.[91] Also in 1998 authorities charged former Northwestern running back Dennis Lundy with perjury for having denied before a grand jury that he fumbled intentionally near the goal line during a close game with Iowa in 1994 in order to protect his bet against Northwestern. Lundy was placing bets with a former Wildcats player who had become a football bookie.[92] The arrests at Northwestern followed closely on the heels of a 1996 gambling scandal at Boston College, in which authorities accused two football players of having bet against their team, and more than twenty-five team members admitted to having bet on games during the college football season, although not necessarily against their own team.[93]

One cannot dismiss these episodes as isolated or aberrant, in light of the results of a survey conducted by two employees of the University of Michigan's athletic department in 1999. The survey, to which 758 Division I college football and basketball players (male and female) responded, found that almost 72 percent of them had bet at least once since entering college. They bought lottery tickets, played cards for money, played bingo, gambled on-line, participated in casino games, bet on sports, and bet on informal golf games and bowling matches in which they had participated.[94] Almost 35 percent reported that they had gambled on sports.[95] More than 3 percent of the athletes (5.2 percent of males) reported that they had provided inside information to gamblers, bet on a game in which they participated, or accepted money in return for performing poorly in a game.[96]

Only 25 percent of the athletes to whom the authors of the survey mailed questionnaires completed and returned them, so it is possible that the respondents were unrepresentative of college football and basketball players with respect to gambling. On the other hand, it is reasonable to assume that some athletes who gambled frequently and who bet large amounts of money did not participate in the survey, because they felt embarrassed or feared being identified. The best evidence for this assumption is that women were almost three times as likely as men (72.4 percent vs. 27.6 percent)[97] to complete and return the survey questionnaire, even though they were less likely to gamble than men.[98] Consequently, this survey may understate, not overstate, the number of college football and basketball players who have provided inside information to gamblers, bet on a game in which they participated, or accepted money for performing poorly in a game. In any event, its results are consistent with statements by the former Arizona State, Northwestern, and Boston College athletes who were implicated in the gambling scandals. They indicated that sports gambling is a common feature of campus culture and that their classmates bet often, asked them for "inside" information regularly, and offered them "free bets," which enabled the athletes to win money if the classmate's wager was successful but to avoid losing money if it was unsuccessful.[99] Their testimony lends some credence to the gaming industry's contention that the NCAA's proposal to outlaw gambling on college sports—even in Nevada, where it is presently legal—would not put student bookies out of business.[100]

Besides, the NCAA's moral authority on the subject of gambling is suspect. The association seeks to end legal gambling on college sports primarily because it wishes to protect the public image of a large commercial enterprise that has made it wealthy and powerful. This desire hardly makes the NCAA the high-minded guardian of amateurism and youthful innocence that it purports to be. Moreover, by developing Division I sports into a commercial enterprise, the NCAA has made some college athletes vulnerable to gamblers. After all, gamblers rarely, if ever, make or take bets on football games between Macalester and St. Olaf or basketball games between Middlebury and Tufts. NCAA officials are hypocritical and foolish if they think that college sports will shed gambling and gamblers while the games remain big-time.

Thus, criminal behavior by college athletes, whether violence against women or sports bribery, is the residue of athletic commerce. The financial imperative to win causes colleges to admit and to retain athletes who are bad campus citizens, and it suggests to them that good athletes need not be good citizens. Consequently, they often behave as if the rules that apply to their classmates do not apply to them. Northwestern athletic director Rick Taylor says: "They think because they're athletes they can get away with anything, and we've got to stop that mentality."[101] The surest way to end this mentality of entitlement is to end the marriage between athletic commerce and higher education.

COACHES AND THE CULTURE OF HYPOCRISY

College coaches perpetuate the mentality of entitlement by making excuses for their athletes' bad behavior, downplaying its seriousness, seeking to postpone court proceedings and the campus disciplinary process as long as possible, and permitting athletes who have been charged with crimes to continue playing, pending the outcome of the judicial process. This behavior by coaches belies their insistence that sports builds character by requiring athletes to discipline themselves and to face adversity. It suggests that coaches are more interested in winning games than they are in teaching self-discipline or personal responsibility.

Former Nebraska football coach Tom Osborne is a case in point. In the fall of 1995, Osborne's star running back, Lawrence Phillips, assaulted his former girlfriend by knocking her to the floor, dragging her down three flights of stairs, and then smashing her head against a wall. Osborne dismissed Phillips from the football team temporarily, but university authorities postponed a disciplinary hearing on the victim's complaint until after the football season. The NCAA permitted Coach Osborne to reinstate Phillips for a November 4 game against Iowa State. Said the coach: "I was a little surprised how long it took [to get Phillips reinstated]."[102] More surprising is the light "punishment" that the university subsequently imposed on Phillips, which included counseling, community service, and *class attendance*. "Since when is going to class at a university a punishment?" asked Judith Kriss, the head of the women's center at Nebraska.[103] Perhaps Phillips thought it was, as he left Nebraska for the NFL soon after helping the Cornhuskers' claim the national championship by beating Florida in the Fiesta Bowl on January 1, 1996.[104]

Phillips's teammate, Christian Peter, also benefited from Coach Osborne's leniency after he was convicted of sexually assaulting the reigning Miss Nebraska. The only penalty that Osborne imposed was to keep Peter out of the annual intrasquad game that marked the end of spring practice. Peter did not miss a regular-season game.[105] The Phillips and Peter cases illustrate why Katherine Redmond, who heads the National Coalition Against Violent Athletes, a victim's advocacy organization, urges colleges to declare athletes who have been charged with crimes of violence ineligible for competition pending the outcome of legal proceedings. Otherwise, Redmond warns, colleges will postpone such proceedings as long as possible. "These athletes are so important to a small town and an educational institution," she says, "that the schools will do anything to keep [them] playing."[106]

Coaches are important, too, and the same double standard that protects a star athlete from being held accountable for otherwise unacceptable behavior can also protect a coach. To paraphrase Ms. Redmond, some colleges will do almost anything to keep a successful coach coaching. That was evident in May of 2000, when Indiana University (IU) declined to fire its long-time basketball coach, Bob Knight, despite his nearly thirty-year history of physically abusive behavior toward his players and his colleagues.

The IU Board of Trustees conducted a seven-week investigation of Knight's twenty-nine-year career in Bloomington after a videotape surfaced that showed the coach's hand on Neil Reed's neck during a practice session in 1997. The investigation concluded not only that Knight had been abusive to Reed but that he had intimidated a secretary in the athletic department in 1988 by hurling foul language and a vase at her, and that he had been verbally and physically abusive to other colleagues on several occasions.[107] Nevertheless, the board determined that "[n]o incident by itself rose to the level of termination," so IU president Myles Brand announced on May 15 that the university would give Bob Knight a "last chance" to coach, although he would miss three games during the 2000–2001 college basketball season and would have to pay a thirty-thousand-dollar fine.[108] He would also coach under a zero-tolerance policy, whereby President Brand and the board could fire him if he had inappropriate physical contact with players or employees at IU or if he failed to behave with "decorum and civility" when representing the university.[109]

During the news conference at which President Brand and the board announced that Coach Knight would retain his job, Brand said, regarding the zero-tolerance policy: "Given the fact that in the past [Knight] hadn't had such guidelines, I believe the ethical approach is to give him one last chance."[110] This statement prompted one journalist to ask: "Does a so-called educator at a state institution need a code of conduct to distinguish between a chair he can throw and a person he might slug?"[111] The chair-throwing reference pertained to an incident at an IU game in 1985 in which Knight hurled a folding chair across the court after he received a technical foul for protesting a referee's call that went against his team.[112]

Even if he did need a code of conduct, Knight was apparently unable or unwilling to follow it. On September 10, 2000, in announcing Knight's termination from IU, President Brand stated that the coach had violated the zero-tolerance policy by engaging in a pattern of "uncivil, defiant, and unacceptable behavior" since the preceding May that had culminated in allegations by a student that Knight had assaulted him physically and verbally after the student had greeted him by saying, "Hey, what's up, Knight?"[113] According to President Brand, Knight had (1) disregarded Brand's personal request to meet with IU athletic director Clarence Doninger; (2) criticized IU officials and trustees publicly and privately; (3) refused to participate in previously scheduled booster club events in Bloomington and Chicago; (4) berated a female university attorney in the presence of others; and (5) refused to cancel a fishing trip to Canada in order to be available to answer the student's claim that Knight had assaulted him.[114] Prior to his termination the coach acknowledged that he had put his hand on the younger man's forearm and said: "I'm Coach Knight or Mr. Knight to you,"[115] in an effort to teach him "manners and civility."[116]

Bob Knight is an extraordinary teacher of basketball, but he is wholly unqualified to teach anybody manners and civility. Journalist Ira Berkow recognized this and exposed Indiana University's hypocrisy in failing to fire Knight in May of 2000 when he observed on the day after Knight's firing: "If an English professor or a dean of students acted as Knight has over the years, he would surely have been out long ago."[117] It is inconceivable that the English professor or the dean of students, no matter how talented either one of them was, would have remained employed at IU after throwing a chair across a classroom or hurling a vase at a secretary. The zero-tolerance policy would have been implicit, if not explicit, in their respective employment contracts, and it would have been in effect for each of them on the first day of work; it would not have begun after twenty-nine years of abusive conduct toward students and colleagues. The same standard should have applied to Bob Knight; but it did not, because he won basketball games and earned money and visibility for IU without violating NCAA rules. Talent and honesty are commendable, but they are not a license to behave abusively. IU could have saved its soul by replacing Knight with an honest, competent, and mannerly coach long before September 10, 2000. It took a step toward redemption that day, but this episode supports, more than it refutes, the view that celebrity protects a successful coach from the swift, certain punishment that another university employee who behaved abusively would receive.

REDEMPTION

Colleges will not redeem their lost souls or see a dramatic reduction in bad behavior by athletes and coaches until they abandon the commercial model of college sports. When colleges abandon the commercial model, the need to win will no longer be paramount, because the general fund, not booster donations, will pay for sports. The pressure to admit and to retain talented athletes who engage in criminal behavior will end. Coaches will cease to be more powerful than the presidents and trustees who employ them, and presidents will promptly fire coaches who abuse athletes verbally and/or physically or impede their academic progress. Coaches will view themselves as teachers instead of as entertainment executives loosely affiliated with colleges. This may appear to be an unlikely prospect, but the financial pressures that attend the colleges' need to comply with Title IX can enable them to recover the souls they have lost to athletic commerce. Chapter 6 will show the road to redemption.

NOTES

1. Donald Chu, *The Character of American Higher Education and Intercollegiate Sport* (Albany, N.Y.: State University of New York Press, 1989), pp. 58–59.

2. Welch Suggs, "Players' Deaths Prompt Questions About 'Balance' in Athletes' Lives," *The Chronicle of Higher Education*, September 7, 2001, pp. A55–A58.

3. Ibid.

4. Ibid.

5. Joe Drape, "Knight Gets 'Last Chance' to Coach at Indiana," *The New York Times*, May 16, 2000, p. A27.

6. Joe Drape, "Citing his Behavior, Indiana's President Fires Coach Knight," *The New York Times*, September 11, 2000, p. D9.

7. *Vallieres v. University of Massachusetts*, No. 2201-0166-A (Hampden Superior Court, filed May 31, 2001).

8. Steve Wieberg, "More Schools Laying Down the Law," *USA Today*, September 18, 1998, pp. 17C–18C.

9. Jeffrey R. Benedict, *Athletes and Acquaintance Rape* (Thousand Oaks, Cal.: Sage Publications, 1998), pp. 27–28.

10. Christopher Flores, "When Athletes Are Accused," *The Chronicle of*

Higher Education, April 19, 2002, pp. A39–A40. *See also* Adam Thompson, "Women at C.U. Party 'Set Up' for Sex," *The Denver Post*, June 13, 2002 [available at http://www.denverpost.com/Stories/0,1413,36%257E669659,00.html]. Late in June 2002, *The Denver Post* reported that the Boulder Police Department had not yet charged any players or recruits with rape, but it had charged four players with contributing to the delinquency of a minor for allegedly supplying recruits with alcohol and marijuana. Coach Gary Barnett stripped two players of their athletic scholarships for the 2002–2003 school year. The university's Judicial Affairs office had charged four football players and five other students with violations of the code of student conduct in connection with the party, but it had not yet completed disciplinary proceedings. Judicial Affairs had punished one player as of this time by "suspending" him from the university, but it chose not to execute the suspension, so he remained eligible to attend classes and play football in 2002–03. He was scheduled to begin a one-year "probation" on December 21, 2002, several weeks after the conclusion of football's regular season. *See* Adam Thompson, "CU Charges 4 Players, 5 Others," *The Denver Post*, June 19, 2002 [available at http://www.denverpost.com/Stories/0,1413,36%257E87%257E682109,00.html] and "CU Punishes Player for Party," *The Denver Post*, June 20, 2002 [available at http://www.denverpost.com/Stories/0,1413,36%257E87%257E684414,00.html].

11. Quoted in Steve Wieberg, "More Schools Laying Down the Law," *USA Today*, September 18, 1998, pp. 17C–18C.

12. James H. Frey, "Deviance of Organizational Subunits: The Case of College Athletic Departments," *Journal of Sport and Social Issues*, 18, no. 2 (May 1994): 110–122. *See also* Murray Sperber, *College Sports Inc.: The Athletic Department vs. The University* (New York: Henry Holt and Company, 1990), p. 258.

13. James H. Frey, "Deviance of Organizational Subunits: The Case of College Athletic Departments," *Journal of Sport and Social Issues* 18, no. 2 (May 1994): 110–122.

14. Ibid.

15. Walter Byers, *Unsportsmanlike Conduct: Exploiting College Athletes* (Ann Arbor, Mich.: The University of Michigan Press, 1995), pp. 216–217.

16. James J. Duderstadt, *Intercollegiate Athletics and the American University: A University President's Perspective* (Ann Arbor, Mich.: The University of Michigan Press, 2000), p. 7.

17. After a six-month investigation of its Academic Center for Athletes, LSU concluded that some of its athletes received improper help with studying and with typing, but that these violations of NCAA rules were minor. As of late September, 2002, the NCAA had not yet decided whether to conduct its own investigation of LSU.

18. Stewart Mandel, "Walking a Fine Line: Distorted Expectations May Explain SEC's Growing Misdeeds," *CNN/Sports Illustrated*, May 20, 2002 [available at http://sportsillustrated.cnn.com/football/college/news/2002/05/19/offseason_beat/]. *See also* Mark Schlabach, "SEC Investigation Alleges Payoffs to ex-Vols QB," *Atlanta Journal-Constitution*, May 7, 2002 [available at http://www.accessatlanta.com/ajc/sports/uga/0502/0508sec.html], Neal McCready, "SEC Investigates Payments to Tee Martin," *Mobile Register*, May 7, 2002 [available at http://www.al.com/news/mobileregister/index.ssf?/xml/story.ssf/ht . . . /1020788101195380.xm], and Greg

Wallace and Taylor Bright, "Culture of Cheating?" *Birmingham Post-Herald*, July 30, 2002 [available at http://www.postherald.com/cheating.shtml].

19. Chris Low, "UT Avoids Sanctions Over Tee Martin," *The Nashville Tennessean*, January 9, 2003 [available at http://tennessean.com/sports/ut/archives/03/01/27473395.shtml?Element_ID=27473395]. *See also* letter from Chris Howand, Assistant Director of Enforcement, NCAA to Doug Dickey, Director of Athletics, University of Tennessee [available at http://www.phillipfulmer.com/ncaaletter.htm].

20. "U. of Georgia Basketball Coach Resigns Amid Investigation of Possible Rules Violations," *The Chronicle of Higher Education*, March 28, 2003 [available at http://chronicle.com/daily/2003/03/2003032801n.htm].

21. Welch Suggs, "Sports as the University's 'Front Porch'? The Public Is Skeptical," *The Chronicle of Higher Education*, May 2, 2003, p. A17.

22. Welch Suggs, "Graduation Rate for Male Basketball Players Falls to Lowest Level in a Decade," *The Chronicle of Higher Education*, September 21, 2001, pp. A34–A37.

23. Billy Hawkins, *The New Plantation: The Internal Colonization of Black Student-Athletes* (Winterville, Ga.: Sadiki Press, 2001), p. 83.

24. John Simons, "Improbable Dreams," *U.S. News and World Report*, March 24, 1997, pp. 46–52.

25. Ibid.

26. Ibid., p. 47.

27. Allen Sack, "Recruiting: Are Improper Benefits Really Improper?" in Richard E. Lapchick and John Brooks Slaughter, *The Rules of the Game: Ethics in College Sport* (New York: The American Council on Education and Macmillan Publishing Company, 1989), p. 79.

28. John Hoberman, *Darwin's Athletes: How Sport Has Damaged Black America and Preserved The Myth of Race* (New York: Houghton Mifflin Company, 1997), p. 77.

29. George H. Sage, *Power and Ideology in American Sport: A Critical Perspective*, 2nd ed. (Champaign, Ill.: Human Kinetics, 1998), pp. 96–97.

30. John Simons, "Improbable Dreams," *U.S. News & World Report*, March 24, 1997, pp. 46–52.

31. Henry Louis Gates, Jr., "Delusions of Grandeur," *Sports Illustrated*, August 19, 1991, p. 78 (quoted in Sage, *Power and Ideology in American Sport*, p. 98).

32. Quoted in Sage, *Power and Ideology in American Sport*, pp. 97–98.

33. Quoted in John Simons, "Improbable Dreams," *U.S. News & World Report*, March 24, 1997, pp. 46–52.

34. Ibid.

35. D. Stanley Eitzen, "Racism in Big-Time College Sport: Prospects for the Year 2020 and Proposals for Change," in Dana Brooks and Robert Althouse, eds., *Racism in College Athletics*, 2nd. ed. (Morgantown, W. V.: Fitness Information Technology, Inc., 2000), pp. 296–297.

36. Hoberman, *Darwin's Athletes*, p. 225.

37. Ibid., p. xxxiii.

38. Gary A. Sailes, "An Investigation of Campus Stereotypes: The Myth of Black Athletic Superiority and the Dumb Jock Stereotype," *Sociology of Sport Journal*, 10 (1993): 88–97.

39. Hoberman, *Darwin's Athletes*, p. 8.

40. Ibid., p. 94.

41. John R. Thelin, *Games Colleges Play: Scandal and Reform in Intercollegiate Athletics* (Baltimore: The Johns Hopkins University Press, 1996), p. 175.

42. One commentator has charged that the football and men's basketball teams at the University of Arkansas operate as "slave" systems in which African Americans, who comprise 70 percent to 80 percent of the members of these teams earn revenues that support the baseball, golf, and tennis teams, which are 95 percent white. *See*: Brian Bolton, "UA Exploits Black Youth," *Northwest Arkansas Times*, July 1, 2002 [available at http://www.nwanews.com/times/story.dhtml?storyID=88344&name= News].

43. Brooks and Althouse, eds., *Racism in College Athletics*, 2nd. ed., p. 146.

44. Allen L. Sack and Ellen J. Staurowsky, *College Athletes for Hire* (Westport, Conn.: Praeger Publishers, 1998), p. 105.

45. Ibid.

46. Hawkins, *The New Plantation*, p. 55.

47. Ibid.

48. Robert J. Rossi and Terry Armstrong, *Studies of Intercollegiate Athletics: Report No. 3: The Experiences of Black Intercollegiate Athletes at NCAA Division I Institutions* (Palo Alto, Cal.: Center for the Study of Athletics, American Institutes for Research, 1992), p. 13.

49. Ibid., p. 19.

50. Ibid., p. 20.

51. Ibid., p. 21.

52. Ibid., p. 22.

53. Ibid.

54. Ibid., p. 30.

55. Ibid.

56. Ibid., p. 52.

57. *Trent et al. v. The University of Massachusett et al.*, Docket No. 99cv12149PBS (United States District Court for the District of Massachusetts, filed October 14, 1999).

58. *Vallieres (and Cernick) v. The University of Massachusetts*, Docket No. 2201-0166-A (Hampden Superior Court, filed May 31, 2001).

59. *Trent et al. v. The University of Massachusetts et al.*, Docket No. 99cv12149PBS (United States District Court for the District of Massachusetts, filed October 14, 1999). Kara, Nicole, and the third plaintiff, Tory Grant, later withdrew their complaint from the federal court for jurisdictional reasons. The suit resurfaced in May of 2001 in a state court in Massachusetts, where it is pending, but with Nicole, her mother, and her stepfather as the only plaintiffs. See note 58 for the title and docket number of the pending case.

60. Peter May, "Hoop Nightmares," *The Boston Globe Magazine*, March 5, 2000, pp. 13–24.

61. Ibid.

62. Ibid.

63. Article 15.3.3.1 of the NCAA Bylaws provides for annually renewable athletic scholarships. See *2002–03 NCAA Division I Manual*, p. 184.

64. Walter Byers, *Unsportsmanlike Conduct: Exploiting College Athletes* (Ann Arbor, Mich.: The University of Michigan Press, 1995), pp. 162–163.

65. Ibid., p. 164.

66. NCAA Constitution, Article 2, Principles for Conduct of Intercollegiate Athletics, 2.9 The Principle of Amateurism, reprinted in NCAA, *2002–03 NCAA Division I Manual* (Michael V. Earle, ed., 2002), p. 5.

67. James Duderstadt, *Intercollegiate Athletics and the American University: A University President's Perspective* (Ann Arbor, Mich.: The University of Michigan Press, 2000), p. 88.

68. Jeffrey R. Benedict, "Colleges Must Act Decisively When Scholarship Athletes Run Afoul of the Law," *The Chronicle of Higher Education*, May 9, 1997, pp. B6–7.

69. Jeffrey R. Benedict, *Public Heroes, Private Felons: Athletes and Crimes Against Women* (Boston: Northeastern University Press, 1997), pp. 126–129.

70. Ibid., p. 188.

71. Todd W. Crosset, James Ptacek, Mark A. McDonald, and Jeffrey R. Benedict, "Male Student-Athletes and Violence Against Women: A Survey of Campus Judicial Affairs Offices," *Violence Against Women* 2, no. 2 (June 1996): 163–179.

72. Todd W. Crosset, Jeffrey R. Benedict, and Mark A. McDonald, "Male Student Athletes Reported for Sexual Assault: A Survey of Campus Police Departments and Judicial Affairs Offices," *Journal of Sport and Social Issues* 19 (1995): 126–140. The results of this study are consistent with the results of a 1993 study conducted at the University of Arizona, which also found an association between participating in varsity sports, particularly football and men's basketball, and various forms of "sexual aggression," which ranged from catcalls and wolf whistles to rape. The Arizona study also examined other possible predictors of sexual aggression and found that alcohol and nicotine use were more highly correlated with such aggression than participation in sports was. *See*: Mary P. Koss and John A. Gaines, "The Prediction of Sexual Aggression by Alcohol Use, Athletic Participation, and Fraternity Affiliation," *Journal of Interpersonal Violence* 8, no. 1 (March 1993): 94–108.

73. Todd W. Crosset, James Ptacek, Mark A. McDonald, and Jeffrey R. Benedict, "Male Student-Athletes and Violence against Women: A Survey of Campus Judicial Affairs Offices," *Violence Against Women* 2, no. 2 (June 1996): 163–179.

74. Ibid.

75. Christopher Flores, "When Athletes Are Accused," *The Chronicle of Higher Education*, April 19, 2002, pp. A39–A40. Recruiting Tony Cole proved to be Jim Harrick's undoing at Georgia. The university reinstated Cole as eligible for basketball when the prosecutor dropped the charges against him, but Coach Harrick refused to lift his suspension from the team. In retaliation, Cole disclosed publicly that Jim Harrick, Jr., the head coach's son and assistant, had given Cole an A in a coaching course he never attended and had given him money in violation of NCAA rules. These revelations forced both Harricks to resign their posts at Georgia and caused the university to announce that its men's basketball team would not play in the 2003 Southeastern Conference and NCAA tournaments, respectively. *See* Welch Suggs, "U. of Georgia Suspends Basketball Coach and Withdraws From Tournaments," *The Chronicle of Higher Education*, March 11, 2003 [available at http://chronicle.com/daily/2003/03/2003031104n.htm] and "U. of Georgia Basketball Coach Resigns Amid Investigation of Possible Rules Violations," *The Chronicle of Higher Education*, March 28, 2003 [available at http://chronicle.com/daily/2003/03/2003032801n.htm].

76. Ibid.

77. Ibid.

78. Deborah Reed, *Where's the Penalty Flag? A Call for the NCAA to Promulgate an Eligibility Rule Revoking a Male Student-Athlete's Eligibility to Participate in Intercollegiate Athletics for Committing Violent Acts Against Women*, 21, no. 1 Women's Rights Law Reporter 41, 45–46 (Fall/Winter 1999). *See also* NCAA Operating By-laws, Article 10.4 Disciplinary Action, reprinted in NCAA, *2002–03 NCAA Division I Manual* (Michael V. Earle, ed., 2002), p. 54. There is an NCAA rule, however, namely, Article 15.3.4.1.2, that permits colleges "to cancel or reduce the financial aid of a student-athlete who is found to have engaged in misconduct by the university's regular student disciplinary authority. . . ." See *2002–03 NCAA Division I Manual*, p. 185.

79. *Brzonkala v. Virginia Polytechnic and State University et al*, 935 F. Supp 772 (W.D. Va. 1996).

80. Ibid.

81. Gil B. Fried, *Illegal Moves Off-the-Field: University Liability for Illegal Acts of Student-Athletes*, 7, no. 1 Seton Hall Journal of Sport Law 69, 72 (1997).

82. Ibid.

83. *Brzonkala v. Virginia Polytechnic and State University et al*, 935 F. Supp. 772 (W.D. Va. 1996).

84. Ibid.

85. Gil B. Fried, *Illegal Moves Off-the-Field: University Liability for Illegal Acts of Student-Athletes*, 7, no. 1 Seton Hall Journal of Sport Law 69, 73 (1997).

86. Ibid.

87. Timothy Davis and Tanya Parker, *Student-Athlete Sexual Violence Against Women: Defining the Limits of Institutional Responsibility* 55, no. 1 Washington & Lee Law Review 55, 104 (Winter 1998).

88. Steve Wieberg, "More Schools Laying Down the Law," *USA Today*, September 18, 1998, pp. 17C–18C.

89. Ibid.

90. Michael Crissey, "2 Former Arizona State Basketball Players Plead Guilty to Conspiring to Shave Points," *The Chronicle of Higher Education*, December 19, 1997, p. A40.

91. Jim Naughton and Jeffrey Selingo, "A Point-Shaving Scandal Rattles a University," *The Chronicle of Higher Education*, April 10, 1998, p. A48.

92. John Sayle Watterson, *College Football: History, Spectacle, Controversy* (Baltimore: The Johns Hopkins University Press, 2000), p. 378.

93. Ibid.

94. Michael E. Cross and Ann G. Vollano, "The Extent and Nature of Gambling Among College Student Athletes," (Ann Arbor, Mich.: The University of Michigan Department of Athletics, 1999), p. 16.

95. Ibid., p. 19.

96. Ibid., p. 23.

97. Ibid., p. 13.

98. Ibid., p. 19.

99. Murray Sperber, *Beer and Circus: How Big-Time College Sports Is Crippling Undergraduate Education* (New York: Henry Holt and Company, 2000), p. 210.

100. Scott Street, "Lobbying Battle Looms Over Plans to End Wagering on College Sports," *The Chronicle of Higher Education*, January 12, 2001, pp. A39–A40.

101. Thomas N. Sweeney, *Closing The Campus Gates—Keeping Criminals Away From the University—The Story of Student-Athlete Violence and Avoiding Institutional Liability for the Good of All*, 9, no. 1 Seton Hall Journal of Sport Law 226, 259–260 (1999).

102. Watterson, *College Football: History, Spectacle, Controversy*, p. 377.

103. Ibid.

104. Ibid.

105. Benedict, *Public Heroes, Private Felons: Athletes and Crimes Against Women*, p. 138.

106. Christopher Flores, "When Athletes Are Accused," *The Chronicle of Higher Education*, April 19, 2002, pp. A39–A40.

107. Joe Drape, "Knight Gets 'Last Chance' to Coach at Indiana," *The New York Times*, May 16, 2000, p. A27; Alexander Wolff, "General Amnesty," *Sports Illustrated*, May 22, 2000, pp. 43–48.

108. Ibid.

109. Ibid.

110. Alexander Wolff, "General Amnesty," *Sports Illustrated*, May 22, 2000, pp. 43–48.

111. Harvey Araton, "At Indiana, The Toadies Are Shocked," *The New York Times*, May 16, 2000, p. A27.

112. Bob Knight and Bob Hammel, *Knight: My Story* (New York: St. Martin's Press, 2002), p. 240.

113. Joe Drape, "Citing His Behavior, Indiana's President Fires Coach Knight," *The New York Times*, September 11, 2000, p. D9.

114. Ibid.

115. Knight and Hammel, *Knight: My Story*, p. 325.

116. Alexander Wolff, "Knight Fall," *Sports Illustrated*, September 18, 2000, pp. 54–57.

117. Ira Berkow, "Degrees of Separation for Coach and Indiana," *The New York Times*, September 11, 2000, p. D9.

CHAPTER 6

SEASONS OF HOPE

TITLE IX AS A CATALYST FOR CHANGE IN COLLEGE SPORTS

CRACKS IN THE FOUNDATION

Previous chapters revealed significant cracks in the foundation of big-time college sports. A catalyst could expand these cracks enough to topple this tawdry Taj Mahal and replace it with a structure that is more modest and more compatible with higher education, especially at athletically marginal Division I colleges. The best potential catalyst for fundamental change in college sports is Title IX, which prohibits discrimination based on sex in education programs that receive federal funds.

Congress enacted Title IX as a part of the Education Amendments Act on June 23, 1972. It states that "[n]o person in the United States shall, on the basis of sex, be excluded from participation in, be denied the benefits of, or be subjected to discrimination under any education program or activity receiving Federal financial assistance...."[1] These words helped to foster a revolution in athletic participation by girls and women in the United States. In 1972, 170,000 men, but less than 30,000 women, played sports sponsored by their respective colleges.[2] By June 23, 2002, the thirtieth anniversary of the enactment of Title IX, 209,000 men and 151,000 women played college sports.[3] In 2001–02 women were 43 percent of the varsity athletes at American colleges, an increase of 403 percent from their virtual invisibility in 1971, the year before Title IX became law.[4]

To be sure, Title IX was not the only spark to ignite the prairie fire of female athleticism that swept across the U.S. in the 1970s and the 1980s. Several other forces—including the greater social acceptance of female athletes that began in the 1960s, the NCAA's challenge to the Amateur Athletic Union (AAU) for supremacy in the training of American Olympians, and a determination by the United States to end the Soviet Union's dominance of women's Olympic sports—also contributed to the growth that occurred during this period in athletic participation by America's female college students.[5] Indeed, Title IX reflected, more than it created, the demand by college women for competitive sports opportunities. Still, Title IX was not just a product of change, it was an agent of change, too. It nudged colleges to improve athletic opportunities for their female students by threatening to cut off federal funds for failure to act and by emboldening female physical educators to pursue those opportunities with unprecedented confidence and forcefulness.[6] According to historian Mary Jo Festle, "Title IX gave women physical educators the legitimacy to advocate for change."[7] It gave them legitimacy because it put the full force and effect of federal law on their side.

The changed social climate that spawned Title IX and the academic and athletic opportunities that flowed from it enabled America's daughters to succeed in venues that had been closed to their mothers and grandmothers. Nobody succeeded in a more grand fashion than Dot Richardson, to whom a Little League coach offered a spot on his roster in 1973, when she was eleven years old and he saw her playing catch in an Orlando, Florida park. Little League officials did not permit girls to play on their teams then, so the coach told Dot, "We'll just cut your hair short and call you Bob."[8] Whether or not the coach welcomed social change, he surely knew athletic talent when he saw it. Dot Richardson became a four-time All-American shortstop at UCLA and the NCAA softball player of the decade for the 1980s. Her home run won the gold medal for the American women at the 1996 Summer Olympic Games in Atlanta. After the Olympics, Dr. Richardson left Atlanta for Los Angeles, where she began a residency in orthopedic surgery at the University of Southern California.[9] Her rich and varied achievements were possible not only because of her considerable talent and effort but also because Title IX and the social change that accompanied it made both organized sports and medical education accessible to the women of her generation.

Still, the high-profile successes of elite athletes are not the true measure of the importance of Title IX. The National Coalition for Women and Girls in Education (NCWGE) recognized this in a report issued on the thirtieth anniversary of the enactment of Title IX. The report stated:

> Olympic medals and professional sports contracts are not what Title IX is all about. Rather, the quest for equal opportunity in sports has always been about the physiological, sociological, and psychological benefits of sports and physical activity participation.[10]

Olympic medals and professional contracts are not what college sports should be about, either. They should confer on all participants the same array of benefits that the NCWGE report identified as the goals of Title

IX. Unfortunately, many athletes do not receive these benefits, because colleges permit commerce to trump education in the governance of intercollegiate athletics. Patricia Viverito, the commissioner of the Gateway Football Conference, said:

> I think we're at a real crossroads. I keep being hopeful that presidents will sort of see the big picture and recognize that we are migrating farther and farther away from an educational model, and that someone is going to right that course and force us to do things in a more reasonable fashion.[11]

The participation model introduced earlier represents an eminently reasonable course correction for college sports. Title IX can facilitate its adoption in Division I and Division II.

Title IX can help to bring fiscal sanity, academic integrity, and personal responsibility to college sports by encouraging colleges to replace the commercial model with the participation model. The trigger for this change is that most colleges cannot afford to support women's sports as generously as they support men's sports, yet Title IX requires them to do so. In other words, the athletic director's dilemma is the reformer's golden opportunity.

Athletic directors are largely responsible for their own predicament. During the 1970s and the 1980s neither the United States Department of Education nor the federal courts enforced Title IX aggressively, in part because it was not possible to do so. Colleges were not required to comply with the regulations that enforce Title IX until 1978, and the Supreme Court ruled in 1984 that Title IX did not apply to college athletic departments unless they received federal funds directly, which they did not. This ruling remained the law until 1988, which means that it was possible to enforce Title IX for only six years during the sixteen-year period from 1972 through 1988. Consequently, athletic departments spent money lavishly on men's sports, especially basketball and football, and shortchanged women's sports.[12] During the 1990s, however, after Congress applied Title IX to athletic departments, the federal courts began to require colleges to comply with it, regardless of the cost. The usual means by which colleges seek to comply is to demonstrate that the percentage of female varsity athletes on campus is "substantially proportionate" to (i.e., within five points of) the percentage of women in the student body.[13] It has been difficult for colleges to comply with Title IX. Despite steady progress during and since the 1990s, in 2000–2001 the percentage of female athletes was within five points of the percentage of female undergraduates at only 71 of the 321 colleges (22 percent) that belong to Division I of the NCAA.[14]

It has also been expensive for colleges to comply with Title IX. The revenue from football and men's basketball has been insufficient to fund existing women's teams or to create new women's teams in order to achieve "substantial proportionality." To make matters worse, non-revenue sports are pricey, especially in Division I, where they cost an average of $220,000 per year apiece in 1999–2000.[15] In the six "equity" conferences (see Chapter 3), the comparable figure was nearly $500,000.[16] Still, colleges refuse to cut the high costs of football and men's basketball, which they continue to believe are potential sources of income with which to fund non-revenue sports. This calls to mind Mark Twain's famous quip that reports of his death had been "greatly exaggerated." The revenue potential of college football and basketball has been greatly exaggerated, too, as Chapter 3 demonstrated.

Men's non-revenue sports, particularly gymnastics, swimming, and wrestling, have been the major casualties in colleges' ongoing battle to balance athletic department budgets and comply with Title IX, while preserving big-time football and basketball. During the 1981–82 academic year 428 college wrestling teams existed in America; by 1998–99, however, only 257 remained.[17] Similarly, in 1981–82, 82 colleges fielded men's gymnastics teams; by 1998–99 only 26 colleges did so.[18] By 2002 that number had declined to 22.[19] Under these circumstances it is not surprising that the National Wrestling Coaches' Association has filed a lawsuit that challenges the constitutionality of the regulations by which the Department of Education enforces Title IX, including the substantial proportionality test.[20] J. Robinson, the wrestling coach at the University of Minnesota, has expressed publicly the sentiments that underlie the suit. Coach Robinson said:

> Boys are being discriminated against because they show more interest in sports. The women feel we're trying to take something away from them and we're not. . . . If women are truly interested in sports, they should be playing more at lower levels—i.e., intramurals and club sports—and they're not.[21]

Some conservative political commentators support this suit because they see the substantial proportionality test as an illegal quota scheme and as an example of "overreaching" by the federal government in the service of political correctness.[22] The wrestling coaches and their political allies contend that men are more interested than women in playing college sports, so colleges should be able to satisfy Title IX by providing both men and women with athletic opportunities that are proportional to their athletic interests, not to their respective percentages in the student body.[23] Supporters of the proportionality standard counter that interest in athletic participation follows the creation of opportunities to participate. Therefore, to base athletic offerings on students' interests will ensure that women continue to participate in sports at a lower rate than men do and at a lower rate than they would participate if more opportunities were made available to them.[24] The Bush administration is conservative, but it has charted a moderate course on Title IX reform during its first two years in office. The Department of Justice moved to dismiss the lawsuit filed by the wrestling coaches,[25] and Secretary of Education Roderick Paige created a Commission on Opportunities in Athletics to "study the effects of Title IX on college sports" and to report its findings to him, which it did in January 2003. Secretary Paige told a Senate committee that his department will review the commission's findings before it decides whether to alter the Title IX regulations, including the substantial proportionality test.[26]

The wrestling coaches and their supporters are right to condemn the elimination of men's non-revenue sports, but they are wrong to blame Title IX, the Department of Education, or the federal courts for the demise of men's teams. The real culprit in this caper is the commercial model of college sports, with its needlessly large football rosters, massive arenas, plush training facilities, extensive intersectional travel to play games and to recruit high school athletes, and princely salaries for bloated coaching staffs. The price tag for such extravagance is so high that the additional cost of sponsoring women's teams strains athletic department budgets to the breaking point and contributes to the deaths of men's non-revenue sports as much as the need to comply with Title IX does.[27] The need to comply with Title IX will continue, so colleges should stop fighting this law and should use it instead to facilitate the development of a new model of college sports. The new model would retain intercollegiate athletic competition, but it would not require colleges to train future professional athletes or to entertain the public. The savings realized from an emphasis on participation instead of commerce would enable colleges to comply with Title IX, balance their athletic budgets, and retain—perhaps even restore—men's non-revenue sports. The promise of a "new season," then, is the replacement of the commercial model by the participation model, with Title IX as the primary catalyst for change.

THE GREAT DEBATES

The importance of Title IX to fundamental change in college sports necessitates a careful examination of its eventful history. The genesis of Title IX was a series of hearings held in 1970 and conducted by the Special Subcommittee on Education of the House of Representatives, which Representative Edith Green (D-OR) chaired.[28] These hearings revealed that discrimination against girls and women was pervasive in elementary, secondary, and postsecondary education. Today, Title IX is probably best known for its impact on high school and college sports, but sports were not the principal concern of the legislators who drafted or debated it in the early 1970s. Indeed, sports received minimal attention during congressional discussions of sex discrimination in education; the advocates for women were concerned primarily about the barriers women faced in seeking admission to undergraduate, graduate, and professional programs and employment in colleges and universities. The comments of Birch Bayh (D-IN), who was the prime mover behind

Title IX in the Senate, illustrate this point. Senator Bayh, speaking on the Senate floor, asked his colleagues:

> How can we possibly justify an arbitrary and compulsory ratio of two and one-half men to every woman at a State university? How can we tolerate discrimination by a land-grant college that refuses all women admission to regular academic sessions unless they are related to employees or students and are pursuing a course of study otherwise unavailable?[29]

He then observed that discrimination not only prevented women from obtaining access to higher education as students but also denied women who had run the academic obstacle course and earned graduate degrees access to employment as professors and college administrators. Senator Bayh observed:

> Today women seeking employment in higher education face an array of obstacles almost as insuperable as those that used to face blacks. [Statistics indicate that] Columbia University annually awards 24 percent of its doctorates to women, but that it has awarded 2 percent of its tenured faculty positions to females; and the last time the Department of Psychology at [the University of California at] Berkeley hired a woman was in 1924. In other words, just as in other professions, an old axiom applies: the higher the rank, the fewer the women.[30]

Discrimination against women in higher education frustrated the late Representative Patsy Mink (D-HI), who was a member of the House when Title IX was under consideration, but her frustration had nothing to do with sports. Several months before her death in September 2002, Representative Mink said of Title IX:

> When it was proposed, we had no idea that its most visible impact would be in athletics. I had been paying attention to the academic issue. I had been excluded from medical school because I was a female.[31]

The legislators' lack of attention to the ramifications of Title IX for sports is one reason why courts, colleges, and commentators have struggled ever since its enactment to determine its intended scope in the sports world. The current debate about the substantial proportionality standard, which is front and center in the lawsuit filed by the National Wrestling Coaches' Association, is the most recent incarnation of this struggle. The other reason why courts, colleges, and commentators have puzzled over the reach of Title IX with respect to sports is that the Congress enacted it as a floor amendment, which means that there is almost no "legislative history" (i.e., witness testimony at hearings, committee deliberations, committee reports) with which to divine its intent.[32] This lack of legislative history helps to explain why it took sixteen years just to determine that Title IX applied to college athletic departments.

The question of applicability to college athletic departments arose early in the history of Title IX. It required a determination of who was a "recipient" of federal funds pursuant to Title IX, which commanded only such recipients to refrain from engaging in sex discrimination. One answer, the "institution-wide" interpretation, held that if any part of a college received federal funds, then every part of that college was a recipient and was obligated to follow Title IX. The underlying rationale for this interpretation, known as the release theory, argued that when one program at a college received federal funds, that program was able to "release" money to other programs at the college. Consequently, the "receiving" program, which could be the athletic department, benefited indirectly from federal funds; therefore, it should be bound by Title IX.[33] The alternative answer, the "program-specific" interpretation, countered that Title IX required only those parts of a college that received federal funds directly to obey its prohibition against sex discrimination.

It would be difficult to exaggerate the implications of this debate for the cause of gender equity in college sports. College athletic departments received little or no federal financial assistance directly. Therefore, if the institution-wide interpretation triumphed, Title IX would bind athletic departments; but if the program-specific interpretation prevailed, Title IX would not, by and large, bind athletic departments. Ultimately, the institution-wide interpretation won the day, but not until 1988. In that year Congress enacted amendments to the Civil Rights Restoration Act that wrote this interpretation of Title IX into federal law, thereby applying Title IX to college athletic departments.[34]

While the debate raged about whether Title IX applied to college athletic departments, regulations designed to put the new law into effect began to take shape. In 1974, Congress authorized the Department of Health, Education, and Welfare (HEW) to promulgate regulations to enforce Title IX. The final regulations, which took effect on July 21, 1975, mandated that colleges comply by July 21, 1978, or risk losing federal financial assistance.[35] When HEW proposed these regulations, the NCAA opposed them and lobbied against them because it feared that a federal mandate in favor of equal athletic opportunities for women would diminish the funds available to operate men's sports, thereby reducing their quality, popularity, and profitability.[36] It even filed a lawsuit in hopes that a federal court would invalidate the proposed regulations, but the lawsuit failed to achieve this objective.[37] The NCAA also supported an amendment offered by Senator John Tower (R-TX) that would have made revenue-producing college sports—namely, football and men's basketball—exempt from coverage by Title IX.[38] The Tower Amendment passed the Senate, but it died in a House-Senate conference committee. Thus, no sport would be exempt from the Title IX regulations.

The regulations raised more questions than they answered in the higher-education community about what constituted compliance with Title IX with respect to sports. After the regulations became law in 1978, many athletic directors complained that they were vague and that they offered scant guidance regarding compliance. On December 11, 1979, HEW responded to these complaints by issuing a "Policy Interpretation" designed to clarify the regulations, particularly their requirement that colleges "provide equal athletic opportunity for members of both sexes."[39] The Policy Interpretation focused its attention on just one of the ten factors that the Title IX regulations had indicated were relevant to a determination of whether a college satisfied the "equal opportunity" requirement. This factor was the only one in the regulations that was broadly evaluative; it required colleges to offer sports and levels of competition that "effectively accommodate[d] the interests and abilities" of both male and female students.[40] During the 1990s this "effective accommodation" test became the most important measure of compliance that the Title IX regulations identified because the federal courts based their decisions in Title IX cases on whether or not the defendant college had accommodated the athletic interests and abilities of its women students effectively. It is the eye of the storm of controversy that continues to swirl around Title IX enforcement in college sports today.

The Policy Interpretation stated that a college accommodated its students' athletic interests and abilities effectively, thereby complying with Title IX, when it satisfied one part of a three-part effective-accommodation test. The college could pass this test by satisfying part one, the substantial-proportionality standard, which required it to show that the percentages of its male and female students who were athletes were substantially proportional to the percentages of men and women in its student body.[41] Failing that, a college could comply with Title IX by demonstrating a "history and continuing practice" of expanding athletic opportunities for the under-represented sex—which usually meant women—in its sports programs.[42] A college that could not satisfy either part one or part two could still comply by showing that its sports offerings, even though they might be limited, accommodated the interests and abilities of its student body fully and effectively.[43]

Today, the Policy Interpretation's three-part effective-accommodation test is the legal standard that determines whether a college is in compliance with Title IX. During the 1990s the three-part test produced a series of courtroom victories for female college athletes and prompted the settlement of other cases on terms that were favorable to female athletes.[44] In the early 1980s, though, the three-part test was not the eye of the Title IX storm; that distinction belonged instead to the question of whether Title IX applied to college athletic departments. The federal courts' preoccupation with this question, the Reagan administration's support for the program-specific interpretation of Title IX, and weak enforcement by the OCR, which took over Title IX enforcement from HEW in 1980, combined to make the 1980s a stagnant decade for the cause of gender equity in college sports.[45] Colleges had expanded athletic opportunities for women significantly in the 1970s, but instead of building on that progress in the 1980s, colleges added only a few sports, typically cross-country, golf, and tennis, which attracted few participants, and gave them minimal financial support.

As if stagnation were not bad enough, the cause of gender equity in college sports nearly slipped into a coma after the United States Supreme Court's decision in *Grove City College* v. *Bell*.[46] In *Grove City*, the Court, siding with the Reagan administration, interpreted Title IX to apply only to programs or departments within a college that received federal funds directly. In so doing, the justices placed college athletics beyond the reach of Title IX because athletic departments hardly ever received federal funds. The consequences of their decision were swift and severe. OCR discontinued approximately forty pending Title IX sports investigations, and it refused to act on new complaints unless the athletic departments named in those complaints received federal funds.[47] One of these investigations was of the University of Maryland, where OCR had found violations of six of the ten factors by which Title IX measured equal opportunity in college sports. *Grove City* forced OCR to abandon this investigation because Maryland's athletic department did not receive federal funds directly.[48] OCR also reduced the scope of an investigation at Auburn after *Grove City*, despite having found violations of seven of the ten factors. As a result of *Grove City*, OCR informed Auburn that it would investigate only discrimination in the awarding of athletic scholarships, to see if the university had misused federal funds.[49]

Grove City remained in force until March 22, 1988, when Congress overrode President Reagan's veto and amended the Civil Rights Restoration Act of 1987, thereby reversing *Grove City* and making the institution-wide interpretation of Title IX the law of the land. The new language defined an educational "program or activity" as "all of the operations of a college . . . ," which brought athletic departments within the reach of Title IX.[50] Henceforth, if *any* office, department, or program within a college received federal funds directly, then *every* office, department, and program within that college had to obey Title IX.

The reversal of *Grove City* in 1988 was as consequential as its announcement had been four years earlier. It triggered the filing of forty-five complaints to OCR that alleged violations of Title IX by college athletic departments,[51] and it facilitated the settlement of a long-standing lawsuit against Temple University on terms that favored the plaintiffs, who were women athletes at Temple.[52] Most importantly, the reversal of *Grove City* shifted the focus of debate from *whether* college athletic departments had to comply with Title IX to *how* they could comply with Title IX, and it substantially relocated this debate from Congress and the Department of Education to the federal courts, where women college athletes would be extraordinarily successful plaintiffs during the 1990s.

The debate about the reach of Title IX was important, but it was not the only debate that raged within the college-sports community during the 1970s and the 1980s. A less visible, but equally significant, debate occurred among the small cadre of women who taught and coached female college students. At issue in this debate was whether women ought to adopt the male model of college sports, with its emphases on winning games and earning money, or whether they ought to create an alternative model that sought primarily to benefit the women who played the games instead of the institutions they represented. Older women physical educators typically rejected the male model, which was contrary to the philosophy to which they had adhered for decades.

This philosophy held that (1) cooperation was preferable to competition; (2) sports should be secondary to a student's academic life, and they should not encourage cheating; (3) sports should not become so important that players had to worry about retaining scholarships and that coaches had to win games and earn profits in order to remain employed; and (4) women of average athletic ability should not be made to believe that their colleges regarded them as less important than teammates who were "stars."[53] It led women physical educators to favor intramural competition, which they believed promoted physical and mental health, while avoiding public displays of athletic prowess. Public displays of athletic prowess had triggered corruption in men's college sports, and they were contrary to traditional ideas about proper female behavior, which the usually conservative women physical educators did not wish to challenge. Thus, according to Allen Sack and Ellen Staurowsky: "The refined and restrained nature of women's sport, so intimately connected to women's education models, replicated the standards of womanly behavior."[54]

Traditional standards of womanly behavior began to change during the 1960s, though, and this change brought an acceptance of, even an appreciation for, female athleticism. In the new environment the traditional opposition by women physical educators to varsity competition among female collegians gradually fell away, setting the stage for the tremendous expansion of athletic opportunities for college women that occurred in the 1970s.[55] Indeed, in 1966 women physical educators founded the Commission on Intercollegiate Athletics for Women (CIAW) for the purpose of providing the intercollegiate athletic competition that women students increasingly desired, but without the "rampant commercialism" and the "almost insane compulsion to win at any cost" that plagued men's college sports.[56] The CIAW sponsored championships for women in several sports.

The CIAW was short-lived because it evolved into a new organization, the Association for Intercollegiate Athletics for Women (AIAW), in 1970.

Unlike the CIAW, which was an organization of women physical educators to which colleges did not belong, the AIAW was a national membership organization to which colleges belonged if they wished to participate in intercollegiate athletic championships for women. Still, the same women who had been leaders in the CIAW were leaders in the AIAW. The AIAW was unique among college-sports governing bodies in that it emerged from, and was affiliated with, an educational association, the Division of Girls' and Women's Sport (DGWS), which, in turn, was a part of the American Association of Health, Physical Education, and Recreation (AAHPER).[57]

Conducting championships was the most visible function that the AIAW performed, but like its male counterparts, the NCAA and the National Association for Intercollegiate Athletics (NAIA), it also published rules for the sports it sponsored, disseminated information, including athletic schedules, and represented its members on matters that related to college sports.[58] In 1972–73, the first year of full-scale operations for the AIAW, 386 colleges held memberships, and their female athletes could participate in AIAW-sanctioned national championships in 8 sports.[59] In 1981–82, the last year of full-scale operations for the AIAW, it conducted forty-one national championship events, which served three divisions and 19 sports.[60] Moreover, between 1973 and 1981, which nearly paralleled the lifetime of the AIAW, the amount of money that colleges spent on women's sports as a portion of their total sports budgets increased by an average of 43.59 percent per college and the number of women's sports increased by an average of 2.73 per college.[61] Women's sports budgets were negligible before 1973, though, so a 43.59 percent average increase still left them much lower than men's sports budgets in 1981.

The AIAW ceased to exist on June 30, 1982, despite having played a pivotal role in the development of college sports for women. Ironically, Title IX was partially responsible for the demise of the AIAW. Title IX surely helped to expand athletic opportunities for college women, but it failed to offer the physical educators and coaches who ran women's college sports what Mary Jo Festle has called "self-determination," that is, a chance to operate the games according to a different model than the men used.[62] Indeed, coaches, athletic administrators, and lawyers generally interpreted Title IX to require "sameness" between men's and women's athletic programs—which pushed women's programs to emulate men's programs, as the latter were the accepted way of doing business in college sports and their patriarchs in the NCAA were unwilling to trade commerce for participation.[63] The implications of this orientation toward sameness became evident early in 1973, when eleven students and three instructors from two Florida colleges filed a lawsuit charging that the AIAW rule that prohibited member colleges from awarding athletic scholarships discriminated on the basis of sex, in violation of the Equal Protection Clause of the Fourteenth Amendment to the United States Constitution. Instead of defending itself in court, the AIAW dropped its scholarship ban. It feared that retaining the ban would result in a loss of member colleges that offered athletic scholarships to men because these colleges would or might think that Title IX required them to offer athletic scholarships to women, too.[64]

The lawsuit was a harbinger of things to come within the AIAW itself. By the mid-1970s one faction continued to favor a participatory model of college sports, which Festle has called "a somewhat more competitive version of the old PE programs," while another faction "wanted to jump whole-heartedly into big-business sports."[65] By the early 1980s it was clear that the big-business faction had won. It won as early as 1980, when the NCAA membership voted to offer five national championships for women in Di-visions II and III during the 1981–82 academic year.[66] The NCAA sought to gain control of women's college sports because Title IX, and the pressure on colleges to fund women's sports that followed its enactment, convinced the association that it had to govern women's sports in order to protect the profitability of men's college sports, and its own economic well-being, in the future.[67] When the NCAA gained control of women's college sports, it elim-inated the AIAW as an organizational rival and extended the reach of the commercial model from the men's games to the women's games.[68]

The NCAA's announcement that it would offer championships for women devastated the AIAW. The NCAA, not the AIAW, would receive the rev-enue to be derived from telecasts of women's college championships. Women's teams would opt to participate in NCAA-sponsored champion-ships because the NCAA, unlike the AIAW, could afford to pay their ex-penses for travel to and from the championship sites.[69] In June of 1981 two hundred colleges, or 20 percent of the AIAW's members, declined to renew their memberships and another 12 percent renewed but indicated that they would not participate in any AIAW championships.[70] The NCAA's superior financial resources—namely, an annual operating budget of more than $20 million, as compared to the AIAW's operating budget of less than $1 mil-lion—enabled it to supplant the AIAW quickly as a sponsor of college sports for women. The AIAW filed suit against the NCAA on antitrust grounds, but lost both at trial and on appeal, as the courts concluded that the NCAA's takeover of women's college sports was not the product of a monopolistic intent.[71]

Thus, by 1988, when Congress finally ended the long-standing debate about the applicability of Title IX to college athletic departments, the debate about the wisdom of intercollegiate athletics for women was over, too. It was clear that the NCAA would govern women's college sports according to the established male model. It was equally clear that Title IX was a double-edged sword for women in sports.[72] Title IX had helped to increase budgets, opportunities to compete, and the visibility of women's college sports, but at the price of adopting a commercial orientation that was fun-damentally incompatible with higher education. In short, Title IX promised women equality in college sports, but it denied them self-determination.[73] During the 1990s women would pursue equality in the federal courts with so much success that a backlash would occur among supporters of men's non-revenue sports, who would charge that colleges sacrificed these sports routinely on the altar of Title IX compliance. The women's courtroom success and the resulting backlash are the subjects of the discussion that follows.

COLLEGE SPORTS ON TRIAL

During the 1990s female college athletes filed several lawsuits in which they alleged that colleges had failed to accommodate their athletic interests and abilities fully. These lawsuits arose out of decisions by the plaintiffs' respective colleges to discontinue specific women's sports because of budgetary shortfalls. Still, the colleges' decisions to drop certain women's sports would not have spawned successful legal challenges had it not been for three federal court decisions that set the table for the Title IX lawsuits by making it possible and worthwhile to pursue gender equity through litigation.[74]

The United States Supreme Court issued two of the table-setting decisions. The first one was *Cannon v. University of Chicago*, in which the High Court ruled that Title IX implicitly entitles an individual who believes that she has been the victim of sex discrimination to file a lawsuit in order to enforce the prohibition against such discrimination.[75] The second Supreme Court decision was *Franklin v. Gwinnett County Public Schools*, wherein the justices ruled that a court may require an educational institution that engages in intentional sex discrimination to pay a plaintiff compensatory and punitive damages besides having to reform its noncomplying program(s) in order to satisfy Title IX.[76] Before *Franklin*, the only penalty to which a college that violated Title IX was subject was the loss of federal financial assistance, which penalty federal regulators had not imposed on any college since Title IX became law in 1972. Thus, *Franklin* gave women college athletes and their attorneys a financial incentive, which they had lacked previously, to challenge in court the failure of colleges to comply with Title IX in sports.

The third table-setting decision, which arose in the college-sports setting, was *Haffer v. Temple University*.[77] The plaintiffs in *Haffer*, who either participated in college sports or wished to do so, complained that Temple had violated Title IX because it "(1) afforded women fewer opportunities than men to compete in intercollegiate sports; (2) allocated disproportionate resources (e.g. coaches, facilities, travel funds and equipment) to men's athletic programs; and (3) allocated disproportionate financial aid to male athletes."[78] *Haffer* occurred before Congress adopted the institution-wide interpretation of Title IX, but the court still concluded that Title IX applied to college-sports programs whether or not they received federal funds directly. The court also rejected Temple's request to dismiss the case without a trial, because there was sufficient evidence of inequitable distributions of participation opportunities, resources, and financial aid to submit the case to a jury. Thus, the court in the *Haffer* case, which the parties ultimately settled out of court, considered the sorts of claims and evidence of sex discrimination that would bring victorious verdicts for female college athletes in the 1990s.

The first of the 1990s Title IX sports cases was *Favia v. Indiana University of Pennsylvania* (IUP), wherein members of IUP's field hockey and gymnastics teams challenged a decision to disband both teams and won a preliminary injunction that forced IUP to reinstate the teams.[79] The trial court later denied IUP's motion to modify the preliminary injunction, which would have enabled IUP to replace the gymnastics team with a soccer team, and the appellate court affirmed the trial court's decision.

The appellate court concluded, for two reasons, that the trial court had not abused its discretion when it denied IUP's motion. First, it was reasonable to try to preserve a gymnastics team that was "at the center" of this litigation. Second, to substitute soccer for gymnastics would have reduced the percentage of IUP's sports budget that funded women's teams without increasing substantially the percentage of its women students who were athletes. The substitution would have increased the percentage of women students at IUP who were athletes from 38 percent to 43 percent, but it would not have achieved substantial proportionality because women were 56 percent of the student body at IUP. Moreover, gymnastics is much more expensive than soccer, so the substitution of soccer for gymnastics would have reduced IUP's expenditures on women's sports dramatically in order to achieve only a modest increase in participation opportunities for women. As a result, IUP would probably have been farther away from, rather than closer to, compliance with Title IX after the substitution because the Policy Interpretation requires not only the "effective accommodation" of students' athletic interests and abilities but also "equivalence" in "athletic financial assistance" and in "other athletic benefits and opportunities."[80]

The *Favia* decision was important because it foreshadowed future developments in Title IX sports litigation, especially the significance of the Policy Interpretation. *Favia* was the first federal court decision to apply any provision of the Policy Interpretation to a Title IX claim in the context of college sports. *Favia* also signaled that defenses based on budgetary constraints, on having offered or disbanded equal numbers of men's and women's teams, and on the absence of discriminatory intent would be ineffective in Title IX sports cases.

In *Roberts v. Colorado State Board of Agriculture*, members of the softball team at Colorado State University (CSU) sued the university after it disbanded their team.[81] The trial court concluded that CSU had violated Title IX, and it issued a permanent injunction that reinstated the team. CSU appealed, and the appellate court affirmed the decision of the trial court, based on the three-part test in the Policy Interpretation.

The plaintiffs satisfied the appellate court that CSU had violated part one of this test, the substantial-proportionality requirement, because without the softball team, there were 10.5 percent more women in the CSU student body than there were on its sports teams, an unacceptable disparity. The plaintiffs also showed that CSU violated part three of the test because the plaintiffs' efforts to get their team reinstated indicated that CSU had not accommodated the athletic interests of its women students fully and effectively. CSU, however, failed to bear its burden, pursuant to part two of the test, to show a history and continuing practice of expanding athletic opportunities for women. It had added eleven women's sports during the 1970s but had allowed athletic opportunities for women to decline by 34 percent during the 1980s.

Roberts was significant because it established that the three-part test was the judicially preferred measure of compliance with Title IX, that the plaintiff bore the burdens of proof under parts one and three, and that the defendant bore the burden of proof under part two in Title IX sports litigation.[82] It also established that a 10.5 percent disparity between female enrollment and female athletic participation failed part one of that test. Finally, it reinforced the conclusions reached in *Favia* that budgetary problems did not relieve a college of its duty to comply with Title IX, that a college could not avoid liability by disbanding an equal number of men's and women's teams simultaneously, and that a plaintiff need not prove discriminatory intent in order to show that the defendant had violated Title IX.

The most pivotal of the Title IX college-sports cases was *Cohen v. Brown University*, which arose from Brown's decision in 1991 to disband its women's volleyball and gymnastics teams.[83] It produced four separate court decisions, two by a federal district (i.e., trial) court in Rhode Island and two by a federal appellate court in Boston. In *Cohen I*, the district court granted the plaintiffs' request for a preliminary injunction, which restored the volleyball and gymnastics teams to varsity status, and Brown appealed. In *Cohen II*, the appellate court affirmed the district court's decision because it concluded that the plaintiffs, who were members of the disbanded teams, would probably prevail on the merits of their lawsuit at trial.[84] The plaintiffs met their burdens of proof under parts one and three, respectively, of the effective-accommodation (three-part) test by demonstrating a disparity between the gender composition of Brown's student body and its athletic teams and the presence of an unmet athletic interest among members of the underrepresented gender. The plaintiffs' efforts to have their teams reinstated reflected this unmet interest. Brown could not shoulder its burden under part two of proving that it had a history and continuing practice of expanding athletic opportunities for women. The appellate court, therefore, sent the case back to the district court for a trial.

In *Cohen III*, the district court concluded after a bench trial (i.e, by judge only, without a jury) that Brown had indeed violated Title IX, and it ordered Brown to submit a plan of compliance. The court subsequently rejected

Brown's plan, whereupon Brown appealed, and the appellate court affirmed the district court again in *Cohen IV*. *Cohen IV* lies at the heart of the current debate about Title IX because it reflects strong support for part one of the three-part test, the substantial-proportionality standard. The appellate court rejected Brown's argument that the substantial-proportionality standard imposed on colleges' athletic-participation quotas for women that exceeded the athletic interests and abilities of women undergraduates. The court held that this standard "merely creates a presumption that a [college] is in compliance with Title IX and the applicable regulation when it achieves [substantial proportionality]."[85] Moreover, the court noted that "the substantial proportionality test is but one aspect of the inquiry into whether an institution's athletics program complies with Title IX."[86] A college could fail to meet it, yet still comply with Title IX by satisfying either part two or part three of the three-part test. This conclusion mirrored the "Clarification" of the three-part test that OCR had issued on January 16, 1996, wherein Assistant Secretary of Education for Civil Rights Norma V. Cantu stated in an introductory letter that substantial proportionality was a "safe harbor," which establishes that colleges that have reached substantial proportionality provide "nondiscriminatory participation opportunities" in sports for their students.[87]

The appellate court in *Cohen IV* also rejected Brown's argument that its duty under Title IX was merely to give women athletic opportunities that reflected their current membership on varsity teams. This "relative-interests" measure of "effective accommodation" is the preferred alternative to substantial proportionality among the critics of the three-part test. The appellate court rejected it in *Cohen IV*, reasoning that to accept it would be to "entrench and fix by law the significant gender-based disparity in athletics opportunities found by the district court to exist at Brown. . . ."[88] This measure would also, in the court's words, "ignore the fact that Title IX was enacted in order to remedy discrimination that results from the stereotyped notions of women's interests and abilities."[89] Athletic "interest and ability rarely develop in a vacuum," the court observed; instead, "they evolve as a function of opportunity and experience."[90] Based on this reasoning, the appellate court upheld the district court's rejection of Brown's proposed plan for Title IX compliance, reversed the district court's order that required Brown to upgrade four women's club sports to varsity sports, and sent the case back to the district court in order to give Brown another chance to submit a plan of compliance.

Brown appealed this decision to the Supreme Court, which declined to hear the appeal.[91] Consequently, the rule of *Roberts* and *Cohen* is the law of the land in Title IX sports cases. Colleges must satisfy one part of the three-part test of "effective accommodation of interests and abilities" in order to comply with Title IX. There are legal and public policy implications of this rule. The principal legal implication has been a vigorous debate about whether Title IX is an affirmative action statute that requires gender-based preferences or quotas or an antidiscrimination statute that requires equal opportunities for both sexes, but not equal numbers of males and females in college sports. Critics of the *Roberts/Cohen* rule charge that Title IX is an antidiscrimination statute that the federal courts have misconstrued as an affirmative action statute that requires substantial proportionality for compliance. Having failed to convince the federal courts, the critics have tried to convince Secretary Paige's commission that the Title IX regulations need a major overhaul.[92]

The principal public policy implication of the *Roberts/Cohen* rule is that college athletic departments must make difficult choices as they try to expand athletic opportunities for women and to preserve athletic opportunities for men at a time when budgets are tight. Congress has not made revenue sports exempt from Title IX; the Supreme Court has declined to consider the issue of Title IX compliance in college sports; and the Department of Education is unlikely to gut the three-part test, because Title IX is politically popular—especially among women, whose votes President Bush will need in order to be reelected in 2004.[93] It is fair to assume, then, that colleges will continue to struggle toward compliance by adding women's teams and by eliminating or capping the rosters of men's non-revenue teams, while preserving football, the supposed cash cow of college sports. OCR's 1996 Clarification of the three-part test states that colleges may "eliminate or cap teams" as a means of achieving substantial proportionality, and several federal court decisions have upheld both practices.[94] Football is not a cash cow at most Division I colleges, however, as Chapter 3 demonstrated. Therefore, football should not be immune from the fiscal restraint that will be necessary if colleges are to comply with Title IX without eliminating men's non-revenue sports. Indeed, football should be the starting point for, and the major focus of, this fiscal restraint, which is a key feature of the participation model of college sports. The following section will explain why reduced rosters and budgets in football are necessary in order to achieve gender equity in college sports.

FOOTBALL FOLLIES

It is especially difficult for Division I colleges that field football teams to comply with Title IX by achieving substantial proportionality because there is no female sport that is even roughly proportionate to football in either roster size or cost. Sportswriter Rick Telander of the *Chicago Sun-Times* summed up this problem well when he wrote that "the Division I football monster, with its swollen numbers and rabid fan base, skews everything."[95] The best evidence of this is that most Division I colleges, particularly those with football teams, have not achieved substantial proportionality. The colleges that are most likely to have achieved substantial proportionality are those that (1) have a relatively small number of female students; (2) can spend large sums of money on women's sports; (3) offer a small athletic program for men and women; or (4) do not field a football team.[96] The first group includes the service academies, engineering schools, and colleges where the academic program mixes coursework and employment.[97] The colleges that have the largest disparities between the percentages of women students on campus and women athletes, respectively, include some of the institutions that play football in Division I-A, the historically black colleges, and smaller institutions that play football in Division I-AA. These colleges share one common feature, namely, they all have many more female students than male students.[98]

Wealth is also a factor in being able to approach or to achieve substantial proportionality, which is why not all of the members of Division I-A have had difficulty in meeting this standard. In 1998–99, at the Division I-A colleges that belong to one of the six "equity" conferences, there was a gap of 8.6 percent, which approaches substantial proportionality, between the percentages of women undergraduates (50 percent) and women athletes (42 percent), respectively, on their campuses.[99] Presumably, this relatively small gap is the happy consequence of large football revenues, which enable profitable conference members to fund women's sports adequately. Conference members who are less successful in sports nevertheless share in the postseason revenues that the powerhouses earn, so there is enough money available to support a large number of sports opportunities for women at every member institution. Colleges that belong to Division I-AAA, whose members do not field football teams, also enjoyed a fairly small gap of 9.8 percent between the percentages of female undergraduates and female athletes on their campuses, without the benefit of football profits.[100]

What football gives, though, football can also take away. A profitable football team can help to support women's sports, but an unprofitable football team starves women's sports by consuming resources that would support women athletes if football were eliminated or funded less generously.[101] For example, at the fifty-three Division I-A colleges that do not belong to an "equity" conference, there was a 12 percent gap between the numbers of women undergraduates and women athletes, respectively, in 1998–99.[102] The gap rose to 14.1 percent at colleges that play football in Division I-AA, where even colleges that succeed on the field lose money on football.[103] These are the types of numbers that spur colleges to eliminate men's non-revenue sports in order to achieve, or even to approach, substantial proportionality.

The elimination of men's non-revenue sports is the least fair and least educationally sound means of resolving the dilemma of Title IX compliance. It destroys teams whose members have long upheld the NCAA ideal of the scholar-athlete by earning high grades, graduating in four years with meaningful degrees, and obeying the law, while preserving teams whose members have mocked that ideal repeatedly. Every potential solution to this dilemma, though, poses problems. Donna Lopiano of the Women's Sports Foundation knows this as well as anyone does. She said that "the easiest solution is to double your resources and give the women the same opportunities as the men." Then she asked, rhetorically: "How many schools can double revenues?"[104]

One school that can, apparently, is the University of Texas at Austin, where Lopiano was once the director of women's athletics. Texas settled a Title IX lawsuit in the late 1990s by promising to add women's sports, and it has done so, establishing women's soccer and softball teams and a women's crew between 1997 and 2002, at a cost of approximately $3 million.[105] Absent such resources, Texas would have had to eliminate men's teams in order to comply with Title IX, as many less wealthy colleges have done. Consider, for example, Miami of Ohio, which plays marginal Division I-A football in the virtually invisible and perennially unprofitable Mid-American Conference. In 1999, Miami dropped its men's wrestling, tennis, and soccer teams in order to comply with Title IX. In response to criticisms of this decision, Miami's president, James C. Garland, discussed his university's struggle with the Title IX dilemma. He said: "We've tried to comply with federal law by the continuing practice of adding women's teams. But any school can only do that for so long, because any time you add a sport, you add . . . expenses."[106]

It is easy to blame Title IX for the elimination of men's teams, but the easy target is not the guilty party in this case. Once again, Donna Lopiano's words are worth heeding. She said:

> It's not Title IX's fault, it's chicken college presidents and athletic directors who won't bite the bullet on the irresponsible spending of their football programs. Their football programs are better funded than most professional sports. Football is pitting the victims against the victims. Until they rise up, men's minor sports will be crying the blues as football keeps laughing to the bank.[107]

There are ample data to support Ms. Lopiano's position. In 2002 a total of one hundred and fifteen colleges fielded football teams in Division I-A and 91 of these colleges spent a larger percentage of their athletic budgets on football than they did on all their women's sports combined.[108] One reason for this, of course, is that football is an extremely expensive sport per participant. Equipment costs alone average about $900 per participant per year, which is much higher than the equipment costs for most other sports.[109] Coaches need not be as expensive as they are, though. Salaries aside, coaches are expensive in Division I-A because colleges are permitted to employ twelve of them, which is four times the number that is allowed in most other college sports.[110] If this number seems excessive, keep in mind that it is only one part of a culture of financial excess that pervades big-time college football. One reflection of this culture was the $919,000 average increase in football budgets that occurred at Division I-A colleges between 1989 and 1993, which translates to 29.53 percent, or nearly twice the increase in the Consumer Price Index (CPI) during the same period. Moreover, the $919,000 figure for football alone dwarfed the increase in the total amount of money that these colleges spent on all women's sports during this period, which was $576,000.[111]

The number of players on the rosters of Division I-A teams is also excessive. A study released in 2001 by the General Accounting Office (GAO), the nonpartisan investigative arm of Congress, revealed that between 1981–82 and 1998–99, football experienced a greater increase in the number of participants than any other college sport, approximately 7,000. Football also had more participants, approximately 60,000, than any other college sport in 1998–99; indeed, football had nearly twice as many participants as its closest competitor among college sports.[112] During this same period the average college football roster, across all four football-playing divisions of the NCAA, increased from 81.6 players to 94 players, with rosters of between 110 and 120 players becoming commonplace in Division I-A.[113] A study published by social scientists Lee Sigelman and Paul Wahlbeck in 1999 revealed that the median Division I-A college had 110 players on its football roster and that its counterpart in Division I-AA had 92 players on its football roster.[114]

Sigelman and Wahlbeck understand the implications of large football rosters for efforts to attain gender equity. "Maintaining football squads this large while maintaining an array of other men's teams," they caution, "makes it extremely difficult to provide women with a proportionate share of participation opportunities."[115] If football roster sizes remain at current levels, then many colleges will achieve substantial proportionality only by expanding athletic opportunities for women dramatically or by shrinking athletic opportunities for men drastically. The first option is prohibitively expensive, and the second option, although legal, arguably enforces the letter of Title IX by violating its spirit.

Football players constitute 40 percent of the male athletes at the median Division I-A college and 41 percent of the male athletes at the median Division I-AA college. Consequently, according to Sigelman and Wahlbeck, the median Division I-A college that seeks to achieve substantial proportionality without reducing the size of its football roster or expanding women's athletic opportunities would have to reduce the number of its non-football-playing male athletes from 167 to just 41, a reduction of 75 percent. The median Division I-AA college that seeks the same result, subject to the same conditions, would have to reduce the number of its non-football-playing male athletes from 135 to 8, a reduction of 94 percent. Put another way, the Division I-A college could achieve substantial proportionality without reducing the size of its football roster by adding 136 athletic slots for women, eliminating 129 athletic slots for men, or shifting 67 athletic slots from men to women. Thus far, most colleges have chosen the last option, which Sigelman and Wahlbeck call "reallocation"; it helps to explain the elimination of men's non-revenue teams in recent years.

There is a better option, though, namely, a substantial reduction in the size of team rosters in football. At the median Division I-A college, Sigelman and Wahlbeck note, a football roster cap of eighty-five players would cut by 30 percent the number of athletic slots that a college would have to add, eliminate, or reallocate in order to realize substantial proportionality. A football roster cap of fifty players would reduce by between 50 percent and 67 percent the number of athletic slots that this college would have to add, eliminate, or reallocate in order to achieve substantial proportionality. This is not a perfect solution, because even after trimming its football roster to fifty players the median Division I-A college would still need to add sixty-three athletic slots for women, eliminate sixty-six athletic slots for men, or reallocate thirty-two athletic slots from men to women. Trimming its football roster, though, would save a college substantial sums of money, which it could use to support additional women's teams without eliminating any men's teams. Indeed, Sigelman and Wahlbeck estimate that for every football-roster slot that is eliminated, it will be possible to create two new athletic slots for women. Based on this assumption, the median Division I-A college after capping its football roster at eighty-five players would have to add only twenty-four athletic slots for women in order to achieve substantial proportionality.[116] The college could add a soccer team or perhaps a cross-country team and a golf team for women, in order to fill the new slots.

By capping its football roster at fifty, the median Division I-A college— indeed, even the seventy-fifth percentile Division I-A college—would achieve, even surpass, substantial proportionality. Roster caps in football would also aid the cause of gender equity at Division I-AA colleges, albeit not as much as they would at Division I-A colleges. By trimming its football roster to eighty-five players, the median Division I-AA college would still fall fifty-five athletic slots for women short of substantial proportionality. By trimming its football roster to fifty players, this college would fall ten athletic slots for women short of substantial proportionality.[117] In the first instance, the savings realized from reducing the size of the football roster would help to fund the additional slots for women; in the second instance, these savings would probably defray the full cost of the additional slots for women.

Thus, an end to the football follies by reducing the size of college football rosters in Division I is essential to the achievement of gender equity at most of these colleges. To be sure, reducing roster sizes makes sense for other reasons, too. College football rosters in excess of one hundred players are ludicrous when professional football teams play longer seasons than the colleges do with fifty-three-man rosters and when most colleges lose money on football. Smaller football rosters would enable colleges to spend their sports dollars to support runners, swimmers, and rowers who actually compete instead of supporting third- and fourth-string football players who rarely see game action. Most immediately, though, smaller football rosters would enable colleges to comply with both the letter and the spirit of Title IX by adding women's sports without eliminating men's non-revenue sports. In the longer term, smaller football rosters will be an important feature of the reform of college sports, for which the Title IX dilemma provides a golden opportunity.

A GOLDEN OPPORTUNITY

The controversy that swirls around the enforcement of Title IX has forced open a window of opportunity for those who would reform college sports in a dramatic fashion. Reform lies in adoption of the aforementioned participation model, which would bring not only gender equity but fiscal sanity, academic integrity, and personal responsibility to college sports. Previous chapters have demonstrated that there is a shortage of the latter three values in college sports at present.

Misplaced values are evident in the recent responses of many colleges to the Title IX dilemma and its attendant financial constraints. They have redoubled their efforts to make football and basketball profitable and to achieve success in the non-revenue sports that their fans care about most, while providing minimal support to their other non-revenue sports and eliminating men's non-revenue sports that lack fan support and make it more difficult to achieve substantial proportionality.[118] This choice for dollars and publicity over participation flies in the face of the NCAA Constitution, which requires each member to conduct its sports programs "as an integral part of the student-athlete's educational experience."[119] The divergence between colleges' behavior and the supposed purpose of college sports, as stated in the NCAA manual, is clear to Brett Nelligan, a former gymnast at the University of Massachusetts, where both the men's team and the women's team were casualties of athletic-department "prioritizing" among sports. He told *The New York Times*:

> I'm a sports management major, and I study the NCAA manual. It says the association's purpose is to invite a learning experience. How are you going to do that if only two sports matter? We should be providing as many opportunities as possible for everyone.[120]

Lawsuits alone will not produce more participation opportunities or the other changes that are necessary in college sports. They are too sporadic and too dependent on facts and circumstances peculiar to each case to be able to effect comprehensive reform. They are also prone to unintended consequences, thereby raising more questions than they answer. For example, the Title IX lawsuits that expanded athletic opportunities for college women in the 1990s by enforcing the substantial-proportionality standard contributed to the elimination of men's non-revenue sports in order to achieve substantial proportionality. This, in turn, sparked the current debate about Title IX enforcement and more lawsuits filed by male athletes whose teams were disbanded as colleges pursued substantial proportionality. Thus, lawsuits are an inefficient means of reforming college sports; they will nip at the heels of the college-sports monster, but they will not bring it to its knees.

Nevertheless, the limitations of lawsuits need not discourage or deter those who would reform college sports. Seven federal appellate courts have upheld the three-part effective accommodation test, including the substantial-proportionality standard, which makes it virtually certain that the Supreme Court will not enter the Title IX debate.[121] When the appellate courts agree about an issue, the Supreme Court usually refuses to review a case that raises that issue.[122] Congress has shown no appetite for changing Title IX, and the Department of Education has indicated that it may revise, but that it will not gut, the effective accommodation test. Undoubtedly, Secretary Paige knows that Title IX is popular with the American public. In a 1997 CBS News Poll, 86 percent of the respondents agreed that "college funding for men's and women's sports should be equal." This view is far more generous to women than is any interpretation of Title IX made by a court or by OCR thus far.[123]

Secretary Paige signaled his disinclination to gut the effective accommodation test when, after receiving the commission's report, which included twenty-three recommendations, he announced that his department would "move forward" on only the fifteen recommendations that the commissioners approved unanimously.[124] Therefore, the department will not adopt the sweeping changes that the wrestling coaches and their conservative political allies favor. Their ideas are reflected in three proposals that the commission considered but did not approve unanimously. Recommendation 15 would measure substantial proportionality by comparing the percentage of women in the student body at a particular college to the number of athletic slots open to women instead of to the actual number of women participating in sports at that college.[125] Recommendation 17 would exclude walk-on athletes from the substantial-proportionality calculation.[126] Recommendation 20 would exclude nontraditional students from the substantial-proportionality calculation.[127] Together these recommendations would weaken the substantial-proportionality standard on the basis of the relative-interests test that the court rejected in *Cohen IV* as likely to "entrench and fix by law" existing discrimination against women in college sports.[128]

The commission neither approved nor disapproved an unnumbered recommendation favored by the wrestling coaches and their allies. It would reconfigure proportionality to mean allotting 50 percent of athletic-

participation opportunities for men and 50 percent for women, with an al-
lowable variance of two or three percentage points.[129] Therefore, it would
preserve inequitable circumstances in which women are, for example, 57
percent of the undergraduates, yet just 47 percent of the athletes, at a particular college, which makes it as problematical as the three relative-interests
recommendations that the commission rejected.

The unanimously approved recommendations from which the department
will presumably select the changes that it favors are generally not controversial. Among these are recommendations to the department to "reaffirm
its strong commitment to equal opportunity" (Recommendation 1), "provide
clear, consistent and understandable written guidelines for implementation
of Title IX" (Recommendation 3), "make clear that cutting teams in order
to demonstrate compliance with Title IX is a disfavored practice" (Recommendation 5), and "encourage educational and sports leaders to promote
male and female student interest in athletics at the elementary and secondary
levels" (Recommendation 7).[130]

Admittedly, some Title IX advocates may view the adoption of three other
unanimously approved recommendations as backsliding. Recommendation
14 would require OCR to "clarify the meaning of substantial proportionality
to allow for a reasonable variance in the relative ratio of athletic participation
of men and women."[131] Recommendation 19 advises OCR to consider "allowing institutions to demonstrate that they are in compliance with part
three of the effective-accommodation test by comparing the ratio of male/
female participation at the institution with [among other things] the interest
levels indicated in surveys of prospective or enrolled students at the institution."[132] Recommendation 21 counsels that "[t]he designation of one part
of the effective-accommodation test as a 'safe harbor' should be abandoned
in favor of a way of demonstrating compliance . . . that treats each part of
the test equally."[133] Nevertheless, these recommendations do not represent
reactionary change. Indeed they reflect OCR's traditional interpretation of
the three-part test, which measures compliance with part one by means of
substantial—not absolute—proportionality, and which encourages colleges
that cannot satisfy part one to satisfy part two or part three instead.

Thus, if Secretary Paige keeps his word, the changes that will most likely
occur in the Title IX regulations will make it easier for colleges to (1) achieve
substantial proportionality by allowing a cushion between the percentages
of women in the student body and on sports teams, respectively, and (2)
satisfy part three of the effective-accommodation test by providing clearer
criteria for complying with it than presently exist. These changes would not
close the gap between the number of women undergraduates and the numbers of women athletes, which Title IX advocates rightly decry, but neither
would they gut the effective-accommodation test that enforces Title IX.

Under these circumstances Title IX can be a catalyst for comprehensive
reform in college sports, but the primary force for change must be a political

movement originating within colleges that uses Title IX as a lever with which to dislodge the commercial model and replace it with the participation model. Colleges would be wise to adopt the participation model, even if Title IX did not exist, because of the financial, academic, and social consequences of big-time college sports. The Title IX dilemma makes its adoption a necessity. The participation model is the subject of Chapter 7.

NOTES

1. Title IX is located at Title 20 of the United States Code (USC), Sections 1681–1688, hereafter designated as 20 USC §§ 1681–1688. The particular language quoted in the text of this chapter is located at 20 USC § 1681(a).

2. Hal Bock, "Title IX—Equalizer or Quota Enforcer?" *The Valley News* (West Lebanon, N.H.), June 23, 2002, p. D5.

3. Ibid.

4. National Coalition for Women and Girls in Education, "Title IX at 30: Report Card on Gender Equity" (Washington, D.C.: NCWGE, 2002), p. 15.

5. Mary Jo Festle, *Playing Nice: Politics and Apologies in Women's Sports* (New York: Columbia University Press, 1996), p. 286.

6. Ibid., p. 287.

7. Ibid.

8. U.S. Department of Education, Office of Civil Rights, "Title IX: 25 Years of Progress" (Washington, D.C.: U.S. Government Printing Office, 1997), pp. 16–17.

9. Ibid.

10. National Coalition for Women and Girls in Education, "Title IX at 30: Report Card on Gender Equity" (Washington, D.C.: NCWGE, 2002), p. 14.

11. Welch Suggs, "Title IX at 30," *The Chronicle of Higher Education*, June 21, 2002, pp. A38–A41.

12. Jeffrey H. Orleans, *An End to the Odyssey: Equal Athletic Opportunities for Women*, 3 Duke Journal of Gender Law & Policy 131, 139 (1996).

13. Ideally, according to the concept of proportionality, if women are 52 percent of the undergraduates at a college, they should also be 52 percent of its athletes. In practice though, the standard is "substantial proportionality," whereby the Department of Education and the federal courts have typically found colleges to be in compliance with Title IX on the issue of athletic participation when the percentage of their women students who were athletes was within five points of the percentage of women in their student populations. In other words, a college at which 52 percent of the undergraduates are women is likely to achieve substantial proportionality if 47 percent of its athletes are women. Still, the Department of Education insists that "[t]here is no set ratio that constitutes 'substantially proportionate,' or that, when not met, results in a disparity or a violation." Valerie M. Bonnette and Lamar Daniel, *Title IX Investigator's Manual* (Washington, D.C.: Department of Education, Office of Civil Rights, 1990), p. 24.

14. Welch Suggs, "Budgets Grow as Colleges Seek to Comply with Gender-Equity Rules," *The Chronicle of Higher Education*, June 21, 2002, pp. A41–A42.

15. Welch Suggs, "Female Athletes Thrive, but Budget Pressures Loom," *The Chronicle of Higher Education*, May 18, 2001, pp. A45–A48.

16. Ibid.

17. Josh Barr, "Title IX Has a Tough Deed at 30: Small Sports Face Financial Inequity," *The Washington Post*, May 9, 2002, p. D1.

18. Ibid.

19. Bill Pennington, "More Men's Teams Benched as Colleges Level the Field," *The New York Times*, May 9, 2002, p. 1.

20. *National Wrestling Coaches Association v. United States Department of Education*, Docket Number 1:02CV00072EGS (United States District Court for the District of Columbia, filed January 16, 2002) [available at www.nwcaonline.com]. *See also* Christopher Flores, "Wrestling Coaches Sue Education Department Over Title IX Enforcement," *The Chronicle of Higher Education*, February 1, 2002, p. A39.

21. Susannah Dainow and Welch Suggs, "Wrestling Coach's Advocacy on Gender Equity Raises Hackles at U. of Minnesota," *The Chronicle of Higher Education*, October 5, 2001, pp. A39–A41.

22. The conservative commentator who has been the most prolific critic of the way in which Title IX is enforced is Jessica Gavora, who is a policy advisor to United States Attorney General John Ashcroft. She has expressed her views in a book, *Tilting the Playing Field: Schools, Sports, Sex, and Title IX* (San Francisco: Encounter Books, 2002), and in several articles, including "The Inequity of Gender Equity," *The Chronicle of Higher Education*, May 3, 2002, pp. B11–B12, and "Title IX Loses Sight of the Goal," *The Washington Post National Weekly Edition*, January 22–28, 2001, p. 23.

23. Jessica Gavora (*see* n. 22) has made this argument, as have numerous lawyers and law students writing in law journals. Among the law journal articles that argue that athletic opportunities should be proportional to student interest are Christopher Paul Reuscher, *Giving the Bat Back to Casey: Suggestions to Reform Title IX's Inequitable Application to Intercollegiate Athletics*, 35 Akron Law Review 117 (2001); Roy Whitehead, Walter Block, and Lu Hardin, *Gender Equity in Athletics: Should We Adopt a Non-Discriminatory Model?* 30 University of Toledo Law Review 223 (Winter, 1999); Jennifer Lynn Botelho, *The Cohen Court's Reading of Title IX: Does It Really Promote a de Facto Quota Scheme?* 33 New England Law Review 743 (Spring 1999); Mark Hammond, *Substantial Proportionality Not Required: Achieving Title IX Compliance Without Reducing Participation in College Athletics*, 87 Kentucky Law Journal 793 (1998–99); Michael Straubel, *Gender Equity, College Sports, Title IX, and Group Rights: A Coach's View*, 62 Brooklyn Law Review 1039 (Fall 1996); George A. Davidson and Carla A Kerr, *Title IX: What Is Gender Equity?* 2 Villanova Sports & Entertainment Law Forum 25 (1995); Walter B. Connolly and Jeffrey D. Adelman, *A University's Defense to a Title IX Gender Equity in Athletics Lawsuit: Congress Never Intended Gender Equity Based on Student Body Ratios*, 71 University of Detroit Mercy Law Review 845 (1994); and Curtis L. Hollinger, Jr., *Are Male College Sports in Jeopardy? A Look at Kelley v. Board of Trustees*," 21 Southern University Law Review 151 (1994).

24. *See*, for example, B. Glenn George, *Title IX and the Scholarship Dilemma*, 9 Marquette Sports Law Journal 273 (1999); Don Sabo, "Women's Athletics and the Elimination of Men's Sports Programs," *Journal of Sport & Social Issues* 22, no. 1 (February 1998): 27–31; and Deborah Brake and Elizabeth Catlin, *The Path of Most*

Resistance: The Long Road Toward Gender Equity in Intercollegiate Athletics, 3 Duke Journal of Gender Law & Policy 51 (Spring 1996).

25. *National Wrestling Coaches Association v. United States Department of Education*, Docket Number 1:02CV00072EGS (United States District Court for the District of Columbia, filed January 16, 2002): Defendant's Motion to Dismiss, filed May 29, 2002 [available at www.nwcaonline.com]. *See also* Welch Suggs, "Defying Rumors, Bush Administration Defends Status Quo on Title IX," *The Chronicle of Higher Education*, June 7, 2002, p. A41.

26. Welch Suggs, "Education Department Announces Panel to Review and Strengthen Title IX," *The Chronicle of Higher Education*, June 28, 2002 [available at http://chronicle.com/daily/2002/06/2002062803n.htm]; "Can a Commission Change Title IX?" *The Chronicle of Higher Education*, July 12, 2002, p. A38; "Federal Commission on College Sports and Gender Equity Hears First Witnesses," *The Chronicle of Higher Education*, August 28, 2002 [available at http://chronicle.com/daily/2002/08/2002082801n.htm] "Federal Commission Discusses Possible Changes in Title IX Enforcement," *The Chronicle of Higher Education*, August 29, 2002 [available at http://chronicle.com/daily/2002/08/2002082901n.htm]; "Smoke Obscures Fire in Title IX Debate as Federal Panel Adjourns," *The Chronicle of Higher Education*, February 1, 2003, p. A31; and "Getting Ready for the Next Round," *The Chronicle of Higher Education*, February 14, 2003, p. A39.

27. Two prominent sportswriters have made this argument in their columns. *See* Rick Telander, "This Battle of Sexes All Wrong," *Chicago Sun-Times*, May 31, 2002 [http://www.suntimes.com/output/telander/cst-spt-rick31.html], and Robert Lipsyte, "Title IX Debate Is About Football," *The New York Times*, May 12, 2002, Section 8, p. 7.

28. U.S. House Committee on Education and Labor, *Discrimination Against Women: Hearings Before the Special Subcommittee on Education, § 805 of H.R. 16098*, 91st Cong., 1st sess., 1970.

29. *Congressional Record*, 92nd Cong., 1st sess., August 6, 1971, p. 30403.

30. Ibid.

31. Josh Barr, "Title IX Has a Tough Deed at 30: Small Sports Face Financial Inequity," *The Washington Post*, May 9, 2002, p. D1 [also available at http://www.washingtonpost.com/wp-dyn/articles/A56845-2002May8.html].

32. Jill K. Johnson, *Title IX and Intercollegiate Athletics: Current Judicial Interpretation of the Standards for Compliance*, 74 Boston University Law Review 553, 557 (1994).

33. Susan M. Shook, Note in *The Title IX Tug-of-War and Intercollegiate Athletics in the 1990s: Nonrevenue Men's Teams Join Women Athletes in the Struggle for Survival*, 71 Indiana Law Journal 773, 778–779 (1996).

34. *See* 20 U.S.C. § 1687(2)(A) (1990), which states that henceforth, under Title IX, the term "education program or activity" means "all of the operations of a college, university, or other post-secondary institution, or a public system of higher education." In other words, Title IX applies to all parts of a college, not just the office(s) or program(s) therein that receive federal funds directly.

35. These regulations appear in volume 45 of the Code of Federal Regulations (CFR) at section 86. Hereafter, they will appear as 45 CFR § 86.

36. Deborah Brake and Elizabeth Catlin, *The Path of Most Resistance: The Long*

Road Toward Gender Equity in Intercollegiate Athletics, 3 Duke Journal of Gender Law & Policy 51, 55 (1996).

37. *NCAA v. Califano*, 622 F.2d 1382 (10th Cir. 1982).

38. The Tower Amendment stated that Title IX "shall not apply to an intercollegiate athletic activity to the extent that such activity does or may provide gross receipts or donations to the institution necessary to support that activity." *Congressional Record*, 93rd Congress, 2nd Session, May 20, 1974, part 12, pp. 15322–15323. This amendment did not require that a sport actually earn revenue in order to enjoy an exemption from Title IX; the potential to earn revenue was sufficient. In this way, it reflected the reality that so-called revenue-producing sports do not earn net revenue at most colleges, including most Division I colleges.

39. 34 CFR § 106.41(C). The Policy Interpretation appears in volume 44 of the *Federal Register* on pages 71413–71423. Congress did not review the Policy Interpretation, so it did not have the force of law. The federal courts have honored it nonetheless as the clearest statement of the enforcing agency's interpretation of the criteria necessary for compliance with Title IX. One reason for this judicial deference may be that the document issued in 1979 was the final version of regulations that HEW had proposed and circulated for public comment one year earlier. The proposed regulations generated more than seven hundred comments, many of which the final document reflected. Still, the lack of congressional review has caused critics of the substantial-proportionality test, which is a part of the Policy Interpretation, to argue that the federal courts' deference to the latter is unjustified. See especially Jessica Gavora, *Tilting The Playing Field*.

40. The nine factors included in the regulations that the Policy Interpretation considered to be less important were equipment and supplies, travel and per diem allowances, scheduling of games and practice times, the receipt of coaching and academic tutoring, the assignment and compensation of coaches and tutors, locker rooms, practice and competitive facilities, medical and training facilities and services, housing and dining facilities and services, and publicity. See 34 CFR § 106.41(C) (2)-(10).

41. 44 Fed. Reg. 71418 (December 11, 1979).

42. Ibid.

43. Ibid.

44. The cases that have made the three-part test the governing standard for measuring "equal opportunity" in sports are *Cohen v. Brown University*, 101 F.3d 155 (1st Cir. 1996), *cert. denied*, 117 S. Ct. 1469 (1997); *Favia v. Indiana University of Pennsylvania*, 7 F.3d 332 (3d Cir. 1993); and *Roberts v. Colorado State Board of Agriculture*, 998 F.2d 824 (10th Cir.), *cert. denied*, 510 U.S. 1004 (1993).

45. Matthew L. Daniel, *Title IX and Gender Equity in College Athletics: How Honesty Might Avert a Crisis*, 1995 Annual Survey of American Law 255, 271 (1995).

46. 465 U.S. 555 (1984).

47. Deborah Brake and Elizabeth Catlin, *The Path of Most Resistance: The Long Road Toward Gender Equity in Intercollegiate Athletics*, 3 Duke Journal of Gender Law & Policy 51, 58 (1996).

48. Festle, *Playing Nice*, p. 221.

49. Ibid.

50. See 20 USC § 1687(2)(A).

51. Diane Heckman, *Women and Athletics: A Twenty Year Retrospective on Title IX*, 9 University of Miami Entertainment & Sports Law Review 1, 15, n. 61 (1992).

52. Temple agreed to improve athletic programs for its female students by adding teams, upgrading facilities, spending more money on existing teams, awarding more athletic scholarships to women, and publicizing women's teams more aggressively between 1988–89 and 1993–94 in return for the plaintiffs' agreement to withdraw their demand for $1.8 million in damages. For a complete discussion of this case, see Christina A. Longo and Elizabeth F. Thoman, Case Comment, *"Haffer v. Temple University: A Reawakening of Gender Discrimination in Intercollegiate Athletics*, 16 The Journal of College & University Law 137, 147–148 (1989).

53. Festle, *Playing Nice*, p. 16.

54. Allen L. Sack and Ellen J. Staurowsky, *College Athletes for Hire: The Evolution and Legacy of the NCAA's Amateur Myth* (Westport, Conn.: Praeger, 1998), p. 62.

55. Ibid., p. 76.

56. Festle, *Playing Nice*, p. 98.

57. Sack and Staurowsky, *College Athletes for Hire*, p. 112.

58. Ibid., p. 111.

59. Ibid., at 122.

60. Ibid., p. 214.

61. Daniel F. Maloney, "Collective Reaction to Injustice in Intercollegiate Athletics: Injustice to Women and Student-Athletes as Test Cases," *Journal of Sport & Social Issues* 23, no. 3 (August 1999): 328–352. The average number by which women's teams per college increased during this period is in dispute. Linda Carpenter, the co-author of *Women in Intercollegiate Sport: A Longitudinal Study*, claims that the correct number is 3.96, not 2.73. Letter to the author from Linda Carpenter, November 4, 2002. I have chosen to use the lower, more conservative figure, while recognizing that it might understate the growth of women's college sports (and the success of the AIAW) during the 1970s and the early 1980s.

62. Festle, *Playing Nice*, p. 288.

63. Ibid., p. 226.

64. Ibid., p. 122.

65. Ibid., p. 182.

66. Ibid., p. 200.

67. Sack and Staurowsky, *College Athletes for Hire*, p. 120.

68. Ibid., p. 124.

69. Letter from Linda Carpenter to the author, November 4, 2002.

70. Festle, *Playing Nice*, p. 210.

71. See *AIAW v. NCAA*, 558 F. Supp. 487 (1983) and 735 F.2d 577 (D.C. Cir. 1984).

72. Ying Wu, "Early NCAA Attempts at the Governance of Women's Intercollegiate Athletics, 1968–1973," *Journal of Sport History* 26, no. 3 (Fall 1999): 585–601.

73. Festle, *Playing Nice*, p. 141.

74. Brian L. Porto, *Completing the Revolution: Title IX as Catalyst for an Alternative Model of College Sports*, 8, no. 2 Seton Hall Journal of Sport Law 351, 367–368 (1998).

75. 441 U.S. 677 (1979).

76. 503 U.S. 60 (1992). Compensatory damages, as their name suggests, are designed to compensate the victim of a physical, financial, or psychic injury for the expenses incurred as a result of that injury. Punitive damages, in contrast, are designed to punish the defendant for reprehensible behavior and to deter its recurrence.

77. 678 F. Supp. 517 (E.D. Pa. 1987).

78. Brian L. Porto, *Suits by Female College Athletes Against Colleges and Universities Claiming that Decisions to Discontinue Particular Sports or to Deny Varsity Status to Particular Sports Deprive Plaintiffs of Equal Educational Opportunities Required by Title IX*, 129 American Law Reports, Federal 571, 580 (1995).

79. 7 F.3d 332 (1993).

80. 44 Fed. Reg. 71415–71418 (December 11, 1979).

81. 998 F.2d 824 (10th Cir.), *cert. denied*, 510 U.S. 1004 (1993). The Colorado State Board of Agriculture is the governing body of Colorado State University.

82. 999 F.2d at 828–831. *See also* Brian L. Porto, *Completing the Revolution: Title IX as Catalyst for an Alternative Model of College Sports*, 8, no. 2 Seton Hall Journal of Sport Law 351, 371 (1998).

83. 101 F.3d 155 (1st Cir. 1996), *cert. denied*, 520 U.S. 1186 (1997). Brown disbanded its men's golf and water polo teams at the same time that it disbanded its women's volleyball and gymnastics teams.

84. The legal citation for *Cohen II* is 991 F.2d 888 (1st Cir. 1993).

85. 101 F.3d at 175.

86. Ibid. at 171.

87. United States Department of Education, Office of Civil Rights, *Clarification of Intercollegiate Athletics Policy Guidance: The Three-Part Test* (Washington, D.C.: U.S. Government Printing Office, 1996), p. 2.

88. *Cohen*, 101 F.3d at 176.

89. Ibid. at 179. A derivative of the "relative interests" approach is the argument made by some critics of Title IX that OCR should count unfilled roster slots on women's teams when comparing a college's athletic-participation opportunities to its female enrollment. In other words, instead of comparing percentages of female athletes and female undergraduates for proportionality purposes, a college could compare the percentage of roster slots on its women's teams to the percentage of women among its undergraduates. According to the critics, this arrangement would take into account the tendencies of women not to "walk on" to college teams (i.e., play without receiving an athletic scholarship) and not to join college teams unless they are talented enough to play regularly in games. See generally Gavora, *Tilting The Playing Field*. OCR rejected this approach in its 1996 "Clarification," which stated that only actual athletes count for proportionality purposes because "participation opportunities must be real, not illusory." The court in *Cohen IV* validated OCR's approach to counting athletes.

90. Ibid.

91. 520 U.S. 1186 (1997). See also Jim Naughton, "Supreme Court Rejects Brown's Appeal on Women in Sports," *The Chronicle of Higher Education*, May 2, 1997, p. A45.

92. Male athletes whose non-revenue teams colleges have eliminated in pursuit of substantial proportionality have been among the most vocal critics of the *Roberts/Cohen* rule. They have filed several lawsuits wherein they have argued that reducing athletic opportunities for men in order to achieve substantial proportionality

is gender-based discrimination that violates Title IX while pretending to enforce it. These lawsuits have been unsuccessful. The courts have held that when women are underrepresented among varsity athletes, Title IX permits colleges to eliminate men's teams in order to achieve substantial proportionality if, after the cuts, the percentage of male varsity athletes remains substantially proportionate to the percentage of males in the student body. If there is substantial proportionality for males after the cuts, a male plaintiff cannot claim that his college has failed to accommodate fully and effectively the athletic interests and abilities of male students, even if the college has eliminated his particular sport. See: *Neal v. Board of Trustees of the California State Universities*, 198 F.3d 763 (9th Cir. 1999); *Boulahanis v. Board of Regents*, 198 F.3d 633 (7th Cir. 1999); *Harper v. Board of Regents, Illinois State University*, 35 F. Supp.2d 1118 (C.D. Ill. 1999); *Kelley v. Board of Trustees*, 35 F.3d 265 (7th Cir. 1994); and *Gonyo v. Drake University*, 837 F. Supp. 989 (S.D. Iowa 1993).

93. The commission that Secretary of Education Roderick Paige established to evaluate the three-part test indicated at its first meeting, which took place in Atlanta on August 28, 2002, that it would not advocate radical changes to Title IX, but that it would consider "tinkering" with the three-part test. Brian W. Jones, the general counsel for the Department of Education, said: "the practical question[s] of, how do we apply the three-part test, and whether we're properly guiding institutions on how to assess the interests of women, are what we have to discuss." Welch Suggs, "Federal Commission Discusses Possible Changes in Title IX Enforcement," *The Chronicle of Higher Education*, August 29, 2002 [available at http://chronicle.com/daily/2002/08/2002082901n.htm]. For a discussion of the political popularity of Title IX, *see* Lee Sigelman and Clyde Wilcox, "Public Support for Gender Equality in Athletics Programs," *Women & Politics* 22, no. 1 (2001): 85–96.

94. United States Department of Education, Office of Civil Rights, *Clarification of Intercollegiate Athletics Policy Guidance: The Three-Part Test* (Washington, D.C: U.S. Government Printing Office, 1996), p. 4. See n. 92 for a list of the cases wherein the federal courts have upheld the capping, or elimination, of men's teams as a means of achieving substantial proportionality.

95. Rick Telander, "This Battle of Sexes All Wrong," *Chicago Sun-Times*, May 31, 2002 [available at http://www.suntimes.com/output/telander/cst-spt-rick31.html].

96. Lee Sigelman and Paul J. Wahlbeck, "Gender Proportionality in Intercollegiate Athletics: the Mathematics of Title IX Compliance," *Social Science Quarterly* 80, no. 3 (September 1999): 518–538.

97. Welch Suggs, "More Women Participate in Intercollegiate Athletics," *The Chronicle of Higher Education*, May 21, 1999, pp. A44–A49.

98. Ibid.

99. Welch Suggs, "Uneven Progress for Women's Sports," *The Chronicle of Higher Education*, April 7, 2000, pp. A52–A57.

100. Ibid.

101. Donald E. Agthe and R. Bruce Billings, "The Role of Football Profits in Meeting Title IX Gender Equity Regulations and Policy," *Journal of Sport Management* 14 (2000): 28–40.

102. Ibid.

103. Ibid.

104. Welch Suggs, "Colleges Consider Fairness of Cutting Men's Teams to

Comply With Title IX," *The Chronicle of Higher Education*, February 19, 1999, pp. A53–A54.

105. Ibid.

106. Ibid.

107. Bill Pennington, "More Men's Teams Benched As Colleges Level the Field," *The New York Times*, May 9, 2002, p. 1.

108. Welch Suggs, "Title IX at 30," *The Chronicle of Higher Education*, June 21, 2002, pp. A38–A41.

109. Lee Sigelman and Paul J. Wahlbeck, "Gender Proportionality in Intercollegiate Athletics: The Mathematics of Title IX Compliance," *Social Science Quarterly* 80, no. 3 (September 1999): 518–538.

110. Ibid.

111. Daniel F. Maloney and Donna Pastore, "Distributive Justice: An Examination of Participation Opportunities, Revenues, and Expenses at NCAA Institutions—1973–1993," *Journal of Sport & Social Issues* 22, no. 2 (May 1998): 127–152.

112. U.S. General Accounting Office, Report to Congressional Requesters: *Intercollegiate Athletics: Four-Year Colleges' Experiences Adding and Discontinuing Teams* (Washington, D.C.: U.S. Government Printing Office 2001), p. 10.

113. Bill Pennington, "More Men's Teams Benched as Colleges Level the Field," *The New York Times*, May 9, 2002, p. 1.

114. Lee Sigelman and Paul J. Wahlbeck, "Gender Proportionality in Intercollegiate Athletics: The Mathematics of Title IX Compliance," *Social Science Quarterly* 80, no. 3 (September 1999): 518–538.

115. Ibid.

116. Ibid.

117. Ibid.

118. Welch Suggs, "Female Athletes Thrive, but Budget Pressures Loom," *The Chronicle of Higher Education*, May 18, 2001, pp. A45–A48.

119. NCAA Constitution, Article 2, Principles for Conduct of Intercollegiate Athletics, 2.2.1, The Principle of Student-Athlete Welfare—Overall Educational Experience, reprinted in NCAA, *2002–03 NCAA Division I Manual* (Michael V. Earle, ed., 2002), p. 3.

120. Bill Pennington, "More Men's Teams Benched as Colleges Level the Field," *The New York Times*, May 9, 2002, p. 1.

121. Welch Suggs, "Defying Rumors, Bush Administration Defends Status Quo on Title IX," *The Chronicle of Higher Education*, June 7, 2002, p. A41.

122. In 2001 the Supreme Court made it harder for plaintiffs to bring civil rights lawsuits, including lawsuits based on Title IX. The High Court held in *Alexander v. Sandoval*, 532 U.S. 275 (2001), that private individuals do not have the right to sue in order to enforce certain regulations that implement Title VI of the Civil Rights Act of 1964, 42 USC § 2000d et seq., unless they can show that they were victims of intentional discrimination. It is not enough to show that one, in fact, received different treatment in a federally funded program based on one's race, even though the regulation(s) involved were racially neutral. After *Alexander*, it will also be necessary for individuals who seek to enforce Title IX in court to demonstrate intentional discrimination because the regulations that implement Title IX, including the substantial-proportionality standard, are authorized by language that is identical to the authorizing language in Title VI. This means that in the future, private in-

dividuals who seek to enforce the substantial-proportionality standard in court must show that their respective colleges intended to discriminate against them. Happily, this requirement is unlikely to bar Title IX suits in college sports because disparities in support for men's and women's college sports result from conscious choices by athletic administrators. For example, the court in *Pederson v. Louisiana State University*, 213 F.3d 858 (5th Cir. 2000) found that LSU had engaged in "intentional gender discrimination" against its female undergraduates with respect to its sports offerings. The evidence indicated that in addition to making sexist comments to female athletes at LSU, the athletic director had (1) told the coach of the women's soccer club that he would add women's varsity sports only "if forced to"; (2) appointed a low-level male staff member in the athletic department "senior woman administrator;" (3) approved larger budgets for travel, personnel, and training facilities for men's teams than for women's teams on a regular basis; and (4) paid much lower salaries to coaches of women's teams than he paid to coaches of men's teams. Plaintiffs in future Title IX sports cases may not be able to show such unabashedly intentional discrimination, but they should not have to do so in order to have their claims litigated. Title IX requires colleges to maintain comparable sports programs for men and women, and coaches and administrators control the recruitment and the funding, respectively, of male and female athletes, so disparities between the support of men's sports and women's sports are likely to result from intentional actions. Thus, *Alexander* is unlikely to bar Title IX suits by female (or male) college athletes in the future.

123. Lee Sigelman and Clyde Wilcox, "Public Support for Gender Equality in Athletics Programs," *Women & Politics*, 22, no. 1 (2001): 85–96.

124. Welch Suggs, "Cheers and Condemnation Greet Report on Gender Equity," *The Chronicle of Higher Education*, March 7, 2003, p. A40.

125. U.S. Department of Education, Secretary's Commission on Opportunity in Athletics, *Open to All: Title IX at Thirty* (Washington, D.C.: Government Printing Office, 2003), p. 41.

126. Ibid., p. 42.

127. Ibid., p. 43.

128. *Cohen v. Brown University*, 101 F.3d. 155, 176 (1st Cir. 1996), *cert. denied*, 520 U.S. 1186 (1997).

129. U.S. Department of Education, *Open to All*, p. 44.

130. Ibid., pp. 37–39.

131. Ibid., p. 41.

132. Ibid., pp. 42–43.

133. Ibid., p. 43.

CHAPTER 7

SEASONS OF PROMISE

A PARTICIPATION MODEL OF COLLEGE SPORTS

KEEP THE GAMES, BUT CHANGE THEIR PURPOSE

John Feinstein glimpsed what college sports can and should be at the conclusion of a men's basketball game during the 1999–2000 season in which Lafayette College defeated Bucknell University 75–73. He recalled that moment in his book, *The Last Amateurs*, which chronicled a season of college basketball in the Patriot League, to which both Lafayette and Bucknell belong.

> When the game ended, I spent some time in each locker room. As the Lafayette locker room emptied, I found myself sitting with junior point guard Tim Bieg and sophomores Reggie Guy and Brian Burke. I can't remember who brought it up, but one of the players looked at me and said, 'So, were you surprised that [John] McCain beat [George] Bush that badly last night?' The next fifteen minutes were spent discussing the New Hampshire primary and its ramifications. As we talked, it occurred to me that this conversation wasn't likely to be taking place in locker rooms in the ACC, the Big Ten, the Big East, or any of the other glamour leagues around the country.[1]

The quality of the Lafayette players' postgame conversation reflects the admissions criteria for athletes at the Patriot League's member colleges, which include West Point, the Naval Academy, Colgate, Lehigh, Holy Cross, and American University in addition to Lafayette and Bucknell.[2] Members of the Patriot League admit athletes on the basis of an academic index that requires each college to create a profile of its students' SAT (or ACT) scores and class rank in high school. Athletes' aggregate profile must fall within one standard deviation of the average test score and class rank of the student body as a whole, and an individual athlete's profile must be no more than two standard deviations below the average for the athlete's class.[3] This is a simpler version of the academic index that the Ivy League uses to ensure that its athletes can hold their own in a competitive academic environment and that they can contribute more to the campus community than breakaway speed or a soft jump shot.

The Patriot League, the Ivy League, and Division III of the NCAA are beacons that light the path to wisdom in the governance of college sports. The path to wisdom requires colleges to seize the opportunity for reform that current legal and financial conditions provide, and to scrap the commercial model of college sports because the financial, academic, and social problems associated with it are too severe and too pervasive for tinkering to rectify.[4] The commercial model must go—to be replaced by the participation model, which will bring fiscal sanity, academic integrity, personal responsibility, and gender equity to college sports, while enabling students to acquire self-knowledge, to develop physical skills, and to enjoy a healthy diversion from the classroom and the laboratory. Thus, its principal beneficiaries will be the students who compete, not the fans who watch them or the media outlets that cover them.

The participation model is not as radical as it might appear to be. It would retain intercollegiate athletic contests. It would also make good on the promise of the NCAA Constitution by ensuring that college sports are an "integral part of the educational program."[5] In short, the participation model would keep the games, but it would change the purposes for their existence and the methods of their administration. It already governs all sports in the Ivy League, twenty-one of twenty-two sports in the Patriot League (where only basketball players can receive athletic scholarships), and all sports in Division III, so the seeds of substantial reform are in the ground. The time has come to plant them on every campus so that the participation model will govern all of college sports.

The participation model is not perfect. Colleges that adopt it may still allow athletic ability to exert undue influence in their decisions about admissions and financial aid. For example, Ivy League colleges allot thirty-five places in their freshman classes each year to football players. The absence of athletic scholarships means that more players at these colleges than at the big-time colleges quit the game during their undergraduate years, so thirty-five football players are admitted annually in order to compensate for the attrition rate.[6]

Division III colleges recruit athletes aggressively, too, even in sports such as tennis and swimming, so that few athletes "walk on" to teams (i.e., try out when they arrive on campus), and many of them earn admission with a coach's assistance.[7] Indeed, says Philip Smith, the retired dean of admissions at Williams College, a Division III school that admits only about 20 percent of its applicants, "[a]thletic recruiting is the biggest form of affirmative action in higher education, even at schools such as ours."[8] He added: "I can name on one finger the number of kids on the Williams hockey team who could make it [i.e., gain admission] on their own without hockey."[9]

Data support the thrust of Smith's argument. In June of 2002 a special faculty committee that studied the status of athletics at Williams reported that the college allocated approximately one hundred slots in the freshman class each year to applicants who were athletes. The committee also reported that each year only about 25 percent of the applicants that Williams identified as "impact athletes" (i.e., likely to play for four years and contribute to a team's success) scored a 1 or a 2 in the college's academic rating system for applicants, which meant that they would probably have been admitted even if they weren't athletes. The remaining 75 percent of the impact athletes scored between 3 and 7 on the college's nine-point scale, which meant that they would almost certainly have not been admitted had they not been athletes.[10]

Several members of the New England Small College Athletic Conference (NESCAC), to which Williams belongs, reviewed and revamped their admissions preferences for athletes during 2002. Their consideration of this issue shows that although a Division III college is not immune from pressure to recruit and to admit athletes in order to maintain competitive teams, it can reverse perceived athletic excesses relatively easily because sports are not essential to its public image or to its financial health. Four members of the NESCAC, including Amherst, Williams, Wesleyan University, and Bowdoin College, announced in 2002 that in considering future applicants, they will reduce the number who are admitted by virtue of an athletic preference.[11] These actions were mild compared to the decision that Swarthmore College, an academically selective Division III school in Pennsylvania, made two years earlier. Swarthmore announced at the end of the 2000 season that it would no longer field a football team because doing so required it to admit a disproportionate number of athletes to its 375-member freshman class. By eliminating football, Swarthmore could reduce the number of "recruited athletes" (i.e., students for whom a sport is the primary extracurricular activity) to a maximum of 15 percent of the student body, and thereby make room for pianists, dancers, and actors who would otherwise have lost out for admission to wide receivers and linebackers.[12] This decision, although painful, was possible because football was not a key to the public image or the financial health of Swarthmore College.

In Division III, the Ivy League, and the Patriot League (except for basketball), not only are colleges free to rein in athletic excesses because their sports are not commercial ventures but students are free to stop playing a sport in order to pursue other interests or to play a sport while still making schoolwork their top priority. Nobody knows this better than sports sociologist Allen Sack, whose sons attended Dartmouth and Wesleyan, respectively. In an article that appeared in *The Chronicle of Higher Education*, Professor Sack wrote:

> My older son attended Dartmouth, where he played lacrosse for one year before deciding that mountain biking gave him more freedom to focus on his academic goals. Giving up lacrosse had absolutely no impact on his financial aid, and his memories of Dartmouth include biking, running, and skiing in New England's rugged White Mountains, as well as intellectual discourse with some of the finest teaching-faculty members in the United States.[13] Professor Sack added: . . . My younger son attended Wesleyan University, where he majored in history and played lacrosse for four years. I know firsthand that when conflicts arose between sport and the demands of the classroom, it was coaches who had to accommodate the needs of players rather than vice versa. Athletes often showed up tardy for practice because of late-afternoon classes; some athletes missed entire seasons because of study abroad. In the absence of athletics scholarships, athletes like my son were able to set their academic and athletics priorities without fear of losing financial aid. It was college sport at its very best.[14]

Indeed, it was *college* sport, namely, sport played by full-time college students whose principal reason for attending college was to obtain a high-quality education. True college sport can exist only when institutions forsake commerce for participation, in which case the financial, academic, and social costs of their athletic programs decline dramatically. Commerce occurs at the University of Texas at Austin, which spent $42 million on twenty intercollegiate teams during the 1999–2000 academic year.[15] Participation occurs at Harvard, which during the same time period spent $6.7 million on forty-one intercollegiate teams.[16] The following section will present a participation model that aims to bring college sport to every institution of higher learning in the United States.

COMPETITION INSTEAD OF COMMERCE

The participation model would preserve the physical and emotional benefits that a student can derive from participation in college sports but would eliminate the pressures that can negate those benefits when the commercial model governs. Toward that end it would pursue six major goals. The goals would generate specific policies that, in turn, would enable colleges and conferences to achieve the goals. A discussion of the six goals follows.

1. Preserve intercollegiate athletic competition.

In a recent article John Gerdy observed that "the most fundamental issue in college athletics is whether an institution, in its efforts to fulfill its public mission of meeting the many challenges facing society, is best served by sponsoring intercollegiate athletics at all—at least as they are currently structured."[17] The participation model would resolve this issue by preserving intercollegiate athletics, but not as currently structured in Division I and Division II of the NCAA. This model derives from the premise that athletic competition liberated from commercial pressures is a valuable adjunct to a liberal-arts education. It can test the body and the spirit in the same way that political philosophy and organic chemistry can test the intellect. Moreover, unlike political philosophy and organic chemistry, athletic competition conducts its tests in public, which can build self-knowledge that a student may be unable to obtain in a classroom or a laboratory.

New York University president Jay Oliva made this point well when he said that "[s]ummoning the guts to compete in the public eye and take one's lumps is an aspect of education that athletics delivers in its purest form."[18] Similarly, former University of Pennsylvania president Sheldon Hackney observed that "[o]ne of the reasons we play sports is that it helps us find out what kind of person we are. It can also help us become the sort of person we choose to be. It is both a revelation and a rehearsal."[19] Anyone who has stood on the free throw line late in a close basketball game in the opponent's gym or who has summoned the last ounce of energy necessary to overtake an opposing runner or skier at the end of a cross-country race has experienced both the revelation and the rehearsal. Years later, the value of the rehearsal will be a revelation as the former college athlete uses the lessons learned in competition to run an organization, to present research findings at an academic conference, or to argue a case in court with skill and confidence.

Competitive sports, then, are similar to musical recitals and theater productions, which also test the muscles and the will in public. All three pursuits demand of the performer a quality that Ernest Hemingway called "grace under pressure," which low-key intramural and club sports typically do not.[20] Viewed in this way, competitive sports are as compatible with the mission of a college or a university as are the glee club, the orchestra, and the theater troupe. Therefore, it would be a mistake to eliminate college sports when many of the same traits that make a successful college athlete also make a successful college student and, later, a productive citizen. Besides, most sports programs at most colleges are constructive adjuncts to the educational process, and most college athletes are pursuing a college education. The problems that Chapters 3, 4, and 5 described are concentrated in the football programs of approximately one hundred colleges and in the basketball programs of perhaps two hundred colleges.[21]

The benefits of athletic competition are powerful reasons for colleges to make varsity sports accessible to more students than they are at present, so that a broader cross section of the campus community can participate. "Perhaps one of the most compelling reasons for de-emphasizing and broadening varsity sports," former University of Michigan president James Duderstadt has written, "is to provide more students with the educational opportunities associated with athletic participation."[22] At Michigan, where the commercial model governs sports, twenty-three varsity teams, ten for men and thirteen for women, provide participation opportunities for only about seven hundred students in an undergraduate student body of twenty-two thousand, or about 3 percent of undergraduates.[23] The commercial model also governs sports at Ohio State, where approximately 1 percent of the class of 1997 played a varsity sport,[24] while at Princeton, where participation trumps commerce, 18 percent of the class of 1997 played a varsity sport.[25]

Thus, the answer to John Gerdy's question about the wisdom of college-sponsored sports teams is to preserve college sports, to expand college sports for women at institutions where they remain underrepresented as athletes, to de-commercialize football and men's basketball, and to not commercialize popular women's sports, notably basketball. Ironically, Gerdy answered his own question best when he made the following observation in his 1997 book, *The Successful College Athletic Program: The New Standard.*

> By the time this year's championship game is played, most people will have forgotten who participated in last year's. What has lasting significance, however, is the way in which athletics can positively affect the lives of those who play and those who watch.[26]

In order to affect lives positively, college sports still need what author Edwin Cady said in 1978 they needed, namely, to be "liberated from [the pressures of] the gate"[27] and to effect a "fresh reconciliation with academe."[28] Only the widespread adoption of the participation model can achieve these goals so that sports enhance rather than hinder education.

2. Eliminate concessions to commercialism and professionalism.

In 1993, Thomas K. Hearn, Jr., the president of Wake Forest University, told a congressional committee that "if there is any silver lining to this awful financial circumstance that we are in, in higher education, then I believe it may be that we are going to be forced to look very hard at all of the things that we have been doing in athletics and determine which of them we can do without."[29] President Hearn's words are as pertinent today as they were when he spoke them. Colleges are still experiencing difficult financial circumstances, yet they continue to spend scarce resources on athletic extravagances that they can surely do without.

One thing that colleges can and should do without is the "athletic scholarship," the oxymoron that is perhaps the most troublesome offspring of the ill-fated marriage between athletic commerce and higher education. Former

NCAA executive director Walter Byers recalls that when the association's annual convention voted in 1956 to award athletic scholarships, he thought that the change "would lead to better days" because it would end informal payments to athletes by members of booster clubs.[30] He now acknowledges that not only did athletic scholarships not end such payments[31] but they actually made matters worse by "encourag[ing] separation of the student-athlete from the student body"[32] and by "promot[ing] self-governance for the athletics department. . . ."[33] Recently, Frank Deford, senior writer for *Sports Illustrated*, sounded a similar theme in a speech to the National Press Club, wherein he said that athletic scholarships "send the message that college, higher education, thinks that sports are more important than art or music or literature."[34] He then asked:

> Why should [athletes] get scholarships for their extracurricular activity, when the college men and women who sing in a glee club or act in campus dramatics or . . . write for the college newspaper or work for the campus radio or television station—why should athletes get scholarships for their extracurricular work when those other equally talented and dedicated students don't?[35]

Presumably, Deford's question was rhetorical, but it warrants an answer nonetheless, and the right answer is that athletic ability should never be the sole determinant of financial access to higher education, nor should it count for more than other talents do when colleges award financial aid to their students. Athletic scholarships enable college coaches, under the guise of offering educational opportunities, to recruit high school seniors to their campuses for primarily nonacademic purposes, and when they enroll as freshmen to monopolize their time with nonacademic activities that stifle educational goals instead of serving them.[36] Therefore, colleges ought to eliminate athletic scholarships so that athletes can study abroad, play in a band, or work in a political campaign instead of feeling compelled to devote most of their nonclass time to sport.

One happy consequence of eliminating athletic scholarships is evident in a conversation that Murray Sperber had with a female discus thrower at Ohio Wesleyan University, a Division III school. The young woman said:

> The Division III philosophy puts academics first. When I told my coaches that I was really interested in studying abroad [during the summer], their answer wasn't, "You're going to miss preseason" [practice], it was "go ahead."[37]

The coaches may have been supportive merely because they were enlightened educators. On the other hand, they may have been supportive because without athletic scholarships, they had no leverage with which to prevent the young woman from studying abroad. In that case, endorsing her plan to spend a summer abroad was arguably the best way to ensure that she returned to school the following fall eager to train and to compete again. Thus, the absence of athletic scholarships gave the track coaches at Ohio Wesleyan an incentive to support the educational aspirations of an athlete even when they conflicted with preseason training.

The elimination of athletic scholarships would mean that colleges would offer financial aid to athletes and to nonathletes alike based on financial need and academic merit only, thereby integrating athletes into the student body.[38] It would also mean that there would be more funds available for women's sports and for men's non-revenue sports. The Ivy League experience illustrates these points. The Ivy League adheres to the participation model more closely than any other Division I conference. Its members have passed up the publicity and the potential television revenues associated with commercialized college sports in favor of offering conference championships for men and women in thirty-three sports, the most in Division I, plus extensive intramural programs.[39] At Harvard, for example, not only are there forty-one intercollegiate teams, but there are also so many junior varsity, club, and intramural teams that approximately 85 percent of undergraduates participate in organized sports.[40] "Athletics are part of the students' education," says athletic director Robert Scalise.[41] On the varsity level, Ivy League football teams do not participate in postseason play in Division I-AA, and most conference games in all sports occur on weekends.[42] Thus, it is not coincidental that Ivy League athletes have the highest four-year graduation rates of athletes in any Division I conference, which are "virtually indistinguishable from the rates of their non-athlete [classmates]."[43]

Admittedly, most American colleges lack the prestige and the wealth that members of the Ivy League enjoy, so they must seek both through sports. Still, most Division I colleges have achieved neither prestige nor wealth through sports, and the pressure to comply with Title IX will continue to make these goals elusive in the future. The elimination of athletic scholarships will reduce this pressure, and it will enable colleges to redirect resources from athletics to education and community service. The prestige acquired through these efforts is likely to last much longer than the flush of a bowl game victory. Harvard could drop football tomorrow with no loss to its prestige, but the University of Nebraska cannot afford to have even one losing season in football because its prestige is wedded to its football prowess.

Some Division I coaches will surely argue that the elimination of athletic scholarships would diminish the quality of college sports, thereby destroying the fans' interest in the games. These predictions are perhaps half right. The games might take on a less professional appearance due to reduced practice time and the defection of some elite athletes and coaches to the professional ranks, but it by no means follows that fans will lose interest in attending games. On the contrary, the games may well become more attractive to spectators who would prefer to watch athletic contests between legitimate undergraduates instead of between semipros who view college as a sweaty apprenticeship in preparation for fame and fortune in the NBA or the NFL.[44]

The second thing that colleges can, and should, do without is autonomous athletic departments. Autonomous athletic departments that depend on off-campus sources of financial support are magnets for corruption because they are more loyal to the "booster coalitions" that fund them than to the colleges of which they are nominally a part.[45] Sports sociologist James Frey has written that "deviant actions become a strategy for dealing with the environmental demand for winning and the requirement that the university not use general fund dollars for athletic program deficits."[46] The best antidote to deviant actions born of athletic department autonomy is for colleges to support their sports teams from their general funds rather than to expect the teams to support themselves from gate receipts, television revenues, and booster club donations.

Indeed, every college should require that all gate receipts, television revenues, and booster club donations enter its general fund for distribution throughout the institution instead of merely within the athletic department. Every college should also list its athletic department as a line item in its budget, and in states where statutes require athletic departments to be self-supporting, colleges ought to lobby vigorously for a change in the law as a means of reining in athletic spending.[47] This change would integrate the athletic department into the college, end lavish spending on football and men's basketball, and free up sufficient funds for women's sports and men's non-revenue sports.[48] It would also spark interest in, and oversight of, sports by faculty because athletics would compete with English, physics, and other academic departments for support. Faculty oversight of sports will be crucial to the successful implementation of the participation model because faculty lack the vested interests in publicity and in athletic revenues that keep athletic directors, NCAA officials, and the presidents of many colleges wedded to athletic commerce. In other words, members of the faculty are more likely than anyone else on campus to believe that when it comes to sports, less is more and small is beautiful.

The third thing that colleges can, and should, do without is coaches who see themselves as entertainment producers instead of as teachers. When coaches see themselves as entertainment producers, they tend to over-emphasize athletic and financial success and to subvert the academic mission of the college of which they are a part.[49] They are also more prone to cheat because, as James Frey has noted, "they are operationally isolated from the university."[50] Under such circumstances, according to Frey, "the norms of the larger institution are meaningless and irrelevant to [coaches] simply because [coaches] do not feel bonded to the university community."[51]

Colleges should adopt three measures to integrate coaches into the campus community. First, colleges should require coaches to have at least a master's degree in physical education or a related field and to coach more than one sport or to teach physical education classes in addition to coaching. A 1993 study by the National Association of Athletic Compliance Coordinators' Committee on Athletics and Higher Education found that only 49 percent of the coaches in Division I possessed a master's degree.[52] This figure must become 100 percent if coaches are to be educators who feel part of the campus community instead of entertainment managers who feel isolated and alienated from it. Toward the same end, colleges should require coaches to participate in an institutional orientation program shortly after they are hired in order that coaches can familiarize themselves with the academic offerings and the campus cultures of the colleges they serve.[53] The teaching requirement will attract to college coaching men and women who perceive themselves to be, and who wish to be, teachers, and the teaching experience will force them to interact with colleagues who do not coach and with students who are not members of their teams. Coaching more than one sport will broaden coaches' professional knowledge and teaching skills, and will expose them to a larger slice of the campus community than they might otherwise see. Moreover, coaches who teach classes or who coach multiple sports will be unable to devote the inordinate amount of time that coaches at Division I colleges currently devote to recruiting.

Second, colleges should make coaches subject to the same personnel policies that govern other professional employees on campus. Colleges should pay coaches' salaries from their general funds, not from athletic department revenues or from booster club donations. These salaries should be comparable to the salaries earned by faculty and staff members whose credentials and responsibilities mirror those of the coaches. Colleges should not permit coaches to pocket the entire proceeds of summer camps or of contracts with athletic-shoe manufacturers or media outlets when the coaches' marketability derives in large measure from their associations with their respective institutions. Instead, colleges should receive the lion's share of the proceeds, and should then pay a portion to the coaches involved.[54]

Third, colleges must improve job security for coaches. It would not be appropriate to make coaches eligible for tenure because the long-standing justification for tenure has been that it ensures academic freedom for faculty in their teaching and research. This justification does not apply to coaches, who usually do not teach and who do not conduct research.[55] Instead, colleges should make coaches who satisfy academic and professional expectations eligible for "rolling" contracts that would be reviewed, and could be renewed, every five years.[56] Under these circumstances coaches would not have to rely on their win-loss records to keep their jobs. Michele Tolela Myers, the president of Dennison University, a Division III school in Ohio, has articulated well the participation model's view of job security for coaches.

She said: "We fire coaches if they are not good teachers, if they are not good coaches, if the players say they aren't doing good jobs—but we don't fire them if they don't have a winning season."[57] This philosophy is essential to the success of the participation model because it reduces the pressures on coaches to win games, to please sports boosters, and to supplement their salaries. Therefore, the best way to ensure that college athletes are students is to enable college coaches to be teachers.[58]

When athletic scholarships end, athletic departments are no longer financially autonomous, and coaches are teachers, colleges will be able to eliminate other vestiges of athletic commercialism and professionalism that they can, and should, do without. One hallmark of the commercial model that must go—even in the Ivy League, the Patriot League, and Division III—is freshman eligibility for varsity competition. Three positive consequences will flow from its demise. First, and most importantly, freshmen will have a full academic year in which to adjust to college classes and to campus life before being expected to devote a substantial block of time to sports. Academically marginal athletes will have a chance to improve their classroom performance, while academically talented athletes will be able to develop interests other than athletics.

Second, when freshmen are ineligible for varsity competition, there will be no need to use scores on standardized tests to determine eligibility for varsity sports, hence, no controversy about the racial implications of doing so.[59] Instead, a simple rule will determine athletic eligibility in the sophomore year; namely, completion of the freshman year with a GPA high enough to avoid academic probation (i.e., 2.0) in courses that will lead to a degree.

Third, the recruiting of high school seniors will be less frantic, pressure-packed, and highly publicized than it is today because college coaches will no longer be able to anticipate that a talented freshman class will turn this year's losing season into next year's conference championship.[60] Finally, freshman ineligibility might well spur elite athletes who care little for the academic aspects of college to forego collegiate competition and to proceed directly to the professional ranks, as many have long done in baseball and some now do in basketball. It could facilitate the establishment of a developmental or minor league in football, too. Thus, athletes who are not interested in school could train for careers in professional sports unencumbered by academic responsibilities, and athletes who are interested in school could be serious students yet still compete in sports.

Another hallmark of the commercial model that must go is spring practice in football, which exists throughout Division I, even in the Ivy League. The end of spring football practice will come as part of a sweeping reform that will limit the competitive season for any sport, including preseason practice, to the length of one academic semester, which is typically fifteen weeks.[61] The football season would run from September through November, the basketball and hockey seasons would run from December through March, and the baseball season would run from March through May. In each instance, the fifteen-week competition period would include postseason playoff games. For example, college basketball teams would be permitted two weeks of pre-competition practice, followed by a twenty-game regular season during an eleven-week period, followed, in turn, by a two-week postseason. The NCAA basketball tournament would include no more than twenty teams, namely, regular-season conference champions and a handful of at-large selections. There would be no postseason conference tournaments preceding the NCAA tournament.[62]

Spring football practice must go not only because it would violate the fifteen-week rule but also because it assigns to football an importance that no college sport deserves. Sports should be secondary to academic life on college campuses, but spring practice suggests that football is such an important college activity that its participants must prepare for the coming season in a formal way four months before the first game. This is the wrong message to send to college students about any sport.

Still another hallmark of the commercial model of college sports that must go is redshirting, the practice of holding an athlete out of competition for one year for the purposes of adding muscle through weight training or improving athletic skills, thereby enabling the athlete to complete his or her athletic eligibility during a fifth year on campus. Redshirting should end because it serves no academic purpose; indeed, it alters the customary four-year course of an undergraduate education primarily to improve the athletic performances of individuals and teams. Redshirting should be permissible only when a student has missed a season of competition in order to recover from an injury or an illness or because of a family emergency, such as the need to support or to take care of a family member temporarily.

Academic assistance programs for athletes housed in athletic departments must go, too. These programs enable athletic departments to exert excessive control over athletes' academic lives, which prevents them from learning to manage their own affairs, subordinates individual academic needs to coaches' priorities, and suggests to athletes that the athletic department will take care of academic matters for them so that they can concentrate on sports. Sometimes, as happened at the University of Minnesota (see Chapter 4), the athletic department does try to take care of athletes academically, with tragic results. These problems will be much less likely to occur when athletes must seek tutoring from the same office on campus that serves their non-athlete classmates, which office reports to the dean of students or the vice-president for academic affairs, not to the director of athletics.[63]

Finally, off-campus recruiting of high school and junior college athletes must go. Coaches could still recruit by means of letters and telephone calls, and recruits could still advertise their skills to college coaches by means of videotapes that show them performing in competition. Coaches could not visit recruits in their homes or in their high schools, though. This change will save colleges substantial sums of money in athletic-recruiting costs. It will also spare the NCAA, or its successor, the trouble of having to regulate off-campus recruiting.[64] It will enable athletes to attend to schoolwork during their senior year of high school and will allow families to live relatively peaceful and orderly lives during the recruiting season. Most importantly, it will signal to both athletes and parents that education, not sport, is the principal campus activity and the major reason to attend college.

3. Pursue gender equity aggressively.

When colleges implement the changes discussed above, several consequences will flow that will make it easier for them to achieve gender equity in sports. One likely consequence is that colleges will have less money to spend on football than they have now because football will have to compete with academic programs for funds. Under these circumstances it will probably be necessary to abandon "two-platoon" football, with its large squads and unlimited substitutions, and to return to "one-platoon" football, in which offensive players remain on the field to play defense when the ball changes hands. College football was one-platoon football until 1965, when the NCAA adopted a "free substitution" rule that ushered in the two-platoon game.[65] Grant Teaff, the president of the American Football Coaches' Association, who has been the athletic director and the head football coach at Baylor University, recognized this likelihood in testimony that he delivered to Congress in 1993. He said:

> [I]f there's going to be more cuts in scholarships, which there could well be, there needs to be a change, . . . for legislation to move away from the type of game we play now which requires more participation—it is two-platoon football—and go back to the one-platoon.[66]

The switch to one-platoon football could reduce the size of college football teams from one hundred or more to fifty, which—considering the estimate by Sigelman and Wahlbeck (see Chapter 6) that for every football-roster slot that is eliminated, it will be possible to add two athletic slots for women—would mean that approximately one hundred new athletic slots would be available to women or to be split between women's teams and men's non-revenue teams.[67]

Another likely consequence of colleges' adoption of the participation model is that professional sports franchises will develop minor leagues in football, in men's basketball, and perhaps in women's basketball in order to ensure a continued supply of well-trained players to the professional ranks.[68] The minor leagues will absorb the high school graduates and the college players who would rather play their sport than attend college and the college coaches who are more interested in athletic entertainment than in teaching. In this way, the minor leagues will de-commercialize college sports further and will remove from the college ranks athletes and coaches who prefer commercialized sport and/or feel threatened by the present movement for gender equity. The presence of minor leagues could also make football and men's basketball slots available to students who might otherwise have been unable to make the team. Thus, men who could not play college sports before could now do so at no cost to women's sports.

This process is already underway in basketball, as the National Basketball Developmental League, which the NBA sponsors, began play in eight southeastern cities in the fall of 2001.[69] Presently, players must be at least twenty years old to play in the league, but one college president, Mary Sue Coleman of the University of Michigan, has recommended reducing the minimum age for eligibility to seventeen or eighteen so that athletes who are uninterested in attending college could enter the developmental league immediately after high school. She said: "I'd much rather have kids who have no interest in college go directly" into the developmental league.[70] They will likely do so in greater numbers if colleges adopt the participation model, perhaps spawning rookie leagues and more advanced leagues, or even age-group-based leagues, in football and basketball, which would be a welcome addition to the minor leagues that already exist in baseball and hockey.

The minor leagues, by virtue of their players' superior talent, could take at least some television coverage away from the colleges, especially if league executives and team owners market the games with energy and imagination. Then, colleges will be sufficiently liberated from the television networks to shorten seasons and to schedule games on weekends only, pursuant to the academic emphasis of the participation model. College hockey teams, for example, have been able to restrict their games to weekends and to maintain a reputation for integrity because there are professional junior hockey leagues that absorb the players who do not wish to attend college.[71]

In the new environment colleges will be able to pursue gender equity aggressively because nobody will view it as a threat to the success and the financial health of football and men's basketball. The participation model will make it possible in the future for many more colleges than can do so today to comply with Title IX by satisfying part one of the effective-accommodation test, the substantial-proportionality standard.[72] In the long run, if not in the short run, colleges should try to comply with Title IX by achieving substantial proportionality. Critics of this standard are mistaken when they charge that it mandates illegal gender-based preferences and quotas. Quotas based on sex are illegal only when they contradict a law that requires institutions to provide opportunities without regard to sex.[73] For example, it would be illegal for a college to establish a minimum or a maximum number of women that could enroll in its engineering school or a minimum or a maximum number of men that could enroll in its nursing school because Title IX requires colleges to provide *academic* opportunities for their students without regard to sex. This requirement is eminently reasonable because there is no biological, psychological, or educational reason why men and women should not study engineering or nursing together.

Sports are a different story, though. Contrary to its prohibition against gender-based quotas in the classroom, Title IX expressly permits colleges to operate separate athletic programs and teams for men and women, so long as both sexes have an equal opportunity to participate in sports. This is eminently reasonable, too, because men are generally bigger, faster, and stronger than women, and, hence, enjoy a substantial advantage in coed competition in sports that favor big, fast, strong athletes. Title IX negates this advantage and fulfills its aim of promoting equal opportunity in sports for both sexes by permitting colleges to establish "separate but equal" athletic programs for each sex. Under these circumstances one legitimate measure of equality is a comparison of the numbers of male and female undergraduates, respectively, who compete in varsity sports. The substantial-proportionality standard is just such a comparison. It seeks to ensure the same result in sports that one would expect to see in the classroom, namely, that men and women participate in numbers that reflect their numbers in the student body.[74] If such a comparison of athletic participation by gender is a quota system, it is a quota system that the law permits because of the lawful segregation by sex that exists in college sports. Thus, the critics of substantial proportionality who charge that this standard violates Title IX because it creates a quota system hoist themselves by their own petard. Their argument explodes in their faces because a gender-based quota system is perfectly legal in the unique context of college sports.

Moreover, the substantial-proportionality standard is more flexible than its critics acknowledge. The "Clarification" of the three-part test that OCR published in 1996 states that OCR will not insist that a college demonstrate numerical proportionality when the number of participation opportunities that it would be necessary to create in order to do so would not be sufficient to sustain a viable team. For example, if at College A, women are 52 percent of the undergraduates and 47 percent of the athletes, and it will be necessary to fill sixty-two additional slots on sports teams to reach substantial proportionality, then College A is not in compliance with Title IX, because sixty-two slots are sufficient to create one or more new teams for women.[75] On the other hand, if women also comprise 52 percent of the undergraduates and 47 percent of the athletes at College B, but because of the small enrollment at College B, it would be necessary to fill only six additional slots there in order to reach substantial proportionality, College B is in compliance with Title IX because six slots are not sufficient to sustain a viable team.[76] Thus, the substantial-proportionality standard is not the slave to numbers that its critics allege.

The critics are also mistaken when they charge that the substantial-proportionality standard violates Title IX by granting preferences or according disparate treatment to one sex. The following language is the basis for this charge. It states:

> Nothing contained in subsection (a) of this section shall be interpreted to require any educational institution to grant preferential or disparate treatment to the members of one sex on account of an imbalance which may exist with respect to the total number or percentage of persons of that sex participating in or receiving the benefits of any federally supported program or activity, in comparison with the total number or percentage of persons of that sex in any community, State, section, or other area. . . . [77]

The substantial-proportionality standard does not violate this language for three reasons. First, contrary to the critics' contention, substantial proportionality does not require *preferential* treatment for women. Instead, as noted above, it merely requires a result that one would expect if sports programs were coeducational and free of gender discrimination, namely, that women would participate in numbers that reflect their numbers in the student body. Second, even if this requirement *were* preferential treatment, it would still not violate Title IX because achieving substantial proportionality is not the only means by which a college can comply with Title IX. This is because, as the appellate court noted in *Cohen IV* (see Chapter 6), substantial proportionality is "a rebuttable presumption, rather than an inflexible requirement," and colleges can still comply with Title IX, absent substantial proportionality, if they can satisfy either part two or part three of the three-part test.[78] Third, Congress intended the language quoted above to prohibit sex-based quotas in college admissions and in faculty hiring, where opportunities should exist for qualified candidates regardless of sex. Accordingly, this language does not pertain to college sports, where Title IX permits separate but equal programs for men and women.[79]

Furthermore, the substantial-proportionality standard wisely rejects the suggestion by its critics that colleges' should provide sports opportunities for male and female students in proportion to their relative interests in playing college sports.[80] If colleges were to substitute relative interests for substantial proportionality, they would comply with Title IX by accommodating the same percentage of the athletic interests and abilities of the underrepresented sex as they did for the overrepresented sex. The principal weakness in the "relative-interests" measure of gender equity lies in its assumption that males are, and always will be, more interested in playing college sports than females are. Based on this assumption, the relative-interests approach would perpetuate the underrepresentation of females in college sports, as the appellate court noted in *Cohen IV*.[81] In contrast, substantial proportionality recognizes that when colleges improve the number and the quality of athletic opportunities for women, more women will participate. Colleges have the power to increase athletic participation by women students because college coaches recruit athletes to fill positions on their teams. Recruiting determines the number of women on college teams nearly as much as women's enthusiasm for sports does.[82]

Another weakness in the relative-interests approach is its failure to recognize that substantial proportionality is merely one part of the three-part effective-accommodation test, part three of which enables a college to comply with Title IX by showing that its athletic program accommodates the athletic interests and abilities of its current students fully and effectively. In other words, the relative-interests approach is, in effect, already available to colleges that cannot achieve substantial proportionality because of a disparity of interest in athletic participation between their male and female students. Thus, if the critics of substantial proportionality are correct, and women are less interested in playing college sports than men are, numerous colleges ought to be able to satisfy Title IX by showing that their athletic offerings for men and women accommodate the interests and abilities of each sex fully and effectively.

The University of New Mexico (UNM) is a good example. In April 2000, OCR reached an agreement with UNM that gave the university a choice of the means by which it will seek to comply with Title IX, namely, by achieving substantial proportionality or by demonstrating that it accommodates the athletic interests and abilities of its female students fully and effectively.[83] If UNM chooses the latter option, it must conduct a detailed survey of its enrolled and admitted students in order to determine their athletic interests and abilities. Whichever option it chooses, UNM must comply with Title IX by July 1, 2003.[84] If, on that date, UNM demonstrates that it is accommodating the athletic interests and abilities of its female students fully and effectively, even though women are more than 50 percent of its students but just 35 percent of its athletes, it can restore one or more of the men's teams (swimming, wrestling, and gymnastics) that it disbanded in 1999.[85] OCR may have been remiss in not emphasizing to colleges that part three is a viable option for Title IX compliance, thereby lending credence to the critics' charge that pursuing substantial proportionality is the only path to the promised land. Still, as the preceding paragraphs demonstrate, the critics are dead wrong when they charge that the Title IX regulations impose a rigid quota system that ignores disparate levels of interest between men and women in playing college sports.

The critics also overstate the adverse impact of the substantial-proportionality standard on the elimination of men's non-revenue teams by colleges during the past two decades. The results of a study conducted by the General Accounting Office (GAO) belie this charge. The GAO conducted a questionnaire survey in which 1,191 colleges participated. The survey asked colleges to provide data concerning their decisions to add and/or to drop athletic teams.[86] Among the 1,191 colleges that completed the questionnaire, 963 added at least one team and 307 discontinued at least one team between 1992–93 and 1999–2000. Among the 948 colleges that added one or more women's teams, 72 percent did so without discontinuing any teams.[87] To be sure, colleges added nearly three times as many women's teams (1,919) as men's teams (702) during this period and discontinued more than twice as many men's teams (386) as women's teams (150) during the same period.[88] Still, 7 of every 10 colleges that added a sport for women did so without discontinuing a sport for men. Therefore, the critics are mistaken when they charge that the pursuit of substantial proportionality forces colleges to rob Peter in order to pay Paula.

Finally, the substantial-proportionality standard is compatible with the aims of the participation model. It connects education to sports by linking college athletes to the student body instead of to the small population that wishes to play college sports and that is capable of doing so. This linkage conveys the message that sports are a part of a college's educational mission.[89] When the participation model is in place, they will be.

In this new environment colleges will achieve substantial proportionality more easily than they can now. The savings realized by replacing commerce with participation will enhance athletic opportunities for women without sacrificing athletic opportunities for men, thereby defusing the current controversy. The controversy will diminish further if OCR reminds colleges that they can use part three of the effective-accommodation test to comply with Title IX, and shows them how to do so. There will be no controversy over substantial proportionality in colleges' awarding of athletic scholarships to men and women because there will be no athletic scholarships.[90] More participation and less controversy will be a refreshing change in college sports.

4. Require personal responsibility from athletes and coaches.

The participation model will also make it easier for colleges to hold athletes and coaches accountable for their actions than it is now because colleges' financial health and public visibility will be considerably less dependent on athletic success than they are under the commercial model. Myles Brand, the former president of Indiana University who became the president and chief executive officer of the NCAA in January of 2003, has said that colleges are "victimized" by the ever-increasing commercialization of their sports programs. "The expectations of alumni and fans push us in that direction, and media contracts push us in that direction, and it intrudes into our decision-making process," he added. In this environment Brand observed, "[y]ou can make sure your basketball coach is held to a level of accountability. But when external forces impinge upon the university, there's a limited amount that I can do. I don't like it, but that's the way it is."[91]

Adoption of the participation model would diminish the power of external forces by severing the tie that binds higher education to athletic commerce. The freedom that results will enable colleges to hold athletes and coaches accountable for academic fraud and for other inappropriate behavior. The governing standard will be what is in the best interest of a college's integrity or of a student's intellectual and personal growth, not what is in the best interest of a team's winning streak or an athletic department's bottom line. Under these conditions it will be easier for colleges than it is today to suspend from practice and competition athletes who have been accused of violating campus rules or the criminal law, pending the outcomes of their cases. Suspension prior to resolution removes from athletic and from college authorities the incentive to postpone disciplinary proceedings until the current season ends or until the accused athlete is no longer eligible for intercollegiate competition. It also signifies that colleges view sports as secondary in importance to education and to their integrity. Sports *are* secondary to education, so colleges should not suspend financial aid to accused athletes, pending the outcome of disciplinary or court proceedings. The chance to pursue a college education is too important to take away from a student until such proceedings are complete and they have established the student's guilt.[92]

Based on these principles, the NCAA or its successor should adopt a rule that suspends from practice and competition any athletes who have been accused of violating campus rules or who have been arrested for breaking the law. Until this rule is in place, colleges should apply the same standard to athletes that they apply to nonathletes who violate campus rules or break the law; if a nonathlete would be suspended from extracurricular activities pending the outcome of disciplinary or judicial proceedings, the athlete who behaves similarly should suffer the same fate. Coaches who violate the terms of their employment contracts or of the faculty and staff handbook should receive penalties that are comparable to the penalties that other college employees would receive for similar transgressions.

Undoubtedly, some coaches and athletes will argue that it is wrong even to suspend an accused athlete from sports prior to the resolution of disciplinary or judicial proceedings because the American legal system presumes that one is innocent until proven guilty. This argument fails for two reasons: First, the presumption of innocence applies in criminal proceedings, but it does not necessarily bind campus disciplinary proceedings, which are separate and distinct from criminal courts. Second, even in criminal courts the presumption of innocence only protects an accused from being fined or imprisoned prior to a determination of guilt; it does not protect against suspension from a college athletic team. Thus, educational and institutional reasons suggest that colleges should suspend accused athletes from practice and competition, pending the outcome of disciplinary or judicial proceedings, and no legal reason suggests otherwise. Undoubtedly, this reasoning will be more persuasive when the participation model is in place and the "external forces" of which Myles Brand spoke are much diminished.

Athletic suspensions, though, are more likely to result from academic failure than from violations of campus rules or from criminal behavior. Therefore, it is important that the participation model hold athletes and coaches accountable for dismal academic performances by individuals and teams. Jon Ericson, who helped to found The Drake Group, a leading reform organization in college sports, argues that the best means of ensuring academic accountability in college sports is for colleges to "disclose the courses enrolled in by team members [of every college team], the average of the grades given in the course, and the instructor of the course. In other words, remove the student's name and include the grades."[93]

Disclosure is important in college sports; without it, myths abound, as the optimistic pronouncements of athletic departments substitute for hard data. The United States Congress recognized this in 1990, when it enacted the Student Right-to-Know and Campus Security Act,[94] and again in 1994, when it enacted the Equity in Athletics Disclosure Act.[95] The former requires colleges that receive federal financial assistance to report their graduation rates to the Secretary of Education annually, including the graduation rates of their athletes, by sport, race, and gender. Colleges must also make this information available to high-school athletes, their families, and their guidance counselors.[96] The latter requires coeducational colleges that receive federal financial assistance to report annually to the Secretary of Education (1) the number of male and female full-time undergraduates on campus; (2) the number of participants on each male and female varsity team; (3) the total operating expenses for each team; (4) the total expenditure for athletic scholarships for males and females, respectively; (5) the percentage of that amount awarded to male and to female athletes, respectively; (6) recruiting expenditures for men's and women's teams; (7) the revenues earned by men's and women's teams; and (8) whether the coaches of these teams are male or female.

Therefore, to require colleges to reveal their athletes' course selections, grades, and professors, without identifying the athletes themselves, would not be a departure from present practices. Like the disclosure of graduation rates, it would enable prospective college athletes, their parents, and their guidance counselors to determine whether athletes would be more likely to get an education at College A than at College B. Moreover, the proposed disclosure is a friend to reform; it will hasten the adoption of the participation model at colleges where it reveals that many athletes "major in eligibility" and leave school without a degree when their athletic eligibility ends. In Jon Ericson's view, disclosure will expose the problem of academic corruption in college athletics "in such a way that denial is no longer possible."[97] Disclosure will also test the academic promises of the participation model after its adoption by showing whether athletes' academic performances improve when and where the new model is in place.

Contrary to popular belief, present law permits the type of disclosure advocated here. Critics of this proposal will argue that it violates the Family Educational and Privacy Rights Act of 1974, which is better known as FERPA or the Buckley Amendment, so named in honor of its principal sponsor in the Senate, James Buckley of New York.[98] FERPA denies federal financial assistance to any college that permits the release of its students' educational records, other than "directory information" (e.g., name, address, telephone number, E-mail address, date and place of birth, photo, major, grade level, extracurricular activities, and so forth), without the written consent of the student if he or she is over eighteen, or the student's parents.[99] Arguably, grades and course selections are not "directory information," which suggests that the proposed disclosure violates FERPA.

A closer look at the statute, though, reveals an exception, which permits colleges to release students' educational records to "other school officials, including teachers within the educational institution . . . who have been determined by such . . . institution to have legitimate educational interests, including the educational interests of the [student] for whom consent would otherwise be required."[100] This means that even if students' grades and course selections are "education records" and not "directory information" within the meaning of FERPA, college registrars may disclose them to a committee of the faculty senate or to members of a college-sports reform group within the faculty who have a "legitimate educational interest" in these records, namely, a desire to see if athletes at their school are being educated. Alternatively, if grades and course selections, absent the students' names, are merely "directory information," there is nothing in FERPA that prevents their disclosure to the public.

These conclusions are consistent with court decisions that have held that education records, or information derived from them, can be disclosed to parties other than the students whose records are involved and their parents in a manner that minimizes the intrusion into student privacy, such as by disclosing only those records that pertain to a certain time period, by redacting names and other personally identifiable information, or by presenting the information in a summary statistical form.[101] Jon Ericson's proposal satisfies these criteria because it would present the pertinent information in a summary statistical form without students' names. The proposal would identify professors who teach athletes each semester, but FERPA protects the privacy of students only; it does not protect professors' privacy.[102] Even under the more restrictive interpretation of FERPA, then, whereby students' grades and course selections are "education records," the Ericson proposal complies with the law.

Thus, the participation model will demand personal responsibility from coaches and athletes by holding them accountable for inappropriate conduct and for academic shenanigans. Suspensions of accused athletes and coaches, pending the resolution of disciplinary or judicial proceedings, will prevent college officials from prolonging these proceedings for athletic purposes. The disclosure of athletes' course selections and grades will prevent colleges from prostituting their academic integrity for athletic purposes with impunity.

5. Promote lifetime sports.

The excesses that plague college sports flow in part from Americans' addiction to *watching* sports. This addiction is part of a sedentary lifestyle that contributes to an epidemic of obesity in this country, which, in turn, results in a variety of diseases and shortened life spans. According to Secretary of Health and Human Services (HHS) Tommy Thompson, "overweight and obesity are among the most pressing new health challenges we face today. Our modern environment has allowed these conditions to increase at alarming rates and become a growing health problem for our nation."[103] Similarly, Surgeon General David Satcher has observed that "overweight and obesity may soon cause as much preventable disease and death as cigarette smoking,"[104] and "could wipe out some of the gains we've made in areas such as heart disease, several forms of cancer, and other chronic health problems."[105]

One of the causes for overweight and obesity is inactivity. Less than one third of Americans satisfy the federal recommendation to engage in at least thirty minutes of moderate physical activity at least five days each week, and 40 percent of American adults engage in no leisure-time physical activity at all.[106] Our schools contribute to this problem, as only one state, Illinois, requires physical education for children and adolescents in grades K–12 and only about one teenager in four nationwide participates in some form of physical education.[107] In 1999, 43 percent of high school students reported that they watched television for two or more hours each day.[108]

The participation model offers a healthy alternative to these trends by encouraging college students to play sports rather than to watch them. It will achieve this purpose in part by de-commercializing football, men's basketball, and women's basketball; reducing roster sizes in football; and eliminating athletic scholarships. These changes will help colleges to distribute their sports dollars among a wider array of varsity (and intramural) teams, thereby enabling more students to participate than can do so today. Colleges should also seek to promote their students' long-term physical and psychological health when they determine the mix of sports to sponsor. A recent study indicates that individuals who are physically active as college seniors will probably be physically active six years after graduation.[109] Accordingly, colleges should sponsor sports that will enable students to be physically active throughout their lives. The mix should include established lifetime sports, such as swimming, skiing, golf, and tennis, and emerging lifetime sports, such as cycling and kayaking. Cycling and kayaking are increasingly popular recreational activities (and Olympic sports) that should become college sports, too. Their opportunity will come when the participation model is in place.

6. Revamp the governance structure in college sports.

Colleges that adopt the participation model deserve a governance structure that reflects their values. It is doubtful that the NCAA can offer such a structure. The association has new leadership, but the early signals indicate that the new leader will hardly be a revolutionary. On October 10, 2002, the NCAA selected Indiana University president Myles Brand as its president and chief executive officer. His term began on January 1, 2003, and will end in 2007.[110] At the news conference announcing his appointment, Dr. Brand indicated that he plans to steer a moderate course that pursues neither more commercialization of college sports nor significantly less. He said: "We want to sustain that very important sense of it being college sports. But I see that as perfectly consistent with broadcast media and the involvement we now have through the large-scale contracts."[111]

Consider also Dr. Brand's record at the University of Oregon during the late 1980s and early 1990s and at Indiana more recently. At Oregon, he opposed faculty-led attempts to de-emphasize big-time sports, and at Indiana, he hired as athletic director Michael McNeeley, who was a top executive of the San Diego Chargers before Brand tapped him to run the Hoosiers' athletic department.[112]

To be sure, colleges that forsake commerce for participation could retain their memberships in the NCAA. They could join Division III, which has been autonomous since 1997, when the association restructured itself, or Division II (also autonomous) could become the new home of larger institutions that adopt the participation model, leaving the small state universities and private liberal-arts colleges in Division III.[113] Either way, these colleges could govern themselves according to the participation model while remaining members of the NCAA. It would be financially beneficial for them to remain in the NCAA because members of Division II receive 4.37 percent of NCAA revenues annually, while members of Division III receive 3.18 percent of those revenues, which support enables both divisions to finance championship events in a variety of sports.[114]

Still, there would be good reasons to leave the NCAA. One reason would be to stop feeding at a trough stocked with the tainted proceeds of commercialized college sports. Division I may become even more commercial in the future because the 1997 restructuring made it autonomous, too. No longer can the members of Divisions II and III vote to curb the insatiable appetites of Division I colleges for new sources of athletic revenue. Beyond that, if colleges that adopt the commercial model establish a new governance association, they could limit its jurisdiction to athletic matters, such as establishing game rules and scheduling postseason championships. Then the regional organizations that are part of the American Council on Education (ACE) and that conduct periodic accreditation reviews of colleges nationwide could govern academic matters related to sports and could withdraw the accreditation of any college where the athletic department fails to follow ACE guidelines relative to sports.[115]

This change could probably not occur within the NCAA because it would likely be seen as an association-wide matter that requires the approval of the Executive Committee, the NCAA's top governing body. Most of the members of the Executive Committee represent Division I, and would presumably oppose restricting NCAA power over academics, even in Division III.[116] Besides, history counsels against trusting the NCAA on this issue. In 1951 a panel of college presidents appointed by the ACE attempted to make this change, but the NCAA, aided by the defection of the panel's chair, blocked it.[117] Thus, the best way for colleges that adopt the participation model to ensure that their national governing body embraces their values would be to leave the NCAA and to create a new governance structure that fits a new model of college sports.

A COLLISION COURSE

College sports cannot continue on their present course indefinitely. Colleges must meet the financial challenges that result from Title IX and from the ever-increasing cost of big-time sports. Even if the Department of Education makes it easier to comply with Title IX, most Division I colleges will struggle to fund sports programs for men and women. Meanwhile, the growing pressure to generate revenue from football and basketball ensures that negative academic and social consequences will persist. According to Murray Sperber, two options are available: college sports can either "move closer to pro sports than ever before" in search of more revenue or educators can "draw clear boundaries that mark them as a part of higher education."[118] To draw clear boundaries is the preferred option. It requires taking advantage of the opportunity that Title IX offers to replace the commercial model with the participation model. This change is long overdue. Chapter 8 will show how colleges can make it happen.

NOTES

1. John Feinstein, *The Last Amateurs: Playing for Glory and Honor in Division I College Basketball* (Boston: Little, Brown and Company, 2000), pp. xxii–xxiii.
2. American University joined the Patriot League after the publication of

The Last Amateurs, and began competing for conference championships in the fall of 2001. *See* Welch Suggs, "The Patriot League's Grand Experiment," *The Chronicle of Higher Education*, March 9, 2002, pp. A40–A41.

3. Welch Suggs, "The Patriot League's Grand Experiment," *The Chronicle of Higher Education*, March 29, 2002, pp. A40–A41. A standard deviation is a measure of how far a particular score is above or below the mean (or average) score in a distribution. One standard deviation above the mean contains 34 percent of the scores in the distribution, as does one standard deviation below the mean. Consequently, assuming a normal bell-curved distribution in which 50 percent of the scores are clustered at the mean, a student whose academic-index score is one standard deviation below the mean of his class would rank below 84 percent of the students in the class. A student whose academic-index score is two standard deviations below the mean of her class would rank below 98 percent of the students in her class. Remember, though, that the colleges in the Patriot League are selective in their admissions, so that a student who ranks at or near the bottom of the class at Colgate or Holy Cross is probably capable of doing adequate, if unspectacular, academic work and of graduating in four years. This is not necessarily true at less competitive colleges that belong to Division I.

4. Brian L. Porto, *Completing the Revolution: Title IX as Catalyst for an Alternative Model of College Sports*, 8, no. 2 Seton Hall Journal of Sport Law 351, 400 (1998).

5. NCAA Constitution, Article 1.3.1, Basic Purpose, reprinted in NCAA, *2002–03 NCAA Division I Manual* (Michael V. Earle, ed., 2002), p. 1.

6. James L. Shulman and William G. Bowen, *The Game of Life: College Sports and Educational Values* (Princeton, N.J.: Princeton University Press, 2001), p. 33.

7. Ibid., p. 58.

8. Edward B. Fiske, "Gaining Admission: Athletes Win Preference," *The New York Times*, "Education Life," January 7, 2001, p. 22.

9. Ibid.

10. Williams College Ad Hoc Faculty Committee on Athletics, *Report on Varsity Athletics* (June 2002) [located at http://www.williams.edu].

11. Welch Suggs, "Tipping the Athletic Scale," *The Chronicle of Higher Education*, March 8, 2002, pp. A37–A39.

12. Welch Suggs, "Swarthmore Kicks Football Out of the College," *The Chronicle of Higher Education*, December 15, 2000, pp. A55–A56.

13. Allen L. Sack, "Big-Time Athletics vs. Academic Values: It's a Rout," *The Chronicle of Higher Education*, January 26, 2001, pp. B7–B10.

14. Ibid.

15. "Sidelines," *The Chronicle of Higher Education*, March 29, 2002, p. A40. *See also* Gordon Witkin and Jodi Schneider, "Special Report: College Sports," *U.S. News and World Report*, March 18, 2002, pp. 50–71.

16. "Sidelines," *The Chronicle of Higher Education*, March 29, 2002, p. A40.

17. John R. Gerdy, "Facing Up to the Conflict Between Athletics and Academics," *Priorities*, 16 (Summer 2001): 1–14.

18. Brian L. Porto, *Completing the Revolution: Title IX as Catalyst for an Alternative Model of College Sports*, 8, no. 2 Seton Hall Journal of Sport Law 351, 400–401 (1998), citing Jeffrey H. Orleans, *The Ivy League as a Model for Intercollegiate Athletics*, a paper presented at the Princeton University 250th Anniversary Symposium on the Academy and Intercollegiate Athletics (November 22, 1996), p. 9.

19. Ibid.

20. Michael Reynolds, *Hemingway: The Homecoming* (New York: W.W. Norton & Company, 1999), p. 11.

21. Brian L. Porto, *Completing the Revolution: Title IX as Catalyst for an Alternative Model of College Sports* 8, no. 2 Seton Hall Journal of Sport Law 351, 401 (1998).

22. James J. Duderstadt, *Intercollegiate Athletics and the American University: A University President's Perspective* (Ann Arbor, Mich.: The University of Michigan Press, 2000), p. 293.

23. Ibid., p. 291.

24. John C. Weistart, *Can Gender Equity Find a Place in Commercialized College Sports?* 3 Duke Journal of Gender Law & Policy 191, 198, n. 21 (Spring 1996).

25. Ibid., pp. 197–198, n. 20.

26. John R. Gerdy, *The Successful College Athletic Program: The New Standard* (Phoenix: Oryx Press, 1997), p. 6.

27. Edwin H. Cady, *The Big Game: College Sports and American Life* (Knoxville: University of Tennessee Press, 1978), p. 233.

28. Ibid.

29. *Title IX Impact on Women's Participation in Intercollegiate Athletics and Gender Equity: Hearing Before the Subcommittee on Commerce, Consumer Protection, and Competitiveness of the House of Representatives Committee on Energy and Commerce*, 103rd Cong., 1st Sess. 33 (February 17, 1993) (Testimony of Thomas K. Hearn, Jr.).

30. Walter Byers, *Unsportsmanlike Conduct: Exploiting College Athletes* (Ann Arbor, Mich.: The University of Michigan Press, 1995), pp. 338–339.

31. Ibid., p. 132.

32. Ibid., pp. 338–339.

33. Ibid.

34. Frank Deford, Speech to National Press Club Luncheon, Washington, D.C., September 5, 2002.

35. Ibid.

36. John R. Gerdy, ed., *Sports in School: The Future of an Institution* (New York: Teachers College Press, 2000), p. 49.

37. Murray Sperber, *Beer and Circus: How Big-Time College Sports Is Crippling Undergraduate Education* (New York: Henry Holt and Company, 2000), p. 255.

38. Brian L. Porto, *Completing the Revolution: Title IX as Catalyst for an Alternative Model of College Sports* 8, no. 2 Seton Hall Journal of Sport Law 351, 403 (1998).

39. Jeffrey H. Orleans, "The Ivy League as a Model for Intercollegiate Athletics," (paper presented at the Princeton University 250th Anniversary Symposium on the Academy and Intercollegiate Athletics, November 22, 1996), p. 4.

40. Gordon Witkin and Jodi Schneider, "Special Report: College Sports," *U.S. News and World Report*, March 18, 2002, pp. 50–71.

41. Ibid.

42. Jeffrey H. Orleans, "The Ivy League as a Model for Intercollegiate Athletics," (paper presented at the Princeton University 250th Anniversary Symposium on the Academy and Intercollegiate Athletics, November 22, 1996), p. 16.

43. Ibid., p. 4.

44. *See* John R. Gerdy, "Hold That Line," *Trusteeship* (September/October 1998): 18–22.

45. James H. Frey, "Deviance of Organizational Subunits: The Case of College Athletic Departments," *Journal of Sport and Social Issues*, 18 (1994): 110–122.

46. Ibid., p. 113.

47. Gerdy, *The Successful College Athletic Program*, p. 129.

48. Brian L. Porto, *Completing the Revolution: Title IX as Catalyst for an Alternative Model of College Sports* 8, no. 2 Seton Hall Journal of Sport Law 351, 405–06 (1998).

49. Ibid. at 406.

50. James H. Frey, "Deviance of Organizational Subunits: The Case of College Athletic Departments," *The Journal of Sport & Social Issues* 18 (1994): 110–122.

51. Ibid., p. 118.

52. Gerdy, *The Successful College Athletic Program*, p. 100.

53. Ibid., p. 66.

54. James J. Duderstadt, *Intercollegiate Athletics and the American University*, p. 270. *See also* Ray Yasser, *A Comprehensive Blueprint for the Reform of Intercollegiate Athletics*, 3, no. 2 Marquette Sports Law Journal 123, 150 (Spring 1993).

55. Wilford S. Bailey and Taylor D. Middleton, *Athletics and Academe: An Anatomy of Abuses and a Prescription for Reform* (New York: The American Council on Education and Macmillan Publishing Company, 1991), p. 83.

56. Ray Yasser, *A Comprehensive Blueprint for the Reform of Intercollegiate Athletics*, 3, no. 2 Marquatte Sports Law Journal 123, 149 (Spring 1993).

57. Jim Naughton, "In Division III, College Sports Thrive With Few Fans and Even Fewer Scandals," *The Chronicle of Higher Education*, November 21, 1997, pp. A41–A42.

58. Brian L. Porto, *Completing the Revolution: Title IX as Catalyst for an Alternative Model of College Sports* 8, no. 2 Seton Hall Journal of Sport Law 351, 407 (1998).

59. Ibid., pp. 143–144.

60. Texas Tech basketball coach Bob Knight was the subject of criticism earlier in this book, but he deserves credit for his critique of freshman eligibility. In Knight's view, "freshman eligibility is a mistake and has contributed enormously to some of today's biggest problems—proliferation of the tout sheets that put a rating on every kid in America, newspaper[s'] and talk shows' preoccupation with recruiting, the high transfer rate of recruited players, the intrusion of shoe companies into recruiting. Give a player a year out of the spotlight, to adjust from high school hype to college reality, and it would be amazing how many pressures would ease." Bob Knight and Bob Hammel, *Knight: My Story* (St. Martin's Press, 2002), p. 304.

61. James Duderstadt has suggested limiting the competitive season for each sport to one academic term. *See* Duderstadt, *Intercollegiate Athletics and the American University*, p. 301. That is probably impractical to do because it would compress the basketball and hockey seasons excessively, but it is certainly possible to limit these seasons to the length of one academic semester.

62. James J. Duderstadt, *Intercollegiate Athletics and the American University*, p. 298.

63. Gerdy, *The Successful College Athletic Program*, p. 76.

64. Ibid., p. 151.

65. Walter Byers, *Unsportsmanlike Conduct: Exploiting College Athletes* (Ann Arbor, Mich.: The University of Michigan Press, 1995), p. 99.

66. *Title IX Impact on Women's Participation in Intercollegiate Athletics and Gender Equity: Hearing Before the Subcommittee on Commerce, Consumer Protection, and Competitiveness of the House of Representatives Committee on Energy and Commerce*, 103rd Cong, 1st Sess. 30–31 (February 17, 1993) (Testimony of Grant Teaff).

67. Lee Sigelman and Paul J. Wahlbeck, "Gender Proportionality in Intercollegiate Athletics: The Mathematics of Title IX Compliance," *Social Science Quarterly* 80, no. 3 (September 1999): 518–538.

68. Brian L. Porto, *Completing the Revolution: Title IX as Catalyst for an Alternative Model of College Sports* 8, no. 2 Seton Hall Journal of Sport Law 351, 408 (1998).

69. Welch Suggs, "Hoop Dreams Without College," *The Chronicle of Higher Education*, April 13, 2001, p. A52.

70. Ibid.

71. Brian L. Porto, *Completing the Revolution: Title IX as Catalyst for an Alternative Model of College Sports* 8, no. 2 Seton Hall Journal of Sport Law 351, 408, n. 329 (1998). *See also* Jim Naughton, "A New Ice Age? College Hockey Hopes for a Surge in Popularity," *The Chronicle of Higher Education*, March 7, 1997, p. A40.

72. Brian L. Porto, *Completing the Revolution: Title IX as Catalyst for an Alternative Model of College Sports* 8, no. 2 Seton Hall Journal of Sport Law 351, 408 (1998).

73. U.S. Department of Education, Office of Civil Rights, *Clarification of Intercollegiate Athletics Policy Guidance: The Three-Part Test* (Washington, D.C.: Government Printing Office, 1996), p. 4.

74. Julia Lamber, *Gender and Intercollegiate Athletics: Data and Myths* 34, nos. 1 & 2 University of Michigan Journal of Law Reform 151, 202 (Fall 2000 and Winter 2001). *See also* Lynette Labinger, *Title IX and Athletics: A Discussion of Brown University v. Cohen by Plaintiffs' Counsel*, 20, no. 2/3 Women's Rights Law Reporter 85, 87 (Spring/Summer 1999).

75. U.S. Department of Education, Office of Civil Rights, *Clarification of Intercollegiate Athletics Policy Guidance: The Three-Part Test* (Washington, D.C.: Government Printing Office, 1996), p. 5.

76. Ibid.

77. 20 USC §1681(b).

78. *Cohen v. Brown University*, 101 F.3d 155, 171 (1st Cir. 1996), *cert. denied*, 520 U.S. 1186 (1997).

79. Deborah Brake and Elizabeth Catlin, *The Path of Most Resistance: The Long Road Toward Gender Equity in Intercollegiate Athletics*, 3 Duke Journal of Gender Law & Policy 51, 85–86 (Spring 1996).

80. *See, e.g.*, Walter B. Connolly and Jeffrey D. Adelman, *A University's Defense to a Title IX Gender Equity in Athletics Lawsuit: Congress Never Intended Gender Equity Based on Student Body Ratios*, 71 University of Detroit Mercy Law Review 845, 882 (1994).

81. *Cohen v. Brown University*, 101 F.3d 155, 176 (1st Cir. 1996), *cert. denied*, 520 U.S. 1186 (1997).

82. Brian L. Porto, *Completing the Revolution: Title IX as Catalyst for an Al-*

ternative Model of College Sports 8, no. 2 Seton Hall Journal of Sport Law 351, 410 (1998).

83. Welch Suggs, "Education Dep't. Offers U. of New Mexico Another Way to Comply With Title IX," *The Chronicle of Higher Education*, May 5, 2000, p. A53.

84. At this writing, in May of 2003, it is not clear which option UNM has chosen. According to Janice Ruggiero, senior woman administrator in UNM's athletic department, "the case has not been resolved," and the university does not intend to disclose its compliance plan until a resolution is achieved. *Email Message to the Author, May 8, 2003. See also* "Commitment to Resolve University of New Mexico Case Number 08992199," Posted May 1, 2000 [available at http://chronicle.com/weekly/documents/v46/i35/4635newmexico.htm].

85. Welch Suggs, "Education Dep't. Offers U. of New Mexico Another Way to Comply with Title IX," *The Chronicle of Higher Education*, May 5, 2000, p. A53.

86. U.S. General Accounting Office, Report to Congressional Requesters, *Intercollegiate Athletics: Four-Year Colleges' Experiences Adding and Discontinuing Teams* (Washington, D.C.: Government Printing Office, 2001), p. 4.

87. Ibid., p. 14.

88. Ibid.

89. B. Glenn George, *Who Plays and Who Pays: Defining Equality in Intercollegiate Athletics*, 1995 Wisconsin Law Review 647, 663–664 (1995).

90. Currently, the Title IX regulations that govern intercollegiate athletics require every college that awards athletic scholarships to achieve substantial proportionality between the percentage of each gender among its athletes and the percentage of its athletic-scholarship budget that it awards to members of each gender. In this case, substantial proportionality means a difference of no more than 1 percent in either direction. Therefore, if women are 42 percent of the athletes at a college that awards athletic scholarships, women athletes must receive between 41 percent and 43 percent of the athletic-scholarship budget in order for the college to comply with Title IX regarding athletic scholarships. *Letter from Dr. Mary Frances O'Shea, National Coordinator for Title IX Athletics, U.S. Department of Education, Office of Civil Rights to Ms. Nancy S. Footer, General Counsel, Bowling Green State University*, July 23, 1998, p. 4.

91. Welch Suggs, "Bob Knight Survives to Coach Another Day," *The Chronicle of Higher Education*, May 26, 2000, p. A58.

92. For an argument in favor of suspending the athletic scholarships of accused college athletes, *see* Jeffrey Benedict, *Public Heroes, Private Felons: Athletes and Crimes Against Women* (Boston: Northeastern University Press, 1997), p. 224.

93. *Remarks by Jon Ericson Before the Knight Foundation Commission on Intercollegiate Athletics*, Willard Hotel, Washington, D.C., October 18, 2000, p. 5.

94. 20 U.S.C. § 1092(e).

95. 20 U.S.C. § 1092(g).

96. Bill Bradley, "The View From the Hill," in Bruce I. Mallette and Richard D. Howard, eds., *Monitoring and Assessing Intercollegiate Athletics* (San Francisco: Jossey-Bass Publishers, 1992), p. 14.

97. *Remarks by Jon Ericson Before the Knight Foundation Commission on Intercollegiate Athletics*, Willard Hotel, Washington, D.C., October 18, 2000, p. 8.

98. 20 U.S.C. § 1232g.

99. 20 U.S.C. 1232g(b)(1).

100. 20 U.S.C. 1232g(b)(1)(A).

101. John E. Theuman, *Validity, Construction, and Application of Family Educational Rights and Privacy Act of 1974*, 112 American Law Reports, Federal 1, 39 (1993).

102. Ibid., p. 26.

103. U.S. Department of Health and Human Services, "Overweight and Obesity Threaten U.S. Health Gains," *HHS News*, December 13, 2001, p. 1 [available at www.hhs.gov/news].

104. Ibid.

105. Ibid., p. 2.

106. Ibid., p. 1.

107. Ibid., p. 2.

108. Ibid.

109. P. B. Sparling and T.K. Snow, "Physical Activity Patterns in Recent College Alumni," *Research Quarterly for Exercise and Sport* 73 (2002): 200–205.

110. Joe LaPointe, "NCAA Selects Indiana's Brand as Its New Chief," *The New York Times*, October 11, 2002 [available at http://www.nytimes.com/2002/10/11/sports/ncaabasketball/11NCAA.html?ex=1035336232&en=dc4d478872].

111. Mark Alesia, "Brand Plans No Overhaul for the NCAA," *The Indianapolis Star*, October 12, 2002 [available at mark.alesia@indystar.com].

112. Murray Sperber, "Will Its New President Bring Real Reform to the NCAA?" *The Chronicle of Higher Education*, October 25, 2002, p. B20.

113. Welch Suggs, "NCAA's New Structure Finds Fans and Foes Among Sports Officials," *The Chronicle of Higher Education*, October 25, 2002, p. B20.

114. Andrew Zimbalist, *Unpaid Professionals: Commercialism and Conflict in Big-Time College Sports* (Princeton, NJ: Princeton University Press, 1999), p. 193.

115. These organizations include the New England, Middle States, North Central, Southern, and Northwest associations of schools and colleges, respectively.

116. Information about the governance structure of the NCAA is available at http://www.ncaa.org/membership/governance.

117. Murray Sperber, *Onward To Victory: The Crises That Shaped College Sports* (New York: Henry Holt & Company, 1998), p. 371.

118. Murray Sperber, "Will Its New President Bring Real Reform to the NCAA?" *The Chronicle of Higher Education*, October 25, 2002, p. B20.

CHAPTER 8

THE NEW SEASON BEGINS

IMPLEMENTING THE PARTICIPATION MODEL

SHORT-TERM PROSPECTS, LONG-TERM GOALS

A popular pastime among academic critics of the existing system in college sports is envisioning the future of college football and basketball. Two alternative visions emerge from this stargazing. One vision is of these games as openly professional and played by athletes who would represent colleges on the field and court, but who would not be required to be students, too. Proponents of this view argue that open professionalism is the only viable alternative to the existing system because Division I colleges, their fans, and sports journalists will not accept a truly amateur system of college sports, such as the participation model represents. Robert Atwell, the president emeritus of the American Council on Education (ACE), is a veteran observer of college sports who envisions their future in this way. He has written:

> It is hopeless to imagine that big-time college sports will ever return to the amateur student-athlete model for which we are so nostalgic. The commercial interests are too powerful, and the booster fanaticism is too overwhelming for any lonely band of university presidents—usually unsupported by their boards or faculty and opposed by alumni and other fans—to overcome them.[1]

Consequently, Atwell argues that big-time sports colleges should free their football and basketball players from academic responsibilities, pay them a "market wage," and then use any profits that they earn to support academic programs and/or non-revenue sports.[2]

James Loughran, the president of St. Peter's College in New Jersey, has endorsed neither open professionalism nor the participation model, but he has urged colleges to choose between these two options instead of continuing to cloak their semiprofessional teams in a thin veil of amateurism. He has written:

> Colleges should either embrace commercialization, . . . or, right now, get out of the business of big-time sports. Why stall another five or seven years until the next Knight Commission pronouncement? If history is our teacher, we only prolong the agony as things deteriorate not just in the athletics arena but throughout our colleges.[3]

Together, the comments of Dr. Atwell and President Loughran present the options that are available for the future of college sports. They also suggest, correctly, that either option would be preferable to the existing system because both alternatives are financially and academically honest, whereas the existing system drips with financial and academic hypocrisy. Still, although honesty may be the best policy, it should not be the only policy that guides college sports. The participation model is as honest as open professionalism is, but unlike professionalism, participation would also bring fiscal sanity, gender equity, and personal responsibility to college sports. Moreover, contrary to Dr. Atwell's grim prediction, the prospects for the widespread adoption of the participation model are hardly "hopeless."

At first blush, it may seem that the widespread adoption of the participation model would require a revolutionary change in Americans' attitudes toward college sports. Still, if the adoption of the participation model represents a revolution in college sports, it will require the reformation that precedes and assists revolutionary change. In 1989 legendary community organizer Saul Alinsky wrote that no revolution could succeed without "the supporting base of a popular reformation."[4] A reformation occurs when large numbers of people become disillusioned with old values and old ways of doing things. They are uncertain of how to change the political, economic, or social conditions that have caused their disillusionment, but they know that "the prevailing system is self-defeating, frustrating, and hopeless."[5] They do not become activists for change, but neither do they oppose their fellow citizens who do. At this point, according to Alinsky, "[t]he time is ripe for revolution."[6]

In college sports the time is not yet ripe for revolution in Division I-A. Disillusionment is growing, but it is concentrated in college faculties and among a small number of journalists. It lacks the critical mass necessary even for reformation, let alone revolution. Under these circumstances, it would be naïve to expect that athletically prominent colleges would adopt the participation model soon. In college sports, as in international politics, unilateral disarmament is unlikely because the entity that disarms will face annihilation by rivals that remain armed.[7] Still, Dr. Atwell overstates his case when he argues that the prospects for true amateurism in college sports are hopeless.

On the contrary, these prospects are bright in conferences in which teams lose money on sports and hardly ever play on television. These conferences should be the first targets of efforts to replace commerce with participation because, as Alinsky learned, a revolution is more likely to succeed when it begins by attacking the most vulnerable targets available.[8]

In other words, it is unlikely that the Big Ten or the SEC will adopt the participation model soon, because several members of each of those conferences are financially successful in sports, and because athletic success is a major component of the public images of those colleges. On the other hand, the Big West, Western Athletic, Sun Belt, and Mid-American conferences, the members of which lose money on sports, and the Mountain West Conference, most of the members of which barely make a profit, might well replace commerce with participation sooner rather than later.[9] Recruiting costs are high for colleges located in the sparsely populated Mountain West because the recruits live far away, mostly in Texas and California, and because scholarships must cover the cost of nonresident tuition. Major television markets are also far away, and the natural environment offers many recreational alternatives to attending college games.

Participation may also replace commerce sooner rather than later at academically rigorous private colleges in Division I-A, such as Rice, Southern Methodist, Vanderbilt, Tulane, Wake Forest, and Northwestern because (1) their high tuition costs make athletic scholarships expensive, (2) they do not need athletic success in order to achieve a favorable public image, (3) they do not have to appeal to sports-loving state legislators for financial support, and (4) their teams are usually mediocre or even weak in football and basketball. If these colleges adopt the participation model, they will probably attract fewer athletes than less expensive state colleges, but they could adjust by severing their current conference ties in favor of playing games against members of the Ivy League and the Patriot League, and against each other. Then, with the state universities of the Mountain West and many of the smaller, private colleges having adopted the participation model, only colleges for which commercialized sports are both a financial success and a cultural necessity would retain the commercial model. Their number would shrink gradually because minor leagues in football and basketball would absorb the best college-age players, making college sports less profitable over time.[10]

If it is unwise for Idaho, New Mexico State, and Rice, which play football in Division I-A, to follow the commercial model of college sports, it is patently ridiculous for the College of William & Mary and Oklahoma Panhandle State University, which play football in Division I-AA and Division II, respectively, to do so. Neither William & Mary nor Panhandle State, nor any other Division I-AA or Division II college, for that matter, earns a profit from sports, yet they sacrifice their academic programs and tarnish their institutional reputations in order to fund athletic scholarships and to keep academically deficient athletes eligible to compete. William & Mary, an academically competitive public institution that dates to colonial times, was in the news at the end of 2002. Together with fifteen sister institutions in Virginia's state college system, it announced that tuition for 2003–04 would rise by 16 percent in order to help offset a projected budget shortfall.[11] William & Mary will make some budget cuts, too, but not in the athletic department, which each student supports with an $885 annual fee, whether or not he or she plays a sport or attends a game. This amount is part of a twenty-six-hundred-dollar "required annual fee" that each student pays to support not only the athletic department but also recreational programs and the student health service.[12]

It is reasonable to expect students to help support recreational activities and medical services. Together, these entities promote physical, mental, and emotional well-being, and all or almost all students will use either or both of them while attending college. It is unreasonable, though, to expect students and their taxpaying parents to support an athletic department at a state college that clings to a commercial model of sports even though it loses money on them, including $300,000 on football in 2001.[13] Perhaps the financial officers at William & Mary bury the athletics fee in the larger "required annual fee" because they sense that if students and parents knew how much they paid every year to support an unprofitable athletic department, they would object. In any event, William & Mary and the rest of Division I-AA should recognize that if they can't play with the big guys, they should start playing with the smart guys by abandoning commerce in favor of participation. William & Mary could do this, according to Professor William Dowling of Rutgers, by joining with Rutgers, James Madison, and the Universities of Massachusetts, Delaware, New Hampshire, and Rhode Island to form the "Independence League," a nonscholarship state-university equivalent of the Patriot League.[14] William & Mary *should* do this, as should athletically marginal Division I colleges across America.

Panhandle State has more reason than William & Mary to try to make a name for itself through sports, as it cannot claim any Founding Fathers as graduates, and its location lacks the cachet of Colonial Williamsburg. On the other hand, Panhandle State has far fewer financial resources than William & Mary has to support an ambitious athletic enterprise, as became evident late in 2002. The Division II Committee on Infractions, citing a "severe lack of institutional control" at the Oklahoma school, put Panhandle State on probation for five years and eliminated 2.5 athletic scholarships for violations of NCAA rules. The violations included allowing athletes who did not meet NCAA academic-eligibility standards to practice, compete, and receive athletic scholarships and allowing athletes who were on academic probation to enjoy the same privileges. According to the committee's report, a principal reason for these violations is that Panhandle State "seems to lack the financial resources to hire and retain qualified personnel to administer its athletics department."[15] As a consequence of low salaries, the report continued, "[t]he athletics administration and coaching staffs have been caught in a virtual 'revolving door' of turnover in the past seven years, which makes it very difficult to establish any degree of consistency in terms of policies and procedures."[16] Therefore, the report concluded, "[u]nless the university can devote greater resources to the administration of its athletics department, . . . [it should] reassess its ability to compete at the NCAA Division II level."[17]

More precisely, it should abandon athletic scholarships and adopt the participation model, which would enable it to pay its coaches higher salaries, improve compliance with NCAA rules, and perhaps even offer more than the four sports for men and four sports for women that it offers now. Alternatively, it should offer only intramural sports and outdoor recreation until it can muster the resources to sponsor intercollegiate teams. Either alternative would allow it to build a reputation for something other than overreaching or mismanagement in athletics.

Thus, the short-term prospects for the participation model are best among the marginal members of Division I-A and in Divisions I-AA and II. Nevertheless, its long-term goal must be to supplant the commercial model among the members of the six major athletic conferences, the so-called equity conferences. This goal may seem to be a pipe dream now because the members of these conferences face less financial pressure from Title IX than athletically marginal colleges do, and they enjoy a favorable public image because of their athletic success. Still, there are good reasons to believe that in the long term, most of today's Division I (including I-A) colleges will adopt the participation model. One reason, as chapter 3 demonstrated, is that athletic success does not guarantee profitability. Recall that even though its football team won the Rose Bowl in 1998, the University of Michigan's athletic department incurred a $2.8 million operating deficit in 1998–99.[18] Second, the steadily increasing price of remaining in the big time could well reduce the number of colleges willing to pay that price in the future. The third reason why participation may trump commerce in college sports in the long term is that there are market forces at work today that will make it difficult, even for athletically successful colleges, to maintain big-time sports programs in the future.

MARKET FORCES FOR CHANGE

Economic conditions will make big-time college sports increasingly expensive to operate in the coming years, thereby expanding the gap between rich and poor colleges and pressuring the latter to abandon athletic commerce. For example, there is growing pressure on colleges to pay athletes who participate in revenue-producing sports. One commentator has proposed that colleges pay $150 per month to athletic-scholarship recipients in football and men's basketball and to a comparable number of athletic-scholarship recipients in women's sports. In his view the underlying premise of such payments would be that "the concept of amateurism, a cornerstone of the NCAA, is essentially a sham due to the commercial nature of the end product."[19] Another proposal is for colleges to incorporate into their athletic scholarships, which now cover tuition, fees, room, board, and course-related books, a fixed amount (e.g., $100 per month) in "laundry money," which athletes could use for incidental expenses.[20] This proposal resurrects an old concept and applies it to the modern context, as athletic scholarships originally included $15 per month in laundry money. The Collegiate Athletes' Coalition (CAC), a Los Angeles–based advocacy group for college athletes, adds that colleges should not only reimburse revenue-generating athletes for their routine out-of-pocket expenses, ranging from laundry to transportation, but should also provide them with health insurance coverage for injuries sustained during off-season training and "voluntary" workouts with their teammates.[21] The CAC also wants the NCAA to remove the $2,000 cap that it places on the amount of money that college athletes can earn from employment during the academic year.

These proposals share one common feature; namely, they would add to the cost of maintaining big-time college sports teams at a time when most colleges, even in Division I-A, do not earn a profit from sports. Moreover, several of these proposals have legal implications that could increase the price tag on big-time college sports by far more than the cost of a monthly stipend or a health insurance premium. For example, if the NCAA decides to permit colleges to pay stipends to athletic-scholarship recipients, it is likely that in many, if not most, states, the athletes who receive stipends would become employees of the colleges that they attend. This status would make them eligible to receive workers' compensation benefits for injuries that they sustain in practice or in competition.[22] It would also increase the premium that a college would have to pay to its state's workers' compensation fund because the fund would be expected to pay benefits to injured athletes in addition to injured faculty and staff members.

Beyond becoming eligible for workers' compensation, college athletes who receive a stipend would be the legal equivalents of graduate teaching assistants, whom the National Labor Relations Board (NLRB) has recognized to be employees of the colleges where they study and work.[23] Under these circumstances colleges would have to pay social security taxes for their athletes, who would have a powerful incentive to unionize and to demand the right to bargain collectively with their employers. Admittedly, just because the NLRB has recognized graduate teaching assistants as college employees does not mean that it would treat college athletes in the same way, even if they receive stipends. Tulane University law professor Gary Roberts has observed that "[c]ollege sports are so ingrained in society that we refuse to give up the ghost of that [amateur athlete] myth. To declare [college athletes] employees would be an assault on an institution that would cause such a hue and cry that it probably would never go through."[24] Moreover, the NLRB is likely to be more susceptible than a court would be to political pressure not to designate college athletes employees because the president appoints (and may reappoint) its members to five-year terms.[25] Still, it is impossible to predict with perfect accuracy what the NLRB would do in a hypothetical case, so the NCAA will take a risk if it approves the payment of stipends to college athletes.

Another aspect of this risk is the potential for colleges that employ athletes to be held legally responsible for injuries resulting from negligent or reckless behavior by athletes that occurs within the scope of their athletic employment. The law recognizes that a "master-servant" relationship exists between an employer and an employee. It holds the master accountable, under the principle of "respondeat superior," for the injurious consequences of the servant's negligent or reckless acts if those acts occur while the employee is on the job and serving the master.[26] In the college-sports context, the most likely scenarios that could lead to institutional liability for the acts of an athlete would involve injuries resulting from fights between athletes during practice or competition, or in the locker room; fights between athletes and fans during competition; or from a violation of game rules, such as a "late hit" in football.

Colleges would probably avoid the adverse legal implications of paying athletes a stipend by adopting the laundry money alternative discussed above. It would be expensive to adopt this proposal, though. If colleges add $100 per month, or $900 per academic year, to their athletic scholarships, they must pay this amount not only to athletes in revenue sports (i.e., football and men's basketball) but also to a comparable number of female athletes, or they will violate Title IX. Therefore, a Division I-A college with eighty-five football players and thirteen men's basketball players on scholarship could have to pay $900 per athlete per year to approximately two hundred athletes, for a total of almost $180,000 per year. An additional expense of this size would be problematic for colleges that barely break even or that lose money on sports now. The total would be smaller if colleges could award stipends proportionally by gender (e.g., to 30 percent of the male athletes and 30 percent of the female athletes), but it would still be sizable.

Questions of fairness would also arise, such as which women athletes would receive the spending money if no women's sport earned a profit. Another open question is whether athletes in revenue sports would merit these funds in years when their teams do not earn a profit. The answer would seem to be no if the premise of awarding spending money is that athletes who earn profits for their colleges ought to share in those profits, at least in some minimal way. Thus, even the laundry money proposal to pay college athletes is fraught with problems, not the least of which is that it would increase the cost of sponsoring big-time sports teams considerably.

Whether or not colleges opt to pay their athletes, and in whatever form they might choose to do so, other costs of big-time college sports are certain to increase. For example, the recent flood of underclassmen to the NBA has increased the cost to colleges of recruiting basketball players. In 1980 only seven college basketball players left school early to enter the NBA draft, but by 1999 twenty-nine players did so.[27] Under these conditions, coaches must recruit more new players every year because they can no longer rely on the services of star players for four years.

The cost to colleges of hiring basketball coaches has also increased in the wake of a federal court decision in 1998 that prohibits colleges from employing "restricted earnings" coaches in basketball. In *Law v. NCAA*,[28] a federal appellate court affirmed the decision of a federal trial court that held that an NCAA regulation limiting certain college basketball coaches to "restricted earnings" of no more than $16,000 annually violated section 1 of the Sherman Antitrust Act, which prohibits "restraints of trade," such as price-fixing and limitations on production.[29] The NCAA regulation, which was known as the "restricted earnings rule," limited basketball coaching staffs at Division I colleges to four members, including the head coach, two assistant coaches, and one restricted-earnings coach (REC), who could earn no more than $12,000 from coaching during the academic year and $4,000 during the summer.[30] It was designed to reduce rapidly increasing personnel costs in big-time college basketball.

Unfortunately for the NCAA, its lawyers could not convince either the trial court or the appellate court that the restricted-earnings rule would contain costs, because there was nothing in the rule to prevent colleges from using the money saved on the salary of the REC to increase the salaries of their other basketball coaches. At the same time, the rule was "anti-competitive," pursuant to the Sherman Act, because it interfered with, and reduced, economic competition among basketball coaches looking for work and among colleges looking for coaches by reducing the price of an assistant coach artificially. These flaws proved to be costly for the NCAA, which, in April of 1999, paid the plaintiffs, who were RECs at Division I colleges during the 1992–93 academic year, $54.5 million to settle the lawsuit.[31] The 310 NCAA member colleges contributed $18.125 million to this amount, and the rest came directly from the association's funds. Even colleges in Divisions II and III, which did not employ RECs, were required to contribute to the settlement fund.[32] Colleges in Division I that did employ them contributed to the fund *and* now pay considerably more money for assistant basketball coaches than they paid prior to the *Law* decision.

The *Law* decision could be a portent of things to come for the NCAA—none of which the association would welcome, but all of which it precipitates by its aggressive commercialism. *Law* is also a break with tradition because for decades the NCAA was immune from judicial scrutiny for possible violations of the Sherman Act. The reason for this informal immunity was the presumption of courts and legal scholars that college sports were amateur activities tied more closely to education than to commerce.[33] This presumption is considerably weaker today than in the past because of plainly commercial behavior by the NCAA, such as moving its men's basketball tournament, including the Final Four, out of campus arenas to larger, metropolitan arenas, where college students are as rare as whooping cranes because they cannot afford to pay the ticket prices.[34] Consequently, if the NCAA continues to act in a way that blurs the difference between college and professional sports, *Law* may turn out to be the opening shot in a long, expensive battle between the NCAA and the antitrust laws. "The more you commercialize what you do," says Professor Roberts of Tulane, "the more you make judges think that antitrust laws apply to you."[35]

The NCAA could be vulnerable to antitrust challenges to its regulations that limit (1) the number of athletic scholarships colleges can award in specific sports; (2) the income that athletes can earn from employment during the academic year; (3) the size of coaching staffs in particular sports; and (4) the expenses that an athletic scholarship can cover.[36] In response, the association must show that the regulation at issue does not restrict economic competition or, at least, that it does not do so unreasonably, as it is needed to ensure a competitive balance between teams and/or to preserve college sports as separate and distinct from professional sports. In order to prove that a restraint of trade is not unreasonable, the NCAA must demonstrate that the regulation at issue is the least restrictive means available of achieving its goals. Unless the NCAA can meet this burden of proof, its members will have to pay more damages to plaintiffs, more money to coaches, and perhaps even more money to athletes.

Nothing would increase the cost of college sports more, though, than a decision by the Internal Revenue Service (IRS) to treat the revenues that some colleges earn from sports as taxable income from an "unrelated business." Historically, the IRS has taken the position that income from paid admissions to college sports events, regardless of the number of attendees or the amount of the gate receipts, is not subject to the Unrelated Business Income Tax (UBIT) because the sports events are related to the educational purposes of the colleges that sponsor them.[37] The Congress took the same position when it enacted the Revenue Act of 1950, which created the UBIT, a tax on the income from businesses that tax-exempt, charitable organizations run that are unrelated to the purposes for which these organizations exist. The IRS continues to take this position even though college sports are considerably more commercial today than they were in 1950.[38] More recently, the IRS has ruled that income that colleges earn from the sale of radio and television rights to broadcast their games is not subject to the UBIT, for the same reason that income from paid admissions is not subject to the UBIT. According to the IRS, radio and television are merely alternatives to live attendance, so if the income from paid admissions is tax-exempt, the income from the sale of radio and television rights should also be tax-exempt.[39]

Colleges benefit not only from the tax-exempt status of their sports revenues but also from the tax deductibility of payments that they receive in return for the right to purchase athletic tickets. There is no tax deduction allowed for the mere purchase of tickets to a college sports event.[40] If, however, one makes a donation to a college athletic department in return for the right to purchase season tickets to the college's home football or basketball games, one can deduct 80 percent of the amount of the donation on a federal income tax return. Assume that a fan of the football team of College A accepts the athletic department's invitation to contribute $1,500 or more to its athletic-scholarship fund in return for the right to purchase two season tickets for home football games. If the tickets cost $300, the fan will write a check to College A for $1,800, which includes the $1,500 donation to the athletic-scholarship fund and the $300 payment for the tickets. The fan cannot deduct the $300 value of the tickets on a tax return, but he or she can deduct 80 percent of the $1,500 donation to the athletic-scholarship fund, or $1,200. In other words, $1,200 of the donation is a charitable contribution under federal tax law.[41]

Colleges benefit immensely from the tax-exempt status of their sports revenues and from the 80 percent deductibility rule. The former permits colleges to retain the profits they earn from sports, and the latter encourages individuals and businesses to support athletic departments, which support might otherwise have to come from institutional funds. Thus, both rules, which are premised on a close association between college sports and a college education, are pivotal to the survival of the commercial model. In their absence, most Division I colleges would have to abandon commerce in favor of participation, and even the colleges that remained in Division I would see their profit margins shrink significantly in the face of federal and state tax liability. It would be good public policy to change these rules because the change would require colleges that derive financial benefits from athletic commerce to bear the burdens of this commerce, too, including the responsibility to pay taxes on their profits.[42]

Nevertheless, it is unlikely that the IRS will decide to subject colleges' sports revenues to the UBIT and to end the 80 percent deductibility rule in the near future. The IRS is subject to political pressure, as was evident in 1997 when it was the target of severe criticism from the public and from members of Congress for its harassment of individual taxpayers.[43] This experience is presumably still fresh in the minds of career IRS employees, and it is likely to dissuade them from changing the tax status of collegiate sports, which is a cultural icon to many Americans. Neither is it likely that President Bush or the Republican majority that took over the Congress in January of 2003 will legislate this change because, by and large, Republicans prefer fewer and lower taxes and wish to reduce the authority of the IRS, not to expand it.[44] The best that supporters of reform can hope for from the federal government is a credible threat by members of Congress to reconsider the tax status of college sports unless the colleges call off the "arms race" in the construction of athletic facilities and increase the graduation rates of their athletes.

Fortunately, though, the success of the participation model does not require the application of the UBIT to revenues from college sports. The NCAA, despite having made numerous pronouncements against government regulation and in favor of cost containment, continues to act in a way that is likely to increase both the regulation and the cost of college sports. The most glaring example of this behavior occurred in 1997, when the association restructured itself in order to give each of its three divisions autonomy. This means that although the association insists that football and basketball players at Florida State, Notre Dame, and UCLA are "amateurs" just like their counterparts at Amherst, Carleton, and Colorado College, the three smaller colleges can no longer act as a brake on the commercial designs of the three larger colleges at the association's annual meetings. Florida State, Notre Dame, and UCLA belong to Division I, the members of which now meet and govern themselves separately from Division III, to which Amherst, Carleton, and Colorado College belong. In other words, the semipros are now both structurally and functionally separate from the amateurs, and they can pursue athletic fame and fortune without interference from less athletically ambitious colleges. Not surprisingly, once the restructuring was complete, the semipros moved quickly to make their club exclusive by imposing tougher and more expensive standards for continued membership in Division I-A (see Chapter 3).

Thus, market forces, along with Title IX, encourage athletically marginal colleges and conferences to abandon athletic commerce in favor of the participation model of college sports. Increased judicial scrutiny of NCAA rules and the ongoing arms race to build bigger and better athletic facilities have raised the cost of the commercial model considerably and will continue to do so, pricing marginal institutions out of the big time. The only fiscally sane alternative for these colleges is to adopt the participation model. When a "critical mass" of Division I colleges adopts the participation model, the colleges that retain the commercial model will become subject to the UBIT, workers' compensation premiums, and social security payroll taxes. Fans will no longer be able to deduct 80 percent of the amount of donations made for the right to purchase season tickets, because the commercial nature of these colleges' football and basketball programs will be transparent. These burdens are likely to shrink the number of big-time teams to two dozen or so, perhaps even fewer over time, as the financial pressures of the marketplace pinch profit margins.

A decline in the number of big-time teams means that opportunities for high school athletes to play college football or basketball in its most competitive form will also decline. The prospect of a reduced talent pool will spur the NBA to expand its Development League and the NFL to establish its own equivalent in order to ensure a steady supply of highly trained players for NBA and NFL teams. In 1991, Commissioner Paul Tagliabue of the NFL acknowledged this likelihood in his answer to a reporter who asked him what would happen if colleges ever refuse to admit high school athletes who do not meet normal admissions standards, which would occur under the participation model. He responded by saying: "Possibly we and the NBA would have to become more heavily involved in minor leagues."[45] If that happens, college will cease to be the exclusive path to the pros in football and basketball, and high school athletes who do not wish to attend college will no longer have to do so in order to pursue their dreams of athletic fame and fortune.

Instead, they can pursue those dreams in age-group-based minor leagues affiliated with, and supported at least in part by, the NBA or the NFL.[46] Each professional league would support two minor leagues, a rookie league for players ages 18–19 who lack professional sports experience and a veterans' league for players ages 19–23 who have played professionally for at least one year. Teams would be located in small-and medium-sized cities distant from the bright lights of the NBA and the NFL and, whenever possible, could play their games in arenas and stadiums sold or leased to them by colleges that have abandoned commercialized sport. Imaginative marketing could make minor league football and basketball profitable, too, just as it has done for minor league baseball, which in 2002 enjoyed the most profitable season in its 101-year history. Attendance at minor league baseball games increased by 29 percent between 1993 and 2002, compared to 3 percent for major league baseball, and in 2001 minor league games drew 38.8 million fans, the largest total since 1949.[47] Creative marketing, assisted by affordable prices that average $6 per ticket, as compared to $19 for a major league ticket, accounts for this success.[48] Teams market their games to young families, and they provide plenty of diversions for children, ranging from fireworks to face painting to nuns dancing the macarena. "What we're selling is fun and affordability," says John Swiatek, the owner of the Washington (PA) Wild Things, who play in the Frontier League.[49] Nobody sells more effectively than Americans, so there is no reason why fun and affordability would not work for minor league football and basketball, too. Ticket prices would be higher for football than they are for baseball because football teams have larger rosters and payrolls than baseball teams, but minor league football could still be fun, more affordable than Division I-A college football, and more family friendly, too.

Players who compete in the rookie league or in the veterans' league would earn not only salaries but also the right to draw a sum of money from a "Futures Fund" at the end of their playing days if they do not sign a contract with an NBA or an NFL team. The amount of money that one could draw from the fund would depend on the number of years that one played minor league football or basketball. It could be a percentage of the player's salary, as John Feinstein has suggested, or it could be equal to the cost for a resident (i.e., tuition, fees, room, board, and books) of a year of college at the flagship state university in the player's (or the team's) home state.[50] The player could use this money to pay for college or vocational training. Once enrolled, the player could play on a college team, but he would lose one year of eligibility in his former pro sport for each year that he played in the minor league. He could play other sports in college for up to four years as long as he remained academically eligible to do so.

As an American, our hypothetical former minor leaguer responds eagerly to market forces. At age eighteen, he wants to play pro basketball or football and to make money. At age twenty-one or twenty-two, having discovered that he is too small or too slow or that his knee is too damaged for the NBA or the NFL, he sets his sights on the market for teachers, nurses, or physical therapists, draws on his "Futures Fund," and enrolls in college, eager to learn. American colleges respond eagerly to market forces, too, which is the last best hope for the reform of college sports. Like athletes who must dream new dreams, colleges that are too small, poor, or academically rigorous to compete in big-time sports must redefine success and pursue it in a new, nonathletic venue. The "Futures Fund" will make this possible for athletes, and the participation model will make it possible for colleges. Indeed, the participation model *is* a "Futures Fund" for colleges.

THE FACULTY MUST LEAD

Faculty members must be the principal advocates for the participation model of college sports, as they are best situated to be its champion for several reasons. First, there is no viable alternative to faculty leadership. It is unlikely that the NCAA would support the replacement of the commercial model with the participation model. The NCAA supported the creation of athletic scholarships and the televising of college football in the late 1950s, and it has advanced the cause of the commercial model ever since then.[51] Moreover, 78 percent of its annual budget comes from television rights to the Division I men's basketball tournament.[52] The NCAA might not resist adoption of the participation model by colleges that lose money on sports, but it would probably resist widespread adoption of the new model as vigorously as it once resisted Title IX.[53]

Neither can college-sports reformers rely on the presidents of Division I colleges for help. If they are not cheerleaders for commercialized college sport, they are either (1) tolerant of it so long as it earns money and attracts students; (2) preoccupied with other issues; (3) powerless against an anti-reform coalition of boosters, athletic administrators, and perhaps trustees and state legislators; or (4) in office for such a short period of time (five years, on average) that they do not have a sufficient opportunity to make major changes.[54]

Second, faculty members bear the chief responsibility for the integrity of the educational process at their respective colleges, as Wilford Bailey and Taylor Littleton noted in 1991. They wrote: "Because the ultimate responsibility for the virtues of honesty and integrity in a college's educational program rests primarily with faculty, university faculties must become more actively involved as a partner in determining the policies for the conduct of intercollegiate athletics."[55]

Third, faculty members do not answer to the sports boosters, the athletic director, the trustees, or to the legislature, as the president must do. Unlike presidents, tenured professors who advocate sports reform will not lose their jobs as a result, although their advocacy may cause them to become social lepers on some campuses.[56] Fourth, they experience the adverse academic consequences of commercialized college sports most directly because they must teach unprepared and uninterested athletes, and they may receive pressure from the athletic department to assign these athletes passing grades.[57] Fifth, they have the most to gain and the least to lose from the reform of college sports. The atmosphere and the resources for education will improve at no cost to faculty members, who rarely own businesses that benefit from college sports and who tend not to brag about their favorite college team at the country club.[58] Indeed, faculty members would probably benefit, by means of salary increases and/or additional funds for their departments, if spending on sports declined significantly.[59]

Sixth and finally, faculty inattentiveness to athletics is responsible in part for the development of big-time college sports and the adverse consequences thereof, so faculty members must begin to undo the damage that their inattentiveness has helped to cause. Ironically, faculty members who, in private, bemoan or condemn the extra income that big-time college coaches earn from radio and television shows and endorsement contracts spend numerous hours drafting grant proposals, conducting research, writing for publication, and consulting, activities that are nearly as unhelpful to undergraduate students as the football coach's endorsement deals are to his players.[60] This arrangement renders faculty members' criticisms of the coach-entrepreneur hypocritical. More importantly, it prevents adequate faculty oversight of athletics, thereby helping to make the coach's entrepreneurial activities, and financial and academic abuses, possible.

In other words, faculty reluctance to take responsibility for overseeing student activities outside the classroom has helped to entrench athletic commerce on college campuses. Faculty members, especially those who are tenured, must look up from their consulting contracts and grant applications long enough to assert themselves on behalf of reform in college sports. They must become less self-absorbed and more interested in undergraduate life. They must also recognize that if unified, they could change the direction of

college sports because they have the primary authority on campus to establish admissions standards, academic standards, curricula, and graduation requirements. There is evidence that this recognition is at hand. In the spring
of 2001 faculty members at eight of the colleges that belong to the Pac-10
conference passed resolutions that condemned the arms race in athletic-
facilities construction and coaches' compensation.[61] Similarly, in November
of 2001 a committee of faculty members at Big Ten universities passed a
resolution that called on their respective institutions to (1) integrate
academic-support programs for athletes into programs that serve the entire
student body, (2) end inappropriate commercialism in college sports, and (3)
slow down the arms race to build elaborate athletic facilities for athletes and
fans.[62]

These resolutions represent halting steps, and they cannot become reality
with faculty support alone. Still, they are hopeful signs because they reflect
the will of faculty members to work together on a conference-wide basis in
order to combat rampant commercialism and professionalism in college
sports. Faculty governing bodies and academic deans should encourage such
actions by rewarding faculty members for their work on college-sports reform in the same way that they are rewarded for publications and for service
to their institutions. Surely, efforts to tame the college-sports monster constitute valuable service to the institution. Therefore, productivity in matters
of athletic governance ought to count in one's favor in decisions about tenure
and promotion, and it should serve as a counterweight to reduced scholarly
output that results from hours spent working on matters of athletic governance.[63] Similarly, department chairs should compensate colleagues who do
yeoman work on athletic governance and reform by reducing their workloads
elsewhere, such as in teaching or advising.[64] A survey of faculty members at
one Big Ten school found that those who said they refrain from participating
in the governance of sports took that stance primarily because they believe
that participation would require too much of their time.[65]

Faculty members not only must unite in favor of athletic reform but must
build a strong national advocacy organization that is dedicated to fundamental change in college sports. Happily, this process is well under way.
Professors from colleges across America have formed the Drake Group,
which calls for reforms in college sports that mirror the components of the
participation model. Specifically, the Drake Group advocates six proposals
that, if adopted, would improve the culture of college sports significantly.
These proposals would (1) retire the term student-athlete; (2) make the location and control of academic counseling and support services for athletes
the same as for all students; (3) establish university policies that emphasize
the importance of class attendance for all students and ensure that the scheduling of athletic contests not conflict with class attendance; (4) replace one-
year renewable scholarships with need-based financial aid or with multiyear
athletic scholarships that extend to graduation (five-year maximum); (5) re-

quire students to retain a grade point average of 2.0 each semester to participate in intercollegiate athletics; and (6) require colleges to disclose such things as a student's academic major, academic advisor, courses listed by academic major, general education requirements, and electives, plus the class GPA, and the instructor in each course the student takes.[66]

By and large, these proposals are compatible with the participation model. One difference is that the model requires the elimination of athletic scholarships, not their replacement by multiyear grants. Still, the Drake Group's preference for need-based financial aid is precisely what the participation model envisions. The model advocates a more limited disclosure of athletes' courses, grades, and professors, but the Drake Group's preference for disclosure of additional information is not philosophically distinct from what the model would disclose. The model does not require a specific grade point average for continued athletic eligibility, but neither does it argue with the Drake Group's insistence that athletes achieve at least a 2.0 GPA *each semester* in order to remain eligible. This requirement differs from the current NCAA rule, which permits colleges to determine academic eligibility for athletics at the beginning of the fall term.[67] Pursuant to this rule, an athlete whose competitive season spans two semesters (e.g., basketball, hockey, cross-country/track) and who has at least a 2.0 GPA at the beginning of the fall semester can compete during the spring semester without obtaining a 2.0 GPA during the fall semester, unless the athlete's college has a stricter rule. The Drake Group is wise to insist that athletes obtain at least a 2.0 GPA each semester in order to compete during the following semester.

Finally, the model does not address the term student-athlete directly, but no supporter of the model will shed any tears at the demise of this term. The NCAA invented it during the 1950s, after the membership approved the awarding of athletic scholarships, because executive director Walter Byers feared that courts would view athletic scholarships as payment for playing sports and would hold that injured athletes on scholarship were entitled to receive workers' compensation benefits.[68] Ironically, the term "student-athlete" was designed to blur the unique hybrid status of college athletes as students/employees of their institutions, but it highlights that status instead because there are no student-musicians, student-dancers, or student-journalists on college campuses. Thus, the Drake Group is correct to seek its retirement, which is why this book has referred to "athletes" or to "college athletes" instead.

It is immaterial whether the Drake Group or another organization ultimately carries the biggest and brightest banner in the march toward college-sports reform. It is vitally important, though, that the organization that assumes this task be the strongest, clearest, most articulate and powerful voice possible for fundamental reform. Therefore, the organization should seek financial assistance from foundations and individuals sufficient to hire a small staff. It should establish a national office, preferably located in Washington, D.C., where it can build relationships with likely allies and monitor proposed governmental initiatives that would affect the cause of college-sports reform and it can lobby for or against those initiatives. It should also establish chapters on campuses and within athletic conferences nationwide because colleges and conferences, not congressional committees, must do most of the heavy lifting in the cause of college-sports reform.

Together, the national office and the campus chapters should craft and implement an educational strategy, a litigation strategy, and a political strategy. The educational strategy will be the principal focus of the organization in its early stages and a continuing priority thereafter. Most of the education will occur outside of Washington, D.C., on college campuses and in surrounding communities. Therefore, it will largely be the responsibility of members of the organization who volunteer their time on the organization's behalf.

This strategy will inform college students, their parents, and the public about the high financial, academic, and social costs of big-time college sports. Its aim will not be to attract converts, but instead, to promote the prerevolution "reformation" of which Saul Alinsky wrote. Informed students, parents, and members of the public might not advocate that participation replace commerce as the main purpose of college sports. Nevertheless, they will be sufficiently dubious about hidden athletic fees and "affirmative action" for power forwards and offensive linemen that they will not resist the adoption of the new model.

The litigation strategy will be the responsibility of the national office, which will hire lawyers to represent the organization's interests in court. The lawyers' job will be to represent clients who wish to challenge violations of Title IX at athletically marginal Division I colleges. The dual purpose of these lawsuits will be to force defendant colleges to comply with Title IX and to encourage them to adopt the participation model as a means of achieving Title IX compliance. Athletically marginal colleges faced with protracted Title IX litigation could adopt the participation model as a condition of a settlement agreement to a lawsuit. Such an agreement would hasten compliance with Title IX and would enable a college to avoid the expense and the negative publicity that are associated with lengthy litigation. If necessary, the litigation strategy could also initiate lawsuits against colleges that refuse to disclose data concerning the academic performance of their athletes.

The political strategy will be the joint responsibility of the national office and of local chapters because the organization will execute it both nationally and locally. On the national level the political strategy will lobby the Congress to enact an "Integrity in Athletics Disclosure Act" that will require colleges to report to the Secretary of Education the courses that college athletes take, their academic majors, the grades they receive, the class average in each course that athletes take, and who their instructors are. These data will supplement the data that the Congress already requires colleges to report concerning athletes' graduation rates and athletic opportunities by gender. The required disclosure of these data will end colleges' refusals to release them on the basis of FERPA, relieve the Department of Education of the burden of deciding whether their disclosure would violate FERPA, eliminate the need for lawsuits to determine whether FERPA prevents their disclosure, and still honor FERPA because disclosure will not identify individual students. In the longer term, when the participation model becomes commonplace among former big-time colleges, the organization will lobby the Congress in favor of legislation that will apply the UBIT to the small cadre of colleges that retains the commercial model of college sports.

Enacting legislation will not be the only focus of the organization's national political strategy, though. The other objective of this strategy will be to build alliances with like-minded individuals and organizations. Potential allies include individual journalists, lawyers, economists, and politicians, who could assist the organization by publicizing and endorsing its agenda, providing it with useful data, and offering their services to the litigation strategy, respectively. Potential allies also include groups that advocate for compliance with Title IX (e.g., National Women's Law Center, Women's Sports Foundation, National Coalition for Girls & Women in Sport), for enhanced educational and professional opportunities for African Americans (e.g., NAACP, National Bar Association), and for improvements in higher education (National Council on Education, American Association of University Professors, etc.). The organization should cultivate alliances with such groups because they are highly visible and practiced in the arts of lobbying and public education. It should also cultivate them because they represent constituencies that will benefit from a model of college sports that treats women equitably, gives African Americans a fair opportunity to get an education, and allows only legitimate undergraduates to represent their institutions in sports.

On the local and regional levels, the political strategy will screen candidates for seats on the athletic governing boards and the college-wide governing boards of individual colleges to determine whether they support the participation model or, at least, specific reforms that are compatible with the participation model. It will oppose the election or the appointment of candidates who are hostile to reform. It will support or oppose candidates for college presidencies on the same grounds. The local political strategy will also advocate the appointment of experienced undergraduate educators as athletic directors and will oppose the appointment of candidates whose professional experiences are limited to big-time college sports and/or professional sports. The former are likely to be considerably more sensitive to the academic and personal-growth needs of college athletes than are the latter. The local political strategy will consult with academic deans and with faculty governing bodies to develop means of rewarding and of protecting against reprisal faculty members who advocate athletic reform on their campuses. Finally, it will unite supporters of the participation model at member colleges within particular conferences in a collaborative effort designed to replace commerce with participation on a conference-wide basis.

The pursuit of fundamental reform in college sports is a political cause. College faculty members who want such reform must build a political organization capable of achieving it. Perhaps the preceding paragraphs will provide a blueprint to guide the builders.

ANSWERS TO THE CRITICS

Advocates of the participation model must answer several criticisms in order to convince skeptics of its wisdom. One likely criticism is that cutting the size of football rosters would reduce opportunities for men to play college sports. The answer is that such cuts would indeed reduce the number of slots available on college football teams, but the "reserves" on Division I teams that have 100 or 120 members rarely play in games under the existing system. In an environment of limited resources, colleges should support male and female runners, swimmers, and rowers who will compete, instead of football players who will sit on the bench. Besides, if boys discover in high school or earlier that the opportunities to play college football are limited, perhaps they will devote their athletic energies to golf, tennis, skiing, track and field, or swimming instead, any of which, unlike football, they will be able to participate in long after graduation from college.

A related criticism is that the reduction in athletic scholarships, in conjunction with the reduction in the size of football rosters, will reduce access to college for African-American men, who receive a disproportionate number of football scholarships. The answer is that there need not be a reduction in access to higher education for African-American men if colleges use a substantial portion of the money that they save by abandoning commercialized sports to assist minority students from low-income families to pay for college. This policy could thereby *increase* access to higher education for African-American men while conveying the message that intellectual skills provide a more viable means of escaping poverty than physical skills.[69] It could also puncture a persistent stereotype by reducing the high percentage of African-American men at Division I colleges who are football players.[70] Thus, although the participation model would probably reduce the number of black college football players in America, it would also probably increase the number of black doctors, lawyers, engineers, and other professionals in America. Anyone who questions the participation model on racial grounds ought to consider whether African Americans are likely to benefit more from producing football players than they are from producing doctors, lawyers, and engineers.

African-American women are likely to criticize the participation model on

two counts. They will argue, first, that the elimination of athletic scholarships would reduce their access to higher education. The answer to this
criticism is the same for black women as it is for black men, namely, that
the participation model will *increase* access to higher education if colleges
spend the money that they save from abandoning commercialized sports on
financial aid for minority students, including African-American women.

They will also argue that the expansion of opportunities for college
women to participate in "emerging sports," such as synchronized swimming,
equestrian, and squash, does not help them because they do not have access
to these sports prior to college. Neither do they benefit from the growth of
more established women's sports, such as soccer, lacrosse, and softball, which
are popular in predominantly white suburban and rural communities, but
are not popular in urban communities, where many African-American
women live.[71] Data appear to support this argument. Black women represent
more than 30 percent of the women who play basketball and nearly 25 percent of the women who participate in track and field at Division I colleges,
but they hold only 2.7 percent of the athletic scholarships in all other sports
combined at predominantly white colleges in Division I.[72]

The short-term answer is that this imbalance of opportunities already exists; the participation model is neither responsible for it nor likely to make
it worse. The NCAA has tried to address this problem by including on its
list of emerging sports, bowling, to which urban black women have more
access than they have to games that require green space. Consequently, in
1999–2000, there were twenty-one women's bowling teams at Division I
colleges, more teams than in any recently-added sport except water polo.[73]
The long-term answer is a sustained effort by the NCAA or its successor,
in partnership with the national governing bodies of various sports and local
organizations, to introduce urban, minority children to sports to which they
would not otherwise have access. This effort is under way. The National
Youth Sports Program, an affiliate of the NCAA, sponsors clinics by college
coaches and athletes in communities throughout the country. Several national sports governing bodies, including the U.S. Tennis Association and
the U.S. Soccer Federation, operate programs designed to introduce their
respective sports to inner-city youth.[74] These activities will continue under
the participation model, whether or not the NCAA survives, because to
achieve gender equity while ignoring racial inequity would be a hollow victory indeed for college sports.

Supporters of Olympic sports will charge that the elimination of athletic
scholarships in these sports will harm America's performance in future
Olympiads. The answer is that this result need not occur if the Amateur
Athletic Union (AAU) and the United States Olympic Committee (USOC)
assume the full responsibility for training future Olympians.[75] Admittedly,
Olympic sports are not nearly as problematical for colleges as football and
basketball are. Still, training Olympians is no more essential to the mission

of higher education than is training professional football and basketball players.

Yet another likely criticism of the participation model is that it would precipitate a revolution when only reform is necessary. This argument is likely to state that "most of what happens in college sports is positive," or an equivalent thereof. Supporters of this argument will probably note that this book has acknowledged that the problems in college sports exist primarily in Division I-A football programs and in Division I men's basketball programs. They will point to outstanding present and former college athletes who are (or were) outstanding students, too. They might cite former University of North Carolina swimmer Richelle Fox, who was ranked fourth in the world in the women's 100-meter butterfly several years ago. Her daily schedule included rising at 5:30 A.M., swimming from 6 until 7:30, and lifting weights until 8:30, all before eating breakfast. After breakfast, Richelle attended classes, ate lunch, underwent physical therapy, and swam again from 3:15 until 6 P.M., after which she ate dinner and then studied. "I couldn't imagine having a whole day to myself," she told a reporter for *The Chronicle of Higher Education*.[76]

Alternatively, they might cite University of Connecticut basketball player Emeka Okafor, who ranked third in the nation in blocked shots in his freshman season (2001–02), but, more importantly, earned a 3.7 GPA while taking eighteen hours of classes during the fall 2001 term, and then took seventeen hours in the spring 2002 term with similar results. The child of Nigerian immigrants, Okafor is wise beyond his years. "Basketball is a gift," he says, "but so is intelligence. I don't want to ever waste either of them."[77]

The maturity and the work ethic of Richelle Fox and Emeka Okafor— and other college athletes like them—are admirable. Nevertheless, it is impossible to ignore the serious problems that are associated with big-time college sports. Just because by virtue of maturity, industry, and strength of character, some athletes succeed academically and athletically in the existing system does not mean that this system is worth preserving. After all, Justice Clarence Thomas overcame poverty and racial segregation to win a seat on the Supreme Court but that hardly makes poverty and segregation benign. Justices Sandra Day O'Connor and Ruth Bader Ginsburg overcame gender discrimination to win their seats on the High Court, but the U.S. should still eradicate gender discrimination. Thus, even if there is more "good" than "bad" in college sports, the bad is hostile to higher education, and it is likely to continue unless participation replaces commerce as the purpose of college sports. When participation replaces commerce, it will be clear that there is more good than bad in college sports because athletes such as Richelle Fox and Emeka Okafor will be more numerous, and less newsworthy, than they are today.

A related criticism that supporters of the participation model should expect is that its adoption would prevent colleges from pursuing excellence in both academics and athletics. This charge assumes, erroneously, that bowl and tournament bids and Olympic medals are as essential to the mission of a college or university as is long-term human development. On the contrary, long-term human development is the purpose for which colleges exist, and they existed in the U.S. for two hundred years before the crews from Harvard and Yale roiled the waters of Lake Winnipesaukee in 1852. Big-time sports do not foster long-term human development. Father Guthrie, the president of Georgetown University, recognized this in 1951, when he announced that Georgetown would drop football. Commercialized sport, he observed, "forms no part of an honest educational system. . . . It has as much reason to subsist on the campus of an educational institution as a night club or a macaroni factory."[78] In other words, the educational value that a college derives from sponsoring powerhouse teams is akin to the educational value that it would derive from sponsoring a lively nightclub or an efficient macaroni factory. The nightclub analogy is particularly apt in light of Murray Sperber's thesis that big-time college sports produces a "beer and circus" mentality among students that results in missed classes, extended weekends, and the excessive consumption of alcohol.[79]

Some critics will charge that the participation model would deprive the public of entertainment that unifies college campuses, builds ties between colleges and off-campus communities, and satisfies a human need for festivals and celebrations.[80] They are mistaken. Big-time sports do not necessarily unify campuses in an era when student fees increase regularly to defray the high costs of maintaining these sports. Chapter 3 showed that sports boosters who support athletic departments rarely support other college departments; therefore, colleges do not necessarily build valuable ties to the public through big-time sports. Besides, college sports under the participation model will be festive and celebratory. The annual men's basketball game between Dartmouth and Princeton at Dartmouth is a prime example. The pep band plays, the crowd alternately roars and sighs, the coaches exhort their players, and when the game ends, I leave feeling excited and exhausted. More importantly, I leave secure in the knowledge that the players will be in class on Monday morning and that they will graduate, having been challenged mentally and physically.[81] For those who remain unconvinced or who crave the big time, professional sports can suffice, without the hypocrisy that plagues college sports.

Hypocrisy is the watchword of the final criticism to be expected. This criticism will come from persons who support fundamental reform in college sports but who believe that it would be sufficient to permit colleges to operate professional sports enterprises in which players would be paid employees, but would not be required to be students. For example, historian John Sayle Watterson has argued that "college football programs should be spun off into university athletic franchises or minor league football teams that play on the university campuses."[82] Surely, the "spin-off" model would end the hypocrisy of the existing system, but it would not end a host of other problems that plague college sports. Under this model, colleges would have to pay taxes on their sports revenues, which would decrease the profit margins of even the most athletically successful colleges and would force less successful colleges to subsidize their athletic departments with institutional funds. Therefore, financial problems would persist, and Title IX compliance would probably suffer as a result. Academic fraud would cease; but social problems would persist, so colleges' reputations would continue to suffer as a result of athletes' off-the-field antics. Thus, the spin-off model would settle for a mere separation between higher education and athletic commerce, even though the circumstances require a divorce.

PARTING THOUGHTS

Colleges and college sports have strayed far from their moorings. "[T]he fundamental focus of [higher education]," writes Professor Stanley Katz of Princeton, "has shifted from the instruction of the young to the creation of useful knowledge."[83] Faculty members devote more time to research than to undergraduate education, coaches have numerous business interests, and institutions pursue excellence and income instead of justice. The dean of the Haas School of business at UC-Berkeley is formally known as the Bank-America Dean of Haas, and college football teams strive for bids to the Nokia Sugar Bowl or the FedEx Orange Bowl.[84] The ringing of cash registers drowns out the protests of students who demand justice in the forms of livable wages for college employees and a refusal to sell college clothing made in sweatshops overseas.[85] Markets create wealth, the students remind their elders, but they do not dispense justice.

Similarly, market mechanisms can help to reform college sports, but they should not govern college sports. They seek short-term gain and care little for long-term human development, which should be the object of sponsoring, or of playing, college sports. The participation model would promote long-term human development. It would expand sports opportunities for women, preserve men's non-revenue sports, and rein in budgets for football and men's basketball. Colleges' responsibilities to train professional athletes and to entertain the public would end. There would be fiscal sanity, academic integrity, personal responsibility, and gender equity in college sports. The NCAA's stated goal that athletics should be an integral part of higher education would become a reality. There would be more justice on campus, at least in the athletic department, which is as good a place as any other to begin. A new season would be under way.

NOTES

1. Robert Atwell, Point of View, "The Only Way to Reform College Sports Is to Embrace Commercialization," *The Chronicle of Higher Education*, July 31, 2001, p. B20.

2. Ibid.

3. James N. Loughran, S.J., "The Divide Between NCAA Athletics and Education: What Do We Do?" *Conversations* 21 (Spring 2002), pp. 11–18.

4. Saul D. Alinsky, *Rules For Radicals: A Pragmatic Primer for Realistic Radicals* (New York: Vintage Books, 1989), p. xxi.

5. Ibid., p. xxii.

6. Ibid.

7. Brian L. Porto, *Completing the Revolution: Title IX as Catalyst for an Alternative Model of College Sports*, 8, no. 2 Seton Hall Journal of Sport Law 351, 411 (1998). *See also* Raymond Yasser, "Athletic Scholarship Disarmament," *The Journal of Sport & Social Issues*, 17 (1993): 70–73.

8. Alinsky, *Rules for Radicals*, p. 133.

9. Porto, *Completing the Revolution*, p. 411; Richard G. Sheehan, *Keeping Score: The Economics of Big-Time Sports* (South Bend, Ind.: Diamond Communications, Inc., 1996), p. 266.

10. Porto, *Completing the Revolution*, p. 412.

11. Marc Fisher, "Academics Play Second String To Athletics," *The Washington Post*, December 8, 2002, p. C01.

12. Ibid.

13. Ibid.

14. This information is available on the Web site of "Rutgers 1000," the organization that Professor Dowling helped to establish at Rutgers in an effort to convince that university to abandon commercialized sport. The Web site is located at [http://members.aol.com/rutg1000/archive.htm].

15. Welch Suggs, "NCAA Punishes Oklahoma Panhandle State U. for Rules Violations," *The Chronicle of Higher Education*, December 19, 2002 [available at http://chronicle.com/daily/2002/12/2002121903n.htm].

16. Ibid.

17. Ibid.

18. James J. Duderstadt, *Intercollegiate Athletics and the American University: A University President's Perspective* (Ann Arbor, Mich.: The University of Michigan Press, 2000), p. 128.

19. C. Peter Goplerud, III, *Pay for Play for College Athletes: Now, More Than Ever*, 38 South Texas Law Review 1081, 1082 (1997).

20. Christopher W. Haden, *Foul! The Exploitation of the Student-Athlete: Student-Athletes Deserve Compensation for Their Play in the College Athletic Arena*, 30, no. 4 Journal of Law & Education 673, 680–81 (October 2001).

21. Bill Briggs, "New Teamsters," *The Denver Post*, December 5, 2002. p. D–01.

22. Goplerud, *Pay for Play for College Athletes*, p. 1094.

23. Tom Farrey, "When Students Are Also Employees," ESPN.com, April 30, 2001 [available at http://espn.go.com/gen/s/2001/0427/1187790.html].

24. Ibid.

25. Ibid.

26. Charlotte M. Rasche, *Can Universities Afford to Pay for Play? A Look at Vicarious Liability Implications of Compensating Student-Athletes*, 16 The Review of Litigation 219, 225 (Winter 1997).

27. Sarah E. Gohl, *A Lesson In English and Gender: Title IX and the Male Student-Athlete*, 50 Duke Law Journal 1123, 1132 (2001).

28. 134 F.3d 1010 (10th Cir. 1998).

29. 15 USC § 1.

30. Richard J. Hunter and Ann H. Mayo, *Issues in Antitrust, The NCAA, and Sports Management*, 10, no. 1 Marquette Sports Law Journal 69, 82 (1999).

31. Ibid., p. 84.

32. Ibid.

33. Ibid., pp. 73–74.

34. Brian L. Porto, *The Legal Challenges to "Big-Time" College Sports: Are They Threats or Opportunities for Reform?* 27, no. 2 The Vermont Bar Journal 41, 42 (June 2001).

35. Hunter and Mayo, *Issues in Antitrust, The NCAA, and Sports Management*, pp. 73–74.

36. Ibid., pp. 74–75.

37. Bertrand M. Harding, Jr., *The Tax Law of Colleges and Universities*, 2nd ed. (New York: John Wiley & Sons, Inc., 2001), p. 96.

38. Porto, *Completing the Revolution*, p. 413, n. 353.

39. Harding, *The Tax Law of Colleges and Universities*, 2nd ed., p. 96.

40. Ibid., p. 183.

41. Ibid.

42. Porto, *Completing the Revolution*, 413.

43. Ibid., p. 414.

44. Ibid., p. 413.

45. Douglas Lederman, "Hogwash, Say Professional-Sports Moguls When Problems in Intercollegiate Athletics Are Laid on Leagues' Doorsteps," *The Chronicle of Higher Education*, March 6, 1991, pp. A29–A30.

46. The idea for age-group-based minor leagues comes from journalist Rick Telander, who suggested more than a decade ago that the NFL establish such a league in football. His proposal differs from the proposal offered here, though, in that his minor league teams would be college teams that retain the commercial model after the marginal teams have abandoned it. *See* Rick Telander, *The Hundred Yard Lie* (New York: Simon & Schuster, Inc., 1989), pp. 213–217.

47. Mitch Frank, "Minor Miracles," *Time*, August 12, 2002, pp. 54–55.

48. Ibid.

49. John Parrotto, "Small-Town Success," *Baseball America*, September 2–15, 2002, pp. 9–13.

50. John Feinstein, "Not Every Athlete Needs to Go to College," *USA Today*, November 13, 1997, p. 15A, cited in Douglas T. Putnam, *Controversies of the Sports World* (Westport, Conn.: Greenwood Press, 1999), p. 218.

51. Porto, *Completing the Revolution*, p. 414. *See also* Arthur H. Fleisher, III, Brian L. Goff, and Robert D. Tollison, *The National Collegiate Athletic Association: A Study in Cartel Behavior* (Chicago: the University of Chicago Press, 1992).

52. Steve Rushin, "Inside the Moat," *Sports Illustrated*, March 3, 1997, pp. 68–83.

53. Porto, *Completing the Revolution*, p. 414.

54. Ibid.

55. Wilford S. Bailey and Taylor D. Littleton, *Athletics and Academe: An Anatomy of Abuses and a Prescription for Reform* (New York: American Council on Education and Macmillan Publishing. Co., 1991), p. 74.

56. Porto, *Completing the Revolution*, p. 415.

57. Ibid.

58. Ibid.

59. James Duderstadt has written: "Few faculty members realize that in most institutions, where intercollegiate athletics operates at a loss requiring institutional subsidy from tuition revenue or state support, this excessive compensation comes directly out of faculty salaries and financial aid available to students." *See* James J. Duderstadt, *Intercollegiate Athletics and the American University: A University President's Perspective* (Ann Arbor, Mich.: The University of Michigan Press, 2000), p. 307.

60. John Sayle Watterson, *College Football: History, Spectacle, Controversy* (Baltimore: The Johns Hopkins University Press, 2000), p. 382.

61. Jody Wilgoren, "Spiraling Sports Budgets Draw Fire From Faculties," *The New York Times*, July 29, 2001, section 1, p. 12; Welch Suggs, "Pac-10 Faculties Seek to Halt the 'Arms Race' in Athletics," *The Chronicle of Higher Education*, May 23, 2001, p. A43.

62. Welch Suggs, "Big Ten Faculty Group Calls for Reforms to Reduce Commercialization of Athletics Programs," *The Chronicle of Higher Education*, November 8, 2001 [available at http://chronicle.com/daily/2001/11/2001110801n.htm].

63. Porto, *Completing the Revolution*, p. 415.

64. Donna Kuga, "Governance of Intercollegiate Athletics: Perceptions of Faculty Members," *Journal of Sport Management* 10 (1996): 149–168.

65. Ibid.

66. Available at http://www.thedrakegroup.org/02props.html.

67. NCAA Operating Bylaws, Article 14, Eligibility: Academic and General Requirements, 14.4.3.1 Fulfillment of Credit-Hour Requirements, reprinted in NCAA, *2002–03 NCAA Division I Manual* (Michael V. Earle, ed., 2002), p. 145.

68. Walter Byers, *Unsportsmanlike Conduct: Exploiting College Athletes* (Ann Arbor, Mich.: The University of Michigan Press, 1995), pp. 69–70.

69. Raymond Yasser, *A Comprehensive Blueprint for the Reform of Intercollegiate Athletics*, 3, no. 2 Marquette Sports Law Journal 123, 139–140 (Spring 1993).

70. Raymond Yasser, "Athletic Scholarship Disarmament," *The Journal of Sport & Social Issues* 17 (April 1993): 70–73.

71. Porto, *Completing the Revolution*, p. 382.

72. Welch Suggs, "Left Behind," *The Chronicle of Higher Education*, November 30, 2001, pp. A35–A37.

73. Ibid.

74. Ibid.

75. *See* Telander, *The Hundred Yard Lie*, p. 220. This proposal is a variation of Rick Telander's recommendation that the AAU and the USOC either subsidize college teams in Olympic sports or assume the full responsibility for the development of elite athletes in these sports.

76. Jim Naughton, "U. of North Carolina Is Proud of Its Balance of Big-Time Athletics and Quality Academics," *The Chronicle of Higher Education*, December 5, 1997, pp. A56–A58.

77. Joe Drape, "Okafor Is Quick Study, On Court and in Class," *The New York Times*, March 24, 2002, p. C16. *See also* Jere Longman, "Academics, and a Game to Back It Up," *The New York Times*, March 26, 2003 [available at http://www. nytimes.com/2003/03/26/sports/ncaabasketball/26OKAF.html? ex = 10496825 . . .].

78. Murray Sperber, *Onward to Victory: The Crises That Shaped College Sports* (N.Y.: Henry Holt and Company, 1998), p. 476.

79. *See generally* Murray Sperber, *Beer and Circus: How Big-Time Sports Is Crippling Undergraduate Education* (N.Y.: Henry Holt and Company, 2000).

80. Porto, *Completing the Revolution*, p. 417.

81. Ibid., n. 374.

82. Watterson, *College Football*, p. 397.

83. Stanley N. Katz, "Choosing Justice Over Excellence," *The Chronicle of Higher Education*, May 17, 2002, pp. B7–B9.

84. Eyal Press and Jennifer Washburn, "The Kept University," *The Atlantic Monthly*, March 2000, pp. 39–54.

85. Katz, "Choosing Justice Over Excellence," p. B8.

BIBLIOGRAPHY

BOOKS

Adler, Patricia A. and Peter. *Backboards and Blackboards: College Athletes and Role Engulfment*. New York: Columbia University Press, 1991.

Alinsky, Saul D. *Rules for Radicals: A Pragmatic Primer for Realistic Radicals*. New York: Vintage Books, 1989.

Andre, Judith and David N. James, eds. *Rethinking College Athletics*. Philadelphia: Temple University Press, 1991.

Bailey, Wilford S. and Taylor D. Littleton. *Athletics and Academe: An Anatomy of Abuses and a Prescription for Reform*. New York: American Council on Education and Macmillan Publishing Co., 1991.

Benedict, Jeffrey. *Athletes and Acquaintance Rape*. Thousand Oaks, Cal.: Sage Publications, 1998.

———. *Public Heroes, Private Felons: Athletes and Crimes Against Women*. Boston: Northeastern University Press, 1997.

Byers, Walter. *Unsportsmanlike Conduct: Exploiting College Athletes*. Ann Arbor, Mich.: The University of Michigan Press, 1995.

Chu, Donald. *The Character of American Higher Education and Intercollegiate Sport*. Albany, N.Y.: State University of New York Press, 1989.

Duderstadt, James J. *Intercollegiate Athletics and the American University: A University President's Perspective*. Ann Arbor, Mich.: The University of Michigan Press, 2000.

Feinstein, John. *The Last Amateurs: Playing for Glory and Honor in Division I Basketball*. Boston: Little, Brown and Company, 2000.

Festle, Mary Jo. *Playing Nice: Politics and Apologies in Women's Sports*. New York: Columbia University Press, 1996.

Fleischer, Arthur H, III; Brian L. Goff; and Robert D. Tollison. *The National Collegiate Athletic Association: A Study in Cartel Behavior*. Chicago: The University of Chicago Press, 1992.

Gavora, Jessica. *Tilting The Playing Field: Schools, Sports, Sex, and Title IX*. San Francisco: Encounter Books, 2002.

Gerdy, John R. *Sports: The All-American Addiction*. Jackson, Miss.: University Press of Mississippi, 2002.

———. *Sports in School: The Future of an Institution*. New York: Teachers College Press, 2000.

———. *The Successful College Athletic Program: The New Standard*. Phoenix: The American Council on Education and the Oryx Press, 1997.

Harding, Bertrand M. *The Tax Law of Colleges and Universities*. 2d ed. New York: John Wiley & Sons, Inc., 2001.

Hawkins, Billy. *The New Plantation: The Internal Colonization of Black Student-Athletes*. Winterville, Ga.: Sadiki Press, 2001.

Hoberman, John. *Darwin's Athletes: How Sport Has Damaged Black America and Preserved the Myth of Race*. New York: Houghton Mifflin Company, 1997.

Hofstadter, Richard. *Anti-Intellectualism in American Life*. New York: Vintage Books, 1963.

Knight, Bob and Bob Hammel. *Knight: My Story*. New York: St. Martin's Press, 2002.

Lawrence, Paul R. *Unsportsmanlike Conduct: The National Collegiate Athletic Association and The Business of College Football*. Westport, Conn.: Praeger, 1987.

Lester, Robin. *Stagg's University: The Rise, Decline, and Fall of Big-Time Football at Chicago*. Urbana, Ill.: The University of Illinois Press, 1995.

Rader, Benjamin G. *American Sports: From the Age of Folk Games to the Age of Televised Sports*, 4th ed. Upper Saddle River, N.J.: Prentice-Hall, 1999.

Rudolph, Frederick. *The American College and University: A History*. Athens, Ga.: The University of Georgia Press, 1962, 1990.

Sack, Allen L. and Ellen J. Staurowsky. *College Athletes for Hire: The Evolution and Legacy of the NCAA's Amateur Myth*. Westport, Conn.: Praeger, 1998.

Sheehan, Richard G. *Keeping Score: The Economics of Big-Time Sports*. South Bend, Ind.: Diamond Communications, Inc., 1996.

Shulman, James L. and William G. Bowen. *The Game of Life: College Sports and Educational Values*. Princeton, N.J.: Princeton University Press, 2001.

Smith, Ronald A., ed. *Big-Time Football at Harvard, 1905: The Diary of Coach Bill Reid*. Urbana, Ill.: The University of Illinois Press, 1994.

———. *Sports and Freedom: The Rise of Big-Time College Athletics*. New York: Oxford University Press, 1988.

Sperber, Murray. *Beer and Circus: How Big-Time College Sports is Crippling Undergraduate Education*. New York: Henry Holt and Company, 2000.

———. *Onward to Victory: The Crises That Shaped College Sports*. New York: Henry Holt and Company, 1998.

———. *Shake Down the Thunder: The Creation of Notre Dame Football*. New York: Henry Holt and Company, 1993.

Telander, Rick. *The Hundred Yard Lie*. New York: Simon & Schuster, Inc. 1989.

Thelin, John R. *Games Colleges Play: Scandal and Reform in Intercollegiate Athletics*. Baltimore: The Johns Hopkins University Press, 1996.

Watterson, John Sayle. *College Football: History, Spectacle, Controversy*. Baltimore: The Johns Hopkins University Press, 2000.

Whitford, David. *A Payroll to Meet: A Story of Greed, Corruption and Football at SMU*. New York: Macmillan Publishing Co., 1989.

Zimbalist, Andrew. *Unpaid Professionals: Commercialism and Conflict in Big-Time College Sports*. Princeton, N.J.: Princeton University Press, 1999.

ARTICLES

Agthe, Donald E. and R. Bruce Billings. "The Role of Football Profits in Meeting Title IX Gender Equity Regulations and Policy." *Journal of Sport Management* 14 (2000): 28–40.

Atwell, Robert. Point of View: "The Only Way to Reform College Sports Is to Embrace Commercialization." *The Chronicle of Higher Education*, 31 July 2001, B20.

Baade, Robert A. and Jeffrey O. Sundberg. "Fourth Down and Gold to Go? Assessing the Link Between Athletics and Alumni Giving." *Social Science Quarterly* 77, no. 4 (December 1996): 789–803.

Benson, Kirsten F. "Constructing Academic Inadequacy: African American Athletes' Stories of Schooling." *The Journal of Higher Education* 71, no. 2 (March/April 2000): 223–246.

Brake, Deborah and Elizabeth Catlin. *The Path of Most Resistance: The Long Road Toward Gender Equity in Intercollegiate Athletics*, 3 Duke Journal of Gender Law & Policy 51 Spring 1996.

Connolly, Walter B. and Jeffrey D. Adelman. *A University's Defense to a Title IX Gender Equity in Athletics Lawsuit: Congress Never Intended Gender Equity Based on Student Body Ratios*, 71 University of Detroit Mercy Law Review 845 1994.

Crosset, Todd W., Jeffrey R. Benedict, and Mark A. McDonald. "Male Student-Athletes Reported for Sexual Assault: A Survey of Campus Police Departments and Judicial Affairs Offices." *Journal of Sport and Social Issues* 19 (1995): 126–140.

Crosset, Todd W., James Ptacek, Mark A. McDonald, and Jeffrey R. Benedict. "Male Student-Athletes and Violence Against Women: A Survey of Campus Judicial Affairs Offices." *Violence Against Women* 2, no. 2 (June 1996): 163–179.

Frey, James H. "Deviance of Organizational Subunits: The Case of College Athletic Departments." *Journal of Sport and Social Issues*, 18, no. 2 (May 1994): 110–122.

George, B. Glenn. *Who Plays and Who Pays: Defining Equality in Intercollegiate Athletics*, 1995 Wisconsin Law Review 647 1995.

Goplerud, III, C. Peter. *Pay for Play for College Athletes: Now, More Than Ever*, 38 South Texas Law Review 1081 1997.

Grimes, Paul W. and George A. Chressanthis. "Alumni Contributions to Academics: The Role of Intercollegiate Sports and NCAA Sanctions." *American Journal of Economics and Sociology* 53, no. 1 (January 1994): 27–40.

Hunter, Richard J. and Mayo, Ann H. *Issues in Antitrust, The NCAA, and Sports Management*, 10, no. 1 Marquette Sports Law Journal 69 (1999).

Katz, Stanley N. "Choosing Justice Over Excellence," *The Chronicle of Higher Education*. 17 May 2002, B7–B9.

Lamber, Julia. *Gender and Intercollegiate Athletics: Data and Myths* 34, nos. 1&2 University of Michigan Journal of Law Reform 151 Fall 2001 & Winter 2002.

Loughran, James N. "The Divide Between NCAA Athletics and Education: What Do We Do?" *Conversations* 21 (Spring 2002): 11–18.

Meyer, Barbara Bedker. "From Idealism to Actualization: The Academic Performance of Female Collegiate Athletes, *Sociology of Sport Journal* 7 (1990): 44–57.

Orleans, Jeffrey H. *An End to the Odyssey: Equal Athletic Opportunities for Women*, 3 Duke Journal of Gender Law & Policy 131 Spring 1996.

Pascarella, Ernest T., Louise Bohr, Nora Amaury, and Patrick T. Terenzini. "Intercollegiate Athletic Participation and Freshman-Year Cognitive Outcomes." *Journal of Higher Education* 66, no. 4 (July/Aug. 1995): 369–387.

Press, Eyal and Jennifer Washburn. "The Kept University." *The Atlantic Monthly* (March 2000): 39–54.

Reed, Deborah. *Where's the Penalty Flag? A Call for the NCAA to Promulgate an Eligibility Rule Revoking a Male Student Athlete's Eligibility to Participate in Intercollegiate Athletics for Committing Violent Acts Against Women*, 21, no. 1 Women's Rights Law Reporter 41 Fall/Winter 1999.

Rhoads, Thomas A. and Shelby Gerking. "Educational Contributions, Academic Quality, and Athletic Success." *Contemporary Economic Policy* 18, no. 2 (April 2000): 248–258.

Sailes, Gary A. "An Investigation of Campus Stereotypes: The Myth of Black Athletic Superiority and the Dumb Jock Stereotype." *Sociology of Sport Journal* 10 (1993): 88–97.

Sigelman, Lee and Paul J. Wahlbeck. "Gender Proportionality in Intercollegiate Athletics: The Mathematics of Title IX Compliance." *Social Science Quarterly* 80, no. 3 (September 1999): 518–538.

Suggs, Welch. "Female Athletes Thrive, but Budget Pressures Loom." *The Chronicle of Higher Education*, 18 May 2001, A45.

———. "Gap Grows Between the Haves and Have-Nots in College Sports," *The Chronicle of Higher Education*, 17 November 2000, A73.

———. "Football's Have-Nots Contemplate Their Place in the NCAA," *The Chronicle of Higher Education*, 30 June 2000, A47–A48.

———. "A Look at the Future Bottom Line of Big-Time Sports," *The Chronicle of Higher Education*, 12 November 1999, A57–A58.

Upthegrove, Tanya R., Vincent J. Roscigno, and Camille Zabrisky Charles. "Big Money Collegiate Sports: Racial Concentration, Contradictory Pressures, and Academic Performance." *Social Science Quarterly* 80, no. 4 (December 1999): 718–737.

Weistart, John C. *Can Gender Equity Find a Place in Commercialized College Sports?* 3 Duke Journal of Gender Law & Policy 191 Spring 1996.

Yasser, Raymond. *A Comprehensive Blueprint for the Reform of Intercollegiate Athletics*, 3, no. 2 Marquette Sports Law Journal 123 Spring 1993.

———. "Athletic Scholarship Disarmament." *Journal of Sport and Social Issues* 17 (April 1993): 70–73.

REPORTS

Rossi, Robert J. and Terry Armstrong, *Studies of Intercollegiate Athletics: Report No. 1: Summary Results from the 1987–88 National Study of Intercollegiate Athletes*. Palo Alto, CA.: Center for the Study of Athletics, American Institutes for Research, 1988.

———. *Studies of Intercollegiate Athletics: Report No. 3: The Experiences of Black Intercollegiate Athletes at NCAA Division I Institutions*. Palo Alto, CA.: Canter for the Study of Athletics, American Institutes for Research, 1989.

———. *Studies of Intercollegiate Athletics: Report No. 7: Academic Performance and College Sports*. Palo Alto, CA.: Center for the Study of Athletics, American Institutes for Research, 1992.

Cross, Michael E. and Ann G. Vollano, *The Extent and Nature of Gambling Among College Student Athletes*. Ann Arbor, MI.: The University of Michigan Department of Athletics, 1999.

Fulks, Daniel L. *Revenues and Expenses of Divisions I and II Intercollegiate Athletics Programs: Financial Trends and Relationships—2001*. Indianapolis: NCAA, 2002.

Knight Foundation Commission on Intercollegiate Athletics. *A Call To Action: Reconnecting College Sports and Higher Education.* June, 2001.

National Coalition for Women and Girls in Education. *Title IX at 30: Report Card on Gender Equity.* Washington, D.C.: NCWGE, 2002.

Savage, Howard J., Bentley, Harold W. McGovern, John T., and Smiley, Dean F., *American College Athletics* (Bulletin Number Twenty-Three). N.Y.: The Carnegie Foundation for the Advancement of Teaching, 1929.

U.S. Department of Education, Office of Civil Rights. *Clarification of Intercollegiate Athletics Policy Guidance: The Three-Part Test.* Washington, D.C.: Government Printing Office 1996.

U.S. General Accounting Office. Report to Congressional Requesters, *Intercollegiate Athletics; Four-Year Colleges' Experiences Adding and Discontinuing Teams.* Washington, D.C.: Government Printing Office, 2001.

COURT DECISIONS

Boulahanis v. Board of Regents, 198 F.3d 633 (7th Cir. 1999).

Brzonkala v. Virginia Polytechnic and State University et al., 935 F. Supp. 772 (W.D. Va. 1996).

Cannon v. University of Chicago, 441 U.S. 677 (1979).

Cohen v. Brown University, 101 F.3d 155 (1st Cir. 1996), *cert. denied,* 520 U.S. 1186 (1997).

Cureton v. National Collegiate Athletic Association, 198 F.3d 107 (3d Cir. 1999); 37 F. Supp.2d 687 (E.D. Pa. 1999).

Favia v. Indiana University of Pennsylvania, 7 F.3d 332 (3d Cir. 1993).

Franklin v. Gwinnett County Public Schools, 503 U.S. 60 (1992).

Gonyo v. Drake University, 837 F. Supp. 989 (S.D. Iowa 1993).

Grove City College v. Bell, 465 U.S. 555 (1984).

Haffer v. Temple University, 678 F. Supp. 517 (E.D. Pa. 1987).

Harper v. Board of Regents, Illinois State University, 35 F. Supp. 2d 1118 (C.D. Ill. 1999).

Kelley v. Board of Trustees, 35 F.3d 265 (7th Cir. 1994).

Law v. NCAA, 134 F.3d 1010 (10th Cir. 1998).

Neal v. Board of Trustees of the California State Universities, 198 F.3d 763 (9th Cir. 1999).

Roberts v. Colorado State Board of Agriculture, 998 F.2d 824 (10th Cir.), *cert. denied,* 510 U.S. 1004 (1993).

INDEX

About the Author

BRIAN L. PORTO is an attorney, a freelance writer, and an adjunct professor at the Community College of Vermont. He holds a J.D. from Indiana University at Bloomington and a Ph.D. in political science from Miami University (Ohio). Dr. Porto has taught at Macalester College (MN) and at Norwich University (VT), and has worked as an attorney in both state government and private practice. During law school he worked as a research assistant at the Center for Law and Sports at the Indiana University School of Law. His writings on the governance of college sports have appeared in the Seton Hall Journal of Sport Law, the Vermont Bar Journal, the Indiana Law Journal, the Journal of Sport and Social Issues, Liberal Education, and in three edited volumes on law and sports. Dr. Porto lives, practices law, and writes in Windsor, Vermont.